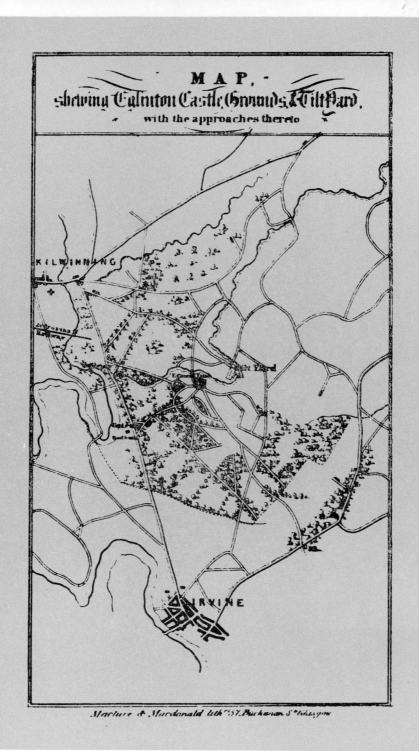

MAP,

shewing Eglinton Castle Grounds & Tilt Yard,

with the approaches thereto

Maclure & Macdonald lith 37 Buchanan S<sup>t</sup> Glasgow

# THE KNIGHT AND THE UMBRELLA

*By the same author*
1  PRESUME: STANLEY'S TRIUMPH AND DISASTER

1. The King's Champion casting his glove at the Coronation
of George IV in Westminster Hall

# THE KNIGHT
## and the
# UMBRELLA

An Account of
THE EGLINTON
TOURNAMENT
1839
by
IAN ANSTRUTHER

GEOFFREY BLES · LONDON

© IAN ANSTRUTHER, 1963

*Printed in Great Britain
by Willmer Brothers & Haram Ltd, Birkenhead
and published by*

GEOFFREY BLES LTD

52 DOUGHTY STREET, LONDON, W.C.I.

33 YORK STREET, SYDNEY

531 LITTLE COLLINS STREET, MELBOURNE

47–53 CASTLEMAINE STREET, BRISBANE

CML BUILDING, KING WILLIAM STREET, ADELAIDE

WYNDHAM STREET, AUCKLAND

10 DYAS ROAD, DON MILLS, ONTARIO

P.O. BOX 8879, PALLSTATE HOUSE

51 COMMISSIONER STREET, JOHANNESBURG

*First published 1963*

*For*
*J. C.*

# Contents

# Illustrations

## Plans

## Endpapers

# Preface

'The good old times—all times when old are good—'
Byron *The Age of Bronze*

The urge to think of times gone by as somehow better than the present day is one of the deepest instincts in human nature. We read in the sixth chapter of Genesis: 'There were giants in the earth in those days; and also after that, when the sons of God came in unto the daughters of men, and they bare children to them, the same became mighty men which were of old men of renown.' This was the world before the Flood and, according to the presumed testament of Noah whose own grandfather was the famous Methuselah, the latter descended from Adam and therefore from God.

The above is merely a handy example, easily matched in other mythologies, of the way in which from the earliest times men have seen their ancestors larger than life. For the same reason, naturally, too—a primitive urge to honour the dead—they have always taken a magnified view of all the things they did.

Throughout Europe in the 19th century but first especially in the British Isles, people began to turn their thoughts to the Middle Ages. The basic reason for this was a feeling of change. New methods of working the land and new processes of manufacture with power supplied by enormous steam engines and quantity achieved by mass

(xi)

production had completely altered the pattern of social life. The Romantic Movement, at the same time, backed by men like Hume and Gibbon who supplied a mass of historical facts, and others like Scott and Bishop Percy who published the ballads of the Middle Ages, revealed to the literate and cultivated world not only the beauties of savage nature but, at least as it appeared to some, the grand simplicity of English medieval life. In a shifting world of factories and steamships, people thought of the past with pride and nostalgia; a mechanical era might lie ahead but nothing, surely, could beat the good old days.

In this atmosphere of change and progress in the year 1838, a young nobleman, the Earl of Eglinton, who longed for the ordered, feudal life and the thrilling combats of his fighting ancestors, decided to revive a tournament. His proposal, now, seems quite ridiculous but at the time it was taken seriously, just as today, in the 20th century, the current fashion for the arts of the Regency, and especially the passion for Georgian architecture with modern villas in the classical style being built by speculators throughout the country, will certainly, in a hundred years, appear to be idiotic. What happened when the tournament took place forms the principal theme behind this book.

The other theme, in a way subsidiary, and yet, in a way, the more important is why he instead of someone else— anyone at all amongst his friends—was the one who actually gave it. There were many people who were just as rich, many who lived in Gothic castles, many who admired the Middle Ages, and many who, better than himself, could have staged such a tournament easily; but the fact remained that it fell to him; and all students of human nature who love the play of chance and character will enjoy watching how these worked and seeing what, in the end, occurred to his scheme.

From the point of view of social history and the general development of the Gothic Revival, the Eglinton Tournament came at a critical moment. The last genuinely 'Gothik' folly of the type invented in the 18th century, it was, too, like the Houses of Parliament—of which the cornerstone had just been laid—the first accurately medieval spectacle of the new Victorian epoch. It forms thus a distinctive landmark between the old and the new, and divides the fashion for the 'picturesque' from the mawkish mania for knights and tournaments and all the trappings of the Middle Ages which first inspired and finally destroyed the country's popular taste.

It was not the first to be held in Europe or, indeed, in the United States (some 18th and 19th century Tournaments are listed in Appendix I), for the Gothic Revival and the Romantic Movement affected people all over the world, but it was the first as well as the last to be held in the United Kingdom; because, in the British Isles at least, the right conditions never appeared again. Not only are such revivals expensive, but also all the feeling in the world for the days gone by and the deeds of chivalry were never enough in later decades to animate even the richest enthusiasts to follow Lord Eglinton's example.

For, in holding such a tournament, he was caught unaware in a net of circumstances; and thus he lost an ancient fortune, not for honour, nor for glory, nor even for the love of a beautiful woman, but simply because he was drowned in the sea of his time.

2. The medieval games at Firle Place, 1827 (artist unknown)

3. Eglinton Castle, from *Survey of Ayrshire*, W. Aiton, 1811

# *Acknowledgements*

Much research is needed to write a book like this especially if, as proved the case, there is no central source of documents; and as a result, over a period, a large number of people have helped me complete it. To record their names would require a page and, for this reason, I do not propose to do so; but to them first, once again, I should like to offer my thanks.

I must, however, mention a few: Mr A. B. Thompson of the Meteorological Office in Edinburgh for providing figures of rainfall in Ayrshire; Dr James Corson, the authority on Scott, for sending me data on the sales of *Ivanhoe*; Mr Kenneth MacKelvie, Chartered Accountant, for helping me to study the Eglinton accounts; Colonel Evelyn Arthur for lending me books; The Marquess of Waterford for bringing me miniatures; The Duke of Atholl for offering me photographs; Sir James Hunter Blair for loaning me letters; Commander Hamilton for giving me papers; Mr and Mrs William Mure for technical advice; Mr Robert Oattes for presenting me with a bowl; Mr James Campbell for the use of a valuable scrapbook.

This last belonged to Joseph Train, the devoted admirer of Sir Walter Scott who wrote that he wished

'to convert into a more permanent form the various accounts of the Tournament contained in the floating periodical literature of the day with the aim of affording at some future period the accurate and interesting details of an exhibition which, although likely to be only incidentally alluded to in the histories of the time, certainly in its object as well as in its execution stood out in bold and prominent relief amid the events of the day.'

The antiquary's foresight has now been justified, and to him also, although long dead, I would like to acknowledge my debt.

It became necessary in the course of the work to put on a suit of armour, and this was arranged by the late Sir James Mann to whom I render particular thanks as I do, also, to William Reid, the expert esquire who armed me.

Next, I should like to thank Mrs Bonnaire for typing the MS a thousand times; Sir James Fergusson, Keeper of the Records of Scotland, for making available the Eglinton muniments; the skilled staff of the London Library and also that of the Library at the War Office for saving me many hours of research; Jocelyn Gibb, my friend and publisher, for spurring me on with genial encouragement; and my wife, Honor, for patience and help.

Finally I come to the two families, those descended from the Lambs of Beauport and the present heir of the 'Tournament Earl'—Miss Harbord of Mousehold, Norwich and William, 17th Earl of Eglinton—on whose private papers this book is based. For rendering me access to their personal archives, giving me their time and hospitality, allowing me to borrow precious volumes, patiently answering innumerable letters, appealing to the press for missing material and, during the many months when it seemed that nothing would ever be written, giving me advice, support and encouragement, I cannot, as every biographer will guess, ever properly express a fraction of my thanks.

# THE EGLINTON TOURNAMENT

'Some people despise and abuse it, and rejoyce that it has cost Lord Eglinton . . . a great sum of money. Others laud it as an original and noble idea, far beyond hunting or shooting or racing, and hold that his Lordship deserves immortality. . . .'

HENRY THOMAS COCKBURN
*Memorials of his Time*
entry dated 15th October, 1839.

# PART ONE

## The Background

### THE CORONATION OF WILLIAM IV 1831
### 'THE HALFCROWNATION'

'As the economy of the age did not allow His Majesty to give his Peers the usual coronation dinner in Westminster Hall, he privately entertained a large party at St. James's.'

*Ann. Reg.*, 1831, p. 155

### QUEEN VICTORIA'S CORONATION 1838
### 'THE PENNY CROWNING'

'The Coronation of Queen Victoria was conducted in most respects after the abridged model of that of her immediate predecessor; the walking procession of all the estates of the realm, and the banquet in Westminster Hall, with all the feudal services attendant thereon, being wholly dispensed with; not, however, without many complaints and various public struggles, as well on the part of the antiquaries, as on that of the tradesmen of the metropolis.'

*Ann. Reg.*, 1838, p. 96, *Chron.*

# Chapter One

THE CORONATION of Queen Victoria, which was held on 28th June, 1838, came at a time of extraordinary progress and change.

The railway age, which for many years had remained a mere dream, had at last become a reality for, during the reign of her uncle and predecessor, William IV, from 1830 to 1837, the power of steam which had been developing steadily for half a century suddenly reached a point of dramatic expansion and, just as suddenly, the homely plod of hoof and sail and the ancient limits of a day's journey started to crumble and vanish.

In 1829 George and Robert Stephenson had successfully demonstrated their famous steam engine 'Rocket', and a year later the first passenger railway in the world had been opened from Manchester to Liverpool. This was followed by the line from Liverpool to Birmingham in 1837, and in 1838, the year of the coronation, by the final, triumphant link from Birmingham to London.

The first official journey over this last route of 112 miles, which had taken ten years to plan and construct and had cost the enormous sum of five million pounds, was performed in four hours and fourteen minutes at an average rate of twenty-six miles per hour. This was twice the speed of the 'Tally-ho', the swiftest stage coach running between the same cities, and from this moment it was clear to everybody that the coaching era was finished.

In the very same summer an identical milestone was reached in the development of steamships. For a number of years small paddle steamers had plied about the coast and across the Channel and once in a while one of them had crossed the Atlantic, but in 1838, the year of the coronation, three gigantic wooden liners, the *Royal William*, the *Sirius* and the *Great Western*, were all launched within a few weeks of each other and began to steam back and forward to the United States regularly.

The most famous of these was the *Great Western*, which was designed by Isambard Kingdom Brunel. She was 212 feet in length, 35 feet in breadth between the paddles, 23 feet in depth, of 2,300 tons displacement, of 750 horses power, as it was described in those days, and of 8½ knots in speed.

She was both the greatest ship in the world and the first in the world to make the crossing by steam alone, which she did steadily in fifteen days and sometimes in twelve and a half. This was four times as fast, at least, as the average time by sail, and from this moment it was clear, too, that the days of sail were over.

These two developments alone, apart from a number of others which were just as important but less spectacular— like the first adoption of Nasmyth's steam hammer, the first commercial use of the electric telegraph, the first employment of the railways for carrying the mails, the first bicycle, even the first expresso steam coffee-pot—convinced everyone, like it or not, that the country stood on the brink of a different epoch.

For this reason, because of the great change in the times, because of the happy contrast between George IV, the last monarch to be crowned with traditional ceremony, and Queen Victoria; because, too, of a useful precedent in the coronation of William IV which had been curtailed because of the riotous state of the country, it was decided to make a change in the coronation.

The antiquated and now pointless ceremonies which had been held previously in Westminster Hall after the service in the Abbey, the public state banquet for the Peers, and the knight in armour, the hereditary King's Champion who challenged all comers to deny the sovereign's right to succession, were abolished. A gay, simple procession from Buckingham Palace, up Constitution Hill, along Piccadilly, down St James's Street, via Pall Mall to Charing Cross, and thence by Parliament Street to the Abbey was arranged to take their place.

This change, however, which was announced in the *London Gazette* on the 10th of April by Lord Melbourne, the Whig Prime Minister, and which was clearly in keeping with the times did not, to a large number of conservative citizens, seem to be necessary in the least.

'I am a plain country gentleman of the old school . . . but my blood is up . . . and I must take leave to ask a few unsophisticated questions,' one of them wrote to the editor of *The Times* three days afterwards.

Was it not typical of the present, penny-wise government of Whigs to pretend they could not afford a few thousand pounds for a coronation when every year they wanted millions on popular reform? And was it not the case that the cancellation of the banquet and the King's Champion was merely a political trick to catch the support of the working classes and snub the old Tory aristocracy?

These were the views of a large number of Englishmen and especially, naturally enough, of the many peers who had taken part in the banquet for George IV and had found it a noble symbol of ancient homage and chivalry. It was a great event, one of the oldest institutions in the monarchy, and the last relic of the days when kings dined in state before their subjects. Furthermore, apart from the ceremony of the Royal Champion, it was the scene of

5

many other feudal customs of equal charm and antiquity.

The Earl Marshal, the Lord High Steward and the Lord High Constable had to ride into Westminster Hall with the first course to escort the dish to the royal table and, once it was served, they had to retire backwards, still mounted on their horses. The Archbishop of Canterbury, as Lord of the Manor of Bardolf, had to present the King with a mess of dilligrout. This was a watery porridge with plums in it, much favoured by William the Conqueror and ordained by him as the manorial fee in perpetuity. The Duke of Atholl, as Lord of the Isle of Man, had to provide the King with two falcons. Thomas Rider, Esq., Lord of the Manor of Nether Bilsington, had to produce three maple cups which were then given to the Mayor of Oxford in exchange for a bowl of wine.

In spite of the interest of these and many other traditional activities—like the washing of hands and the strewing of herbs to prevent pestilence—nothing compared to the ceremony of the King's Champion which had been performed by the same Lincolnshire family of Dymoke for nearly six centuries.

Immediately after the first course the Champion had to appear in full armour on a caparisoned charger, just as he would for a tournament, preceded by two trumpeters, two esquires holding his shield and lance, and escorted by the Lord High Constable and the Earl Marshal. The Knight Marshal, the Earl Marshal's deputy, had to clear the way and, after a flourish of trumpets, the Lancaster Herald called on all persons of any degree whatsoever to declare themselves and fight if they disputed the claim of the new sovereign to ascend the throne.

The Champion then threw down his gauntlet, which was picked up and returned to him by the Herald after a pause of a few moments.

This was performed three times—at the entrance to the hall, at the centre and at the top end before the King's table. After the last challenge the King drank to the Champion from a gold cup which he handed to the Champion and from which the latter drank to the King in return. When he had drained the cup he was allowed to keep it as his fee. After this he shouted 'Long life to his Majesty the King', and then, bowing to the Monarch, backed his horse away from the royal table. He had to continue backing all the way down the hall to the entrance. This was an extremely difficult feat, especially in full armour.

As invariably happens in public life when a large body of people are discontented, one man at last came forward and became their official spokesman. In this case it was Charles William Stewart, 3rd Marquess of Londonderry, the half-brother of the famous Lord Castlereagh, himself a distinguished soldier and diplomatist and friend and staff officer of Wellington during the Peninsular War.

On the day following the Prime Minister's cancellation of the banquet in Westminster Hall he spoke in the House of Lords. He deplored, he said, the abrogation of so many ancient ceremonies. The great changes in the present time ought to inspire the Government to keep the old traditions instead of putting an end to them.

These remarks had no result and a month later he presented a petition to the same effect from five hundred merchants of the City of London, for the City, too, like the Lords of Manors, enjoyed many ancient privileges at coronation banquets of which, now, they were being deprived.

Finally, on the 28th of May, when none of these moves had any effect whatever, he asked the Prime Minister not to crown the Queen at all. What was the point of doing so, he asked furiously, glaring across the floor of the House of

Lords at the Government's spokesman, Lord Fitzwilliam. Let the noble Earl present a motion to abolish the coronation altogether and then—ha ha, bitterly!—let him present another to abolish himself.

But Lord Londonderry was well known as a root and branch reactionary, to such a degree, in fact, that a mob of enraged reformers had once torn him off his horse in Hyde Park; so the Government took no notice of him. There were the strongest possible reasons for not having an old fashioned coronation and Lord Melbourne and other members of the administration made them clear to the public convincingly.

The banquet for George IV, seventeen years earlier, had cost the enormous sum of twenty-five thousand pounds. Now, the exchequer was short of funds and the last budget, just declared, had shown a deficit of one and a half millions. Therefore, all departments had to economise, and certainly nothing at all could be spared for what, in fact, with George IV, had only developed into an orgy.

Added to this was the great changeover to mass production in industry. Thousands of people were out of work and at this moment fifty-thousand weavers were literally starving. It was clearly impossible, under these circumstances, to hold a public state banquet for the peers, let alone for the Queen to partake of it with them.

As to the appearance of the King's Champion—at the coronation of George IV, a clanking youth, who had challenged no one except the antiquaries because he had carried the wrong shield—there was every chance that the whole ceremony would simply become a pantomime. For this had happened during the past on three different and calamitous occasions.

At the coronation of William and Mary in 1689 the Champion had lost his Champion's glove. An old crone had picked it up, laughed mysteriously, and disappeared with it. A romantic stranger, whom all the Jacobites knew to be Bonnie Prince Charlie, had done the same thing at the coronation of George III in 1761. He had seized the Champion's glove from the floor, thrown another, and immediately vanished.

In 1685, at the coronation of James II, the Champion had suffered a truly immortal humiliation. He had flung his glove to the ground so furiously that he had flung himself to the floor in pursuit of it. He had lain on his back like a winded beetle. In the first moment of frightful silence the Queen had snorted and the King had actually laughed.

Lord Melbourne recalled these incidents pointedly. No Government could risk this sort of catastrophe, he said. He was quite sure that on reflexion every sensible person would agree with him.

Thus it came about that Queen Victoria was crowned with only simple pageantry. The state banquet in Westminster Hall, the romantic challenge by the Royal Champion and all the other picturesque ceremonies were done away with. Like the feudal homage they represented, they became themselves things of the past.

In spite, however, of the Prime Minister's reasonable hope that everyone who thought about his arguments would agree with him, many people refused to do so, especially the old Tory aristocracy, and particularly one of them—a dashing, wealthy nobleman of twenty-six, head of an ancient Scottish family; Archibald William Montgomerie, the 13th Earl of Eglinton.

He was perfectly mortified at being deprived of the coronation banquet and all its feudal solemnities. For apart from being a true product of his times, born at the high tide of the romantic movement, steeped in the myths

9

and lore of chivalry and thoroughly addicted to medieval ceremonies, it so happened that his step-father, Sir Charles Lamb—who had brought him up like a son—was the Earl Marshal's deputy, the Knight Marshal of the Royal Household, and ought to have marshalled the Champion for Queen Victoria.

So as well as feeling annoyed at being done out of the banquet, to which he had looked forward all his life and to which his rank entitled him, he was highly irritated at being denied the fun of watching his step-father, clad in a scarlet dress slashed with blue and a scarlet cloak and blue stockings, clear the floor of Westminster Hall for the Champion. He was also perfectly incensed at missing the spectacle of the Champion himself, a veritable knight in armour, in flesh and blood, casting his steel gauntlet as though at a tournament.

Therefore, after the coronation in the summer of 1838, he returned home to his Ayrshire seat, a vast, modern, Gothic castle, thoroughly exasperated at missing these famous ceremonies. For the worst of it was that Queen Victoria was very young and very unlikely to die before him; and so he had almost certainly lost the only chance of his life.

During the first week of August a guest* or neighbour whose name is forgotten but which ought to be written in black, funereal Gothic type in the family records and cursed for ever, made a suggestion which slightly cheered him up.

At his next private race meeting at Eglinton Park, annually held in the spring at Bogside, he might add to the

* This was possibly Henry Gage, the Knight of the Ram at the Tournament, a friend and exact contemporary of Lord Eglinton's and a neighbour of the latter's step-father in Sussex. Gage's father, Viscount Gage, had held a party of this nature at his home, Firle Place, in 1827.

amusements by instituting medieval games. One of his friends could appear in armour and perform the ceremony of the challenge, while others could run at rings and tilt at quintains.

This idea, at which Lord Eglinton laughed and to which he agreed, started an extraordinary rumour: that in the spring he planned a medieval tournament; and because of the great number of people like himself who were sorry about the Champion; because, too, of the spell of the Gothic Revival which made them interested in medieval life; and because, finally, of a frivolous hoax in the *Court Journal* the year before which had announced a tournament at Windsor Castle for the Queen's accession, practically everybody believed it.

They wrote in hundreds to congratulate him and ask for details, while the *Court Journal* and other popular society newspapers ironically welcomed the return to the age of chivalry.

At first, Lord Eglinton simply laughed at all this. But after a day or two he began to think about it.

For unluckily for him, his step-father, Sir Charles Lamb, who was still smarting, too, at being done out of the ancient ceremonies, thought the idea was captivating. Because, as Knight Marshal of the Royal Household, he could then appear in correct regalia, holding his baton and leading his marshalmen, and perform his authentic medieval role as a principal umpire of a tournament.

It happened, also, that Sir Charles's son, Lord Eglinton's half-brother, a dreamy artistic boy who naturally knew Lord Eglinton intimately, shared his father's enthusiasm—although for entirely different reasons. For oddly enough, by a strange and unhappy twist of fate, he had nursed a passion for tournaments all his life—in fact was positively obsessed by them—and even as a man, at the age of twenty-three, lived entirely in a private world of shining knights and chivalry.

So, pushed along by his step-father and half-brother, who looked for the fun and none of the expense, Lord Eglinton announced that the rumour was correct.

What was more, he said, he would follow it up with a medieval banquet. There would be roast peacocks, boars' heads, barons of beef and bowls of dilligrout, with every other antiquated delicacy, and afterwards a dance to the strains of lutes and harpsichords. By doing this he might even discredit the Government. For such an act of private hospitality would mock their parsimony at the coronation and would surely make Lord Melbourne blush with shame.

In taking this decision, Lord Eglinton embarked on the greatest folly of the century. He soon discovered that however cheap and commonplace it might have been to arrange a tournament in the age of chivalry, however simple for the heralds to announce it and however easy for a knight to take part in it, in the age of steam it was hardly a possibility.

The organisation of all the participants—all of whom had to be enlisted—and of armour, lances, costumes and tents—all of which had to be made—required a staff of hundreds, while the cost of mounting and equipping even one single combatant proved to be astronomical.

Being a spoilt, impulsive young man, immensely rich and used to having his smallest wish even at the slightest pretext, he simply waved his hand when all this became evident and said he would do it anyway.

And he carried it through to the end, even though he had to postpone it, had to pledge a large part of his ancestral estate to pay for it, had to suffer the ridicule of the press throughout the world and, finally, to endure an ultimate affliction of Providence.

Any ordinary person would have been crushed by all this, but Lord Eglinton almost thrived on it. Beneath a delectable manner he was a man of fine courage, too, with plenty of pride, common sense and capability. For the first time in his life he was really put to a test and, although the trial was absurd and the defeat agonising, he displayed such extraordinary cheerfulness and sportsmanship that in the end the jeers were drowned by a murmur of congratulations.

He became as a result, and by general acclamation, the most popular nobleman in Scotland, and this position he held for the rest of his life. He was loaded with honours in the world of sport, and, later on, when Lord Melbourne's government was out and the Tories in office, with coveted political distinctions.

Twenty years afterwards and not long before his comparatively early death—by then twice Lord Lieutenant of Ireland, patron of the Turf, Derby winner and for many years 'the excellent and justly popular nobleman' of his epitaph in Burke's *Peerage*—he wrote an account of his life.

He composed it privately, just for his family, in neat, close handwriting, in a small locked leather diary, and only recorded those details of his career which he thought had been interesting. Of the year 1839 and its great *débâcle*—the one event for which he is now remembered and for which at the shallow edge of social history he is certain of immortality—he wrote merely, 'I gave a tournament at Eglinton.' That, except for a few irrelevant remarks, was the only mention he made of it.

He said nothing at all of the difficulties, humiliations, notoriety and disappointments, nor did he mention the cost. Throughout his life he spent his money in a golden shower so he probably never assessed it. And although, in fact, the expense was gigantic, compared to his losses afterwards on bets, wagers, carriages and racehorses, it was certainly only a drop in the bucket.

But there was, too, possibly another reason for hardly mentioning the tournament. For him, at least, it had broken the spell of the Gothic Revival, the magic enchantment of the Age of Chivalry, the charmed aura of his vanished youth; and he himself, in a way like Orpheus, by looking back, had caused the death of the thing he loved the most.

In wearing armour, couching a lance, paying *devoirs* to a Queen of Beauty and trying to evoke the days of tournaments, he had learnt nothing of medieval habits and only discovered a prosaic truth:

That the past can never be brought to life, and that ancient pastimes and decorative arts should never be imitated in a different age.

Lord Melbourne had been proved to be right. The olden days were not so good and to revive chivalry in the Age of Steam was only to invite an absurd catastrophe.

# Chapter Two

THE FAMILY of the Earls of Eglinton, the Montgomeries of Eagleshame and, through the female line, the
Setons of Seton, had one of the oldest Norman pedigrees
in Scotland, which stretched back to a French knight
called Mundegumbri who settled in what is now Ayrshire
in the twelfth century.

It was always supposed that the Mundegumbris came
from France with William the Conqueror, and were in
descent from the ancient French family of Montgommerie,
but the only certain fact was that this particular Mundegumbri acquired the lands of Eagleshame from the High
Steward of Scotland at some time after 1157. He was
called Robert, and he married the High Steward's
daughter, Marjory, so perhaps the lands were her dowry.
He died about 1178.

For the next two hundred years his successors lived the
life of small but important landlords, fighting in local feuds,
attending the Scottish court, supporting the King at war
and all the while, by purchase and marriage, slowly increasing the family property and influence.

In 1388 the 9th descendant, Sir John Montgomerie,
fought in the famous battle of Otterburn and captured
Harry Hotspur, the renowned son of the Earl of Northumberland. For this exploit he was immortalised in Scottish
ballad and forced his captive, by way of ransom, to build a
castle at Polnoon on the Eagleshame estate. He did well
in domestic matters, too, for he married the only daughter
of a neighbouring landlord, Sir Hugh Eglinton, and

15

through her gained the Eglinton and Ardrossan estates.

One more generation passed and then the family became enobled. Sir Alexander Montgomerie, 11th of Eagleshame, who was a Privy Councillor, a Lord of Parliament, and three times the King's representative at treaties of peace with England, was created the 1st Lord Montgomerie by James II in 1445.

This gave the family a position of much greater authority and it was not long before they took advantage of it. Lord Montgomerie's eldest son died before him and never succeeded, but his grandson and great grandson both inherited his ability and strength of character, and the latter, by supporting the future James IV in the struggle against his father, gained a position of Royal favour which finally earned him the Earldom in 1506. He, too, like his great grandfather, was a Lord of Parliament, a Privy Councillor and a constant holder of many high and important appointments throughout his life; and during sixty years of influence he greatly increased the family estates. In him, Hugh Montgomerie, 1st Earl of Eglinton and 13th holder of the lands of Eagleshame, the direct descendants of Robert Mundegumbri reached their peak after a steady climb of seventeen generations.

Then there was a change. In 1612, the 5th Earl, the great grandson of the 1st Earl, died childless. Perhaps this was the result of too much family ambition, for his uncle who was the heir-apparent but without sons, broke the rules of blood relationship and married the Earl to his eldest daughter.

Whatever the cause, the 5th Earl left no descendants and thus, after more than four hundred and fifty years, the male line of the Mundegumbris became extinct.

In those days, however, there were more ways than one of keeping a great family intact and before he died the Earl obtained a Crown Charter to name an heir in the female line.

His maternal aunt, Lady Margaret Montgomerie, had three sons by her husband, the 1st Earl of Winton, and he chose the last of these, Sir Alexander Seton.

In this way the family preserved their identity. For although in lineal terms they became Setons, they kept their own name of Montgomerie and all their old estates and privileges.

In the end they came out better than before. One hundred and fifty years later the Setons themselves became extinct, with their own ancient baronies of Seton and Tranent and their earldom of Winton.

Then the Montgomeries claimed these honours because of the fact that in birth they were really Setons. They still kept the name of Montgomerie, however; for the Crown Charter gave them the right and just because of a little blood they saw no reason to insult their ancestors and substitute the name of Seton for their own noble Norman patronymic.

The chapter of family history which opened now with the new heir, Sir Alexander Seton, continued without a break to the 13th Earl of Eglinton who gave the Tournament. Sir Alexander did not inherit entirely without opposition, for in spite of the Crown Charter, his right to the Earldom was challenged by James VI and he had to struggle hard to establish it. He was obliged, too, to make a large payment to a neighbouring peer, Lord Balfour of Burleigh, who had laid claim to part of his estate of Kilwinning. Also, in compensation to the last Earl's wife, as Dowager Countess and eldest child of the former heir-presumptive, he was forced to raise a substantial sum in hard cash, equivalent to thirty-two thousand pounds today (1960).

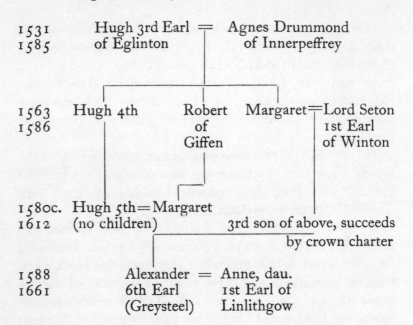

| | | | | |
|---|---|---|---|---|
| 1531<br>1585 | Hugh 3rd Earl<br>of Eglinton | = | Agnes Drummond<br>of Innerpeffrey | |
| 1563<br>1586 | Hugh 4th | Robert<br>of<br>Giffen | Margaret | =Lord Seton<br>1st Earl<br>of Winton |
| 1580c.<br>1612 | Hugh 5th<br>(no children) | =Margaret | | 3rd son of above, succeeds<br>by crown charter |
| 1588<br>1661 | Alexander<br>6th Earl<br>(Greysteel) | = | Anne, dau.<br>1st Earl of<br>Linlithgow | |

But 'Greysteel', as he came to be called because of his quiet but dangerous temperament, brushed aside the financial difficulties and, showing a princely disregard for the inconvenience of debt, which appeared again in many succeeding generations, pledged his entire property to obtain the funds.

'God send us some money, for they are little thought of that want it,' he is said to have prayed many years afterwards.

Although this transaction placed him in great financial straits for the rest of his life, he lived to see his titles and estates firmly established with every hope of passing them on to his children.

This ambition was doubly fulfilled. Through him, two hundred years later, the male line of the family was saved

*Diagram showing the descent of Lord Eglinton
from 'Greysteel'*

| | | |
|---|---|---|
| 1588<br>1661 | Alexander ═ Anne, dau.<br>6th Earl ǀ 1st Earl of<br>of ǀ Linlithgow<br>Eglinton<br>(Greysteel) | |

1613    Hugh 7th                James (4th son)
1669                                   1st of Coilsfield

1640    Alexander 8th              Hugh
1701

1658    Alexander 9th            Alexander
1729

1726
1796    *Archibald 11th  →  →  →  Hugh 12th Earl
            (no sons)                   of Eglinton
                                       1739
                                       1819

            1787 Mary ═ Archibald 1773
            1848                1814

### ARCHIBALD WILLIAM 13th Earl
### who gave the
### Tournament

* Succeeded his brother, 10th Earl, not shown.

from extinction a second time. His eldest son's direct descendant, the 11th Earl, had no sons and his fourth son's direct descendants became the successors. The eldest children of these two branches married and the fourth son of this union became Lord Eglinton who gave the Tournament.

'Greysteel' was famous not only for saving the family Earldom but also for living a vigorous life himself. As a man, a soldier, a politician and a courtier, he was held in the highest regard by his contemporaries. He was one of the many Scottish peers who renewed the Covenant against Charles I, and he fought against him with great distinction in several battles during the Civil War. Like many others, however, he disapproved of his execution and he lost faith in the aims of the Commonwealth and began to support the cause of Charles II. He was captured in 1651 and kept in prison at Berwick for nine years, forfeiting all his possessions, but he survived until the Restoration and was then released and given back his estates.

His life spanned the whole era which witnessed the ultimate decline of chivalry and saw the beginnings of modern thought. As a boy he certainly must have worn armour and taken part in tournaments, and as an old man he may well have found it hard to believe that such pastimes had ever been fashionable. He was thus, in his own life, in his own time and by hereditary achievement, the first head of the modern family. He married the daughter of the 1st Earl of Linlithgow who bore him five sons and he died in 1661 at the age of seventy-three.

From now on, for the next six generations, right up to the time of Lord Eglinton who gave the Tournament, two interwoven themes formed the pattern of family development. The first of these was consolidation and increase of all that 'Greysteel' had left them, and the second, always dragging close behind, was the need to find enough money to achieve it.

There are many papers about debts from this time onwards in the family archives. Some of these are classified 'good', others 'doubtful' and some 'desperate'. Seven years after 'Greysteel's' death his son had to sell £29,000 worth of property to meet some urgent creditors, and three generations and eighty years had to pass before every one of them was satisfied.

'Greysteel's' great-grandson, the 9th Earl, brought the family to solvency. But he no sooner did this than he borrowed huge sums himself and passed the burden on to his successors.

From this moment, in the early years of the reign of George I, the family debt was perpetual. Long minorities, faithful trustees and Acts of Parliament made no difference to it. It was like the sea which washed away the Eglinton Harbour at Ardrossan. It rose and fell and imperceptibly sucked the soil from the roots of the family tree.

The most interesting feature of the family history from the time of 'Greysteel's' death to the succession of Lord Eglinton's paternal grandfather at the end of the 18th century was the fact that for one hundred and twenty years the estates were managed by only three members of the family. This came about because 'Greysteel's' grandson was not interested in estate management and handed over the whole property to his son on his eighteenth birthday. This son who became the 9th Earl controlled the estates for fifty-three years, first with such economy that all the debts were extinguished and then with such enthusiasm that every one of them was resuscitated.

In a way, he was quite justified in acting in this manner, for all the projects for which he borrowed money— enclosure, drainage, building and especially planting trees—greatly increased the potential value of the estate. All that his children had to do was to live the way he had done himself—at first plainly for forty years, paying off the debts, and then on a moderate scale with their unencumbered income.

His sons, however, found this philosophy tiresome and each succeeding generation only accepted the convenient parts of it, taking loans as fast as they could and admonishing their children to pay them back.

The 9th Earl was responsible, too, for a special Will which in later years brought an irreparable family disaster. He entailed the lands which he had bought himself—Dundonald, Kilmaurs, Glassford and Southennan, on his children generally, male or female. The great danger in this arrangement lay in the chance that one of his heirs might have only daughters. For if an Earl died with daughters but no sons, the old Eglinton estates and titles would pass to the nearest male relatives but the new lands of the 9th Earl would remain in line to his own female children. So the new heir would only inherit half the total estate.

This precise event happened in 1796 with Lord Eglinton's father and mother, for his mother became heiress to the 9th Earl's new estates and his father, a cousin, the heir-apparent to the old family lands and Earldom; since the two married, the whole inheritance was kept intact.

In the 19th century, however, it happened a second time and the old titles and estates and the new lands again became separated. The estate was split and ever since the two valuable parts have remained in different possession.

After the death of the 9th Earl in 1729, only two earls remained before the succession changed to 'Greysteel's' younger line, the Montgomeries of Coilsfield.

These two were brothers, Alexander the 10th and Archibald the 11th, and they both showed particular ability combined with all the best traits of their ancestors. They were manly, generous, amusing and hospitable; intelligent farmers, distinguished courtiers and efficient holders of many important administrative posts. The 10th Earl, especially, made real contributions to Scottish agriculture by adopting the latest methods on his estates and breaking down many old-fashioned prejudices by the success of his experiments.

Some people thought him a crank because he tried to discard his peerage, finding the House of Lords frustrating and believing that he could be more useful in the House of Commons.

He was not really a peer, he said, because he had lost his patent, and therefore he ought to be treated as a commoner.

The Dean of the Faculty of Advocates in Edinburgh, however, ruled that the loss of patent was no proof of loss of nobility and doubtless the Earl's heir, his brother Archibald, was extremely glad to hear it; but for some time he renounced his title and called himself Mr Montgomerie.

'Don't forget horse howing if you love Scotland,' he wrote to his brother when the latter was on the eve of a duel, his passion for agriculture making him forgetful of the possibility of his brother's death.

But the 10th Earl himself was the one to lose his life. He was shot by a poacher on his own estate in 1769 and died, unmarried, at the age of forty-six.

With the succession of Archibald Montgomerie, 11th Earl, Lord Eglinton's maternal grandfather, the senior male line of the Setons came to an end. Almost two hundred years had passed since 'Greysteel' had staked his career to uphold the Montgomerie titles and estates and not one of his children, grandchildren, great-grandchildren,

23

great-great-grandchildren had shown themselves unworthy of it. They had lived honourably and usefully, serving their country and increasing their estates, and if they had also borrowed money, there were few landowners who had behaved differently, and at least they had never done so for themselves but always in the best interest of the family.

When the 11th Earl died, only four years before the beginning of the 19th century, the family had reached their highest level of magnificence. They were rich, grand, influential and popular and could look back on 700 years of ancestry with frank and open pride.

The one thing they lacked was an up-to-date castle. The ancient house at Eglinton—'strong but rude', according to a contemporary—was small and old fashioned and altogether unfitted for modern life.

Luckily the new Earl who now succeeded happened to have a penchant for architecture and had just built a delightful small house on his own estate at Coilsfield.

The moment his cousin died he sent for an architect.

It was no good, late in life and rather unexpectedly becoming Earl of Eglinton, Lord Montgomerie and twenty-fourth holder of the lands of Eagleshame if he had to live in a ruin.

He realised he would have to find some money; but if twenty-four generations had managed to do so, he felt convinced that he could find some, too.

In Hugh Montgomerie, 12th Earl, and Lord Eglinton's paternal grandfather, all the family characteristics burst forth uncontrollably. He had spent many years in the Army, seeing active service in America, and had then retired to his family home of Coilsfield and become a Member of Parliament. Since he was only a third cousin of his two predecessors, he might have expected to receive only a third part of their ancestral temptations, but instead he inherited three times the force of every one of them. The excitement of being the Earl unhinged him and, having passed fifty-seven years of his life in comparative simplicity, he now determined to live as he really liked.

As well as delighting in architecture, he particularly enjoyed surveying and civil engineering, having, in the latter part of his career, been Government Inspector of military highways in Scotland and having, with great pleasure and regardless of cost, surveyed and constructed dozens of roads and bridges.

He now, therefore, surveyed and inspected the Eglinton Estates and at once he observed the need for several improvements.

First, he demolished Eglinton Castle to the ground and rebuilt it, ignoring the architect, in a style, as his factor put it, 'uncommonly elegant and peculiarly his own.'

Next, he rejuvenated his accounts by taking control of the richer half of the family estate which had just passed by tail general to his cousin, the late Earl's eldest daughter. He arranged her marriage to his eldest son and appointed himself trustee of her settlement.

Then he embarked on a major work of hydraulic engineering. He commenced a gigantic harbour on his estate at Ardrossan on the Firth of Clyde designed to hold a hundred ships of all sizes, and began a canal at Glasgow at the same time by which to connect his harbour direct to the city. The idea behind this was that ships could then avoid the longer tidal route of the river and be towed conveniently straight to the centre of the metropolis.

Two things went wrong with these arrangements. Every winter the sea destroyed the work he had done in the summer and every year the hazards of navigating the river by sail were diminished by the increased efficiency of steamships.

The whole magnificent project became a failure. The canal was never finished; the harbour was hardly advanced beyond a breakwater, and the only thing that was ever completed was a charming small house at Ardrossan called The Pavilion—a kind of luxury surveyor's office from which he issued his instructions.

In spite of all these disasters, however, the scheme was sound in its day and the very best experts were used to survey it. The chief of these was Thomas Telford, the famous designer of many other canals and dockyards whom the Earl had known personally for many years.

This canal (wrote Telford afterwards), is a striking instance of the risk which exists in an active nation of undertaking any new work which requires much time in completion; for although it may be very hopeful when projected, yet so rapid has of late years been the progress of invention that some novelty is frequently introduced which totally alters the case, and interferes with former establishments; for instance, no person in 1805 suspected that steam boats would not only monopolise the trade of the Clyde, but penetrate into every creek where there is water to float them in the British Isles . . .*

This was certainly true; but long after the general scheme was abandoned, enormous sums had to be poured into the enterprise. The sea kept silting up the harbour and washing it away, and more and more money had to be spent on simply preserving the foundations.

The old Earl was annoyed by set backs, but not in the least dispirited. Steam ships or sail, he remained convinced that in the end it would pay the family to finish the harbour, if nothing else. He borrowed money again and again and, like so many of his ancestors, justified himself by saying

* Life of Thomas Telford by himself, 1838, p. 69.

that the only thing his successors would have to do would be to live simply for the next forty years and then enjoy the fruits of his investment; for he himself had lived like this as a young man and he knew the value of economy.

Happily, too, in this case he was in a position to insist on it. His son was dead and his grandson, the future Lord Eglinton who gave the Tournament, was only a baby, so he tied him up with knots of trustees and forced him to live beside him at Eglinton Castle.

The old man loved the child tyranically, beating him and giving him candy. In after years Lord Eglinton described him: he was 'little, ugly, hardheaded and irritable,' his nose stuffed with quids of tobacco, and still wearing his hair in the old-fashioned military pigtail. He spent his days racing and hunting and his evenings entertaining his friends; when he was alone he wrote poetry*, played the violin or read about his forbears in the peerage.

Lord Eglinton was happy with him for, although his mother had married again and was living in England, her place was filled by a loving spinster aunt. Like most other boys of his generation, he was brought up on tales of knights and chivalry and he passed his childhood contentedly in the castle, dreaming of days gone by and filling the bright new rooms with the ghosts of his medieval ancestors.

And although Eglinton Castle was only twenty years old, it was just the place in which to imagine past generations of the Montgomeries. It was built in the latest romantic style like a medieval fortress, with turrets, battlements, castellations and a moat.

---

* He is said to have written the Canadian Boat Song:
  'From the lone shieling of the Misty Island
  Mountains divide us, and a waste of seas,
  Yet still the blood is strong, the heart is Highland,
  And we in dreams behold the Hebrides.'

The old Earl was immensely proud of it, far prouder than if he had finished twenty harbours and canals from Glasgow. For it stood for the things he valued most—the respectable wealth, noble status and genuine medieval origin of the family.

It is not easy to maintain a dynasty successfully, and more than male heirs or money, luck or even a Crown Charter are necessary. A sense of history is needed, too, to appreciate the inherited honours and to play the part of tenant-for-life constructively. Without this historical instinct—the enjoyment of family possessions, the pride in past achievements and perhaps, too, ambition to add to them—no succession is likely to last for many generations.

But the heirs of the Montgomeries had all possessed this instinct and none more strongly than the 12th Earl who built the castle.

When he died at the age of eighty in 1819, there were only forty-two earls in Scotland and his creation was older than all but six of them. Twenty-four generations lay behind him, and also three flourishing cadet branches, all with their own estates.

Eglinton Castle was indeed a fine home for the head of such a dynasty—a massive symbol of all their characteristics, their antiquity, importance, generous hospitality and perhaps, as well, their disregard of economy.

Its antique elevations, beautiful round hall and spacious, comfortable rooms gave just the right impression. They gave a feeling of graceful nobility and of all those honours and achievements which their founder Robert de Mundegumbri must have wished for his descendants six hundred and sixty-two years earlier when he married the High Steward's daughter and acquired the nearby lands of Eagleshame.

The medieval lines of Eglinton Castle gave one other

impression, too, which became extremely important to Lord Eglinton.

At this time, in the last years of the Regency, the Gothic idiom was overwhelming the 18th century taste for

*Table of Debts left by the Earls of Eglinton*
*1665–1819*

| Ref: | Earl | Date of debt | Merks Scots | £ Stg | £ Stg 1952 |
|---|---|---|---|---|---|
| | Greysteel 6th, died 1661. No record | | | | |
| Slip 1079 | 7th | 1665 | M.328,484 | £20,000 | £140,000 |
| | 8th | No record | | | |
| | 9th | c1700 | | NIL | NIL |
| Slip 7571 | 9th | 1729 | | £18,000 | £126,000 |
| Slip 7571 | 10th | 1769 | | £60,000 | £360,000 |
| Slip 7571 | 11th | 1796 | | £40,000 | £160,000 |
| Trust A/C | 12th | 1819 | | £269,000 | £720,000 |

1. Scots pound = one twelfth of pound Sterling = 1/8d.
2. Merk = two thirds of a Scots pound = 1/3d.
   (Both these statements come from the O.E.D. under 'pound' and 'mark', and the equation of Scots to Sterling pounds is taken at the date of the union of the crowns, 1603).
3. Conversion to the 1952 equivalent. The tables used for this conversion are those in *Economica*, November, 1956, 'Seven centuries of the prices of consumables'.
4. The Slip numbers refer to documents in the Scottish Record Office.

Classical simplicity, and the more romantic and picturesque a building looked, the better it pleased the fashionable imagination.

Already the 19th century craze for the Middle Ages was almost universal. Medieval history absorbed the writers of the western world and architecture stood on the brink of the Gothic Revival.

Thus the antique design of Eglinton Castle was a massive symbol of social taste as well, of the taste of the times and the mood of the family, their contemporary outlook and modern ways, which set them up in the front of fashion, themselves a symbol of Gothic enthusiasm.

In this form Lord Eglinton was to immortalise them. For the Gothic mood was expressed in many other ways besides historical novels, poetry and architecture.

It appeared in politics, machinery, dress, conversation and in every other field of the national existence. A strange medieval fever swept over the European continent. The days of chivalry obsessed the minds of everybody and knights in armour stirred a thousand dreams.

4. Lady Jane Montgomerie and the infant 13th Earl of Eglinton
(by Raeburn, c. 1816)

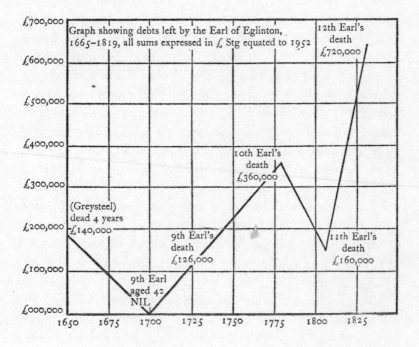

£700,000

Graph showing debts left by the Earl of Eglinton, 1665–1819, all sums expressed in £ Stg equated to 1952

12th Earl's death £720,000

£600,000

£500,000

£400,000

10th Earl's death £360,000

£300,000

(Greysteel) dead 4 years £140,000

£200,000

9th Earl's death £126,000

11th Earl's death £160,000

£100,000

9th Earl aged 42 NIL

£000,000

1650  1675  1700  1725  1750  1775  1800  1825

31

**D**

# Chapter Three

LORD EGLINTON was born on the 29th of September, 1812, at the Casa Mistretta, Palermo, the fourth and last legitimate child of the 12th Earl's heir, Lord Montgomerie. He was christened Archibald William by the Rev. Eyre Obins, Chaplain to Lord William Bentinck, the British Minister to the Sicilian Court and Commander in Chief in the Mediterranean. In the same week and in the same house a daughter was born to his father's mistress, and this child was called Elizabeth. Lord William Bentinck with General and Mrs Campbell of Inverneil became the children's godparents.

Lord Eglinton's father, Lord Montgomerie, the eldest son of the 12th Earl, was then aged thirty-nine, a man of charm and good looks but of no great personality who left little mark on his contemporaries. A Major General in the Royal Glasgow Regiment, he was placed in charge of the British Mission during the absence of Lord William the following year, but 'The poor man,' according to the latter, was 'reduced to death's door by the anxiety and annoyance he has experienced from these people.'* His health failed and, forced to sail for home, he died of consumption at Alicante on the 4th of January, 1814, at the age of 41, and was buried at Gibraltar.

The rest of the family who had travelled, too, reached Scotland safely, including the future Lord Eglinton; being

---

* The Bentinck Papers, Nottingham University, Bentinck to Admiral Hallowell, 23rd Oct. 1813.

then still an infant and having an elder brother, Hugh, who became the heir, no one took any notice of him.

The next year his mother married again. From the point of view of the Tournament, this proved an event of the utmost importance, for his mother's choice, Charles Lamb, as well as being heir to a baronetcy, together with several estates including the one in which he lived called Beauport, near Battle in Sussex, and a comfortable income of £12,000 per year, was due to become the Knight Marshal of the Royal Household.

This appointment carried a salary of £2,000 per year and—at least according to Sir Charles—conferred precedence over all other baronets in the Kingdom. In medieval times, as deputy to the Earl Marshal, it had been a valuable position, giving access to many of the Earl Marshal's prerogatives, including the arrangement of court functions and the judgment of combats and disputes of chivalry. It was now only a sinecure but it came to life at the time of a coronation. Then the Knight Marshal had to ride in the royal procession and manage the ceremony of the Champion in Westminster Hall.

But Lord Eglinton's grandfather who knew the Lambs, and did not like them, was not impressed by Sussex baronets or indeed by anything else. Having always approved of Lord Eglinton's mother because, as the family's richest heiress, she had sensibly married his eldest son and properly given him several grandsons, he was now thoroughly displeased with her. If she married an Englishman like Lamb, the whole income from her enormous fortune would be lost to the Eglinton Trust for the rest of her life.

This would not do when every penny of it was needed to support his harbour, the biggest single investment the family had and from which her eldest son would eventually benefit.

He explained the matter as patiently as he could, reminding her of his position as head of the Montgomeries and trustee of her marriage settlement. If she wanted to marry again she must choose another cousin and keep her fortune within his control. If she persisted in espousing Lamb she would only commit an act of selfishness for which she alone must take the consequences.

He did not bother to explain this threat but the moment she married Charles she discovered his intentions. Under a medieval Scottish law, known as Tutory Dative, she was forced to place her sons under the guardianship of their next male agnate over the age of twenty-five—in this case Lord Eglinton's grandfather—and leave them behind at Eglinton Castle. They were to be looked after by their Aunt Jane, her late husband's sister. Their mother could see them whenever she wished but, since her home was now 450 miles away in Sussex, this privilege was virtually meaningless. It only served as a cruel reminder that in reality she would hardly see them at all.

Thus her marriage to Charles Lamb had two results for Lord Eglinton. It caused him to lose his mother at an early age and in effect become an orphan; and it gained him a step-father in later years who, because of his inherited position, was one of the few people in the world who was personally interested in reviving a tournament.

Two years after this, his elder brother died of croup and left him the Eglinton family title of Lord Montgomerie and made him heir to the earldom and both his mother's and grandfather's estates. Although he was only four years old at the time, he never forgot the terrible effect which this tragedy had on his grandfather.

' I remember to this hour the storm of grief by which the old man was struck down,' he wrote in his diary forty-four years later.

The old earl erected a monument to the dead child and inscribed it with the characteristic elegance of his own vanished 18th century.

TO THE MEMORY OF HIS BELOVED GRANDSON,
HUGH
WHO DIED THE 13TH JULY 1817,
AT THE AGE OF SIX YEARS AND A FEW MONTHS:
A CHILD OF PROMISE.
ON THIS SPOT, ONCE HIS LITTLE GARDEN,
THIS STONE IS ERECTED
BY HIS AFFLICTED AND DISCONSOLATE GRANDFATHER,
HUGH EARL OF EGLINTON.

He made no mention of the child's mother and it is unlikely that he even thought about her. Life for him, at the age of seventy-seven, was too short to bother with sentimentality. There was only time for matters of real importance. He raised a further £150,000 by sales and mortgages and, with one last exasperated turn of energy, flung it all into the harbour at Ardrossan.

The effect on Lord Eglinton's character of this bereavement was no more than anyone might have expected. Suddenly becoming the direct heir of a 750 year old dynasty, he soon became unmanageable. His aunt Jane who looked after him was 'affectionate, warm hearted, pious, excellent in every relation of life . . . a bright example of every precept she inculcated,' but she was no good as a disciplinarian. She dressed him up like a courtier in sky blue suits with gold frogs, and adored him, petted him and allowed him to do whatever he liked.

Each birthday she composed him an ode, and this year's, which ran to eighteen stanzas, contained the following:

*I*

'All hail, dear boy! whose merits claim
This tribute from a Bard ethereal:—
(I own my calling; but my name
Is like my nature—*immaterial*!)

*II*

'Of all the Sylphs who dwell in air
(Not AYR, for female Sylphs so noted)
Few tend the objects of their care
So well as I—your own devoted!

*III*

'Your playful JOLIE\*, but for me
Would grow so fierce, you could not trust her,
And worthless would your DIAMOND† be
Did not my care preserve his lustre.'

*XVI*

'I mark your Mother's happy smile,
I see your fond Aunt's flush of pleasure,
And watch your Grandsire's eyes, the while
He gazes on his cherished treasure!'

*XVIII*

'Farewell, dear boy! my song must end,
Your fond and faithful Sylph remember
Thro' life; for *every* month your *friend*,
And *Poet Laureate* for *September*!'

From this it seems that he did at least see his mother
occasionally. It was no wonder that, growing up in the
beams of so much doting attention, he remembered this
time of his childhood with happiness.

The year after this, in 1819, his grandfather died and
he came into his inheritance at the age of seven as the
13th Earl of Eglinton. His mother certainly must have
hoped that now she would get possession of him; but it

---

\* A favourite dog.    † His pony.

turned out otherwise. Under his grandfather's will he was left to his Aunt Jane and five tutors to live at Eglinton for the next seven years until he reached the age of fourteen. After that he could live with whom he liked although the tutors would still be responsible for him. This, too, was to have an important influence on his character. He was not used to having five apparently aged men telling him what to do with himself. Whenever he had the chance he tried to annoy them. He was backed up in this by his mother. She maintained a polite and sufficient relationship with them but swore she would have a revenge.

It was only now, when the old Earl was dead, that the family found out the terrifying state of his finances. Under his will which he had drawn up when Lord Eglinton had become his heir in 1817, he had left £1,000 a year to Aunt Jane and £4,000 a year to his harbour. After dealing with a few other small annuities to servants and specifying other annual expenses as might be necessary—such as the upkeep of Eglinton Castle for which he allocated £700—he instructed his trustees to pay the balance of income each year against his debts. Only when they had settled everything could the Trust be liquidated and the management of the estate be handed over to Lord Eglinton.

The very first glance at the balance sheet showed this to be impossible. It was simply a repetition of the old family philosophy of expecting the heir to live on a bean for forty years until, towards the end of his life, he became solvent and could start to spend freely. At the present rate of nett income, it would have taken at least thirty years to discharge the debt without any allowances for emergencies. The gross income for the first year, 1820, was £27,435; the minimum expenditure was £17,881; the outstanding debt was more than a quarter of a million.

The trustees—or tutors, as they were known in Scotland—originally appointed under the will were as follows:

Sir David Hunter Blair, aged 52, a neighbour and friend of Lord Eglinton's grandfather; Lt. General James Montgomerie, aged 65, Lord Eglinton's great uncle; Richard Alexander Oswald of Auchincruive, aged 49, Lord Eglinton's uncle by marriage; Alexander West Hamilton of Pinmore, aged 55, Lord Eglinton's first cousin once removed by birth and also by marriage; George Russell, Writer to the Signet (Solicitor), aged about 42, of the firm of Tod & Hill in Edinburgh. Alexander West Hamilton acted as agent to the trustees and held the title of Commissioner.

Their first decision, taken at once, was to disregard the testator's instructions and cease all except the most vitally essential payments to the harbour. At this moment it was a pure white elephant. No ships of any size could berth in it. The canal from Glasgow had never been finished so that nothing could reach it from the land.

This necessary and sensible economy was the best of many which the tutors were forced to take during the next twelve years and no group of five men, faced with many vexatious problems, ever sacrificed their time more freely or sensibly, or ever received less appreciation from those to whom they gave it.

The greatest difficulty which confronted them was the calamitous depression in agriculture which followed the end of the Napoleonic war. Nearly all the Eglinton fortune came from farm rents and in 1817, when the will had been drawn, all land and farm produce had been more valuable than at any time in living memory, due to the usual shortages produced by war. During this year, many farm leases had fallen in and these had naturally been renewed at the currently augmented level. All plans set out in the will had been based on this inflated income.

But when the war came to an end food was once more easily imported and farm prices began to drop.

The annual rental value of one of the Eglinton farms called Caprington, for example, fell from £390 in 1819 to £285 in 1827 and this latter figure was fixed, according to a note in the Trustee's Minute Book, after the farm had been 'much improved by the tenant.'

Each year between 1820 and 1827 the Trustees were forced to allow abatements of rent, often as much as 20 per cent, and only by the most extraordinary care and economy were they able to end these years with any surplus. West Hamilton, the Commissioner, generously declined all his fees although he was entitled to £300 per year, and this selflessness was typical of all of them.

Each year they managed to balance the books and to put aside seven or eight thousand pounds towards the mortgages. The worst year of all, and one of national crisis, was 1826. After this things got easier, so far as the management of the estate was concerned; but then they had to deal with Lord Eglinton. On the 12th of September he reached the age of fourteen and was, according to Scottish law, partially able to manage his own affairs. He could make decisions so long as the Trustees approved of them. This meant, in other words, that he could legally make a nuisance of himself. That he meant to do so was fairly quickly seen.

Apart from Aunt Jane's birthday eulogies there are few papers about his childhood before this point. He was taught lessons first of all by a small Irish tutor called John Kerr who was left £100 in the 12th Earl's will and who also wrote him long birthday paeons. They were no good and Aunt Jane must have laughed at them. Kerr was followed by a tall Englishman who was succeeded by a petulant Welshman. Then there was school. Lord Eglinton

39

remembered nothing about his tutors in later years except their relative size, but the fact that he got through three of them in three summers shows that he was difficult. The Trustees thought so, certainly, and when he was nine, in 1821, they recorded in the Minute Book that it was time he went to school. He was too young to go to Eton and they sent him to one at Mitcham, probably Richard Roberts', one of the two small boarding academies there which prepared the sons of gentlemen for public school, though its name is not recorded. Here, for the first time, 'Young Hopefull' as he described himself sardonically, discovered what life from home could be like.

Even at this distance of time I shudder at the very thought of it (he wrote in his diary forty years later) and I cannot understand how I could have been kept there so long, but I suppose my just complaints were not credited. A more selfish, ill tempered, niggardly brute than the Master (there was but one for 18 boys) never existed, and any interference of his wife was always to our detriment. We were abused and cudgelled, we had no amusements, we were half starved and washing was unknown. For breakfast three small pieces of dry bread and a mug of milk was the allowance, for supper one piece with a smaller quantity of milk, and for dinner one plate of meat and a helping of pudding. On Friday evenings two foot-pans, without any change of water, did service for the whole eighteen boys, and on Saturday our necks and arms were washed, but all other portions of our bodies were left to the chance of what might happen in the holidays.

At the end of four years he left and spent the summer at Richmond with his Aunt Jane before going to Eton. He began to develop his lifelong interest in the turf and appeared for the first time in the Racing Calendar, winning a match against Sir James Boswell of Auchinleck for 100 gns over half a mile with a grey mare called Violet, ridden by a famous jockey called Tommy Lye. He began, too, to show signs of the family carelessness about finance, and Sir David Hunter Blair, the principal Trustee, had to remind him about economy. But this was the final summer before his fourteenth birthday and he paid no attention to him.

His mother, with whom he stayed, too, during these holidays, encouraged him in this attitude and made mischief between him and the Trustees deliberately. She did not blame Sir David for having kept her child because, after all, he was only doing his duty, but she did blame him for nagging the boy about money before he had actually got into debt. Being extremely rich herself, she had never bothered about this sort of thing. She thought it was ridiculous and only likely to make a person grow up extravagant. Quite unexpectedly, at this moment she was given a chance to cozen the Trustees out of a useful slice of capital, and both she and her husband, Charles, laughed so much about it that they nearly gave themselves apoplexy. Having worked out the necessary tactics, she made the Trustees a proposition. With all the innocence of their own honesty they discussed it at a meeting and, finding it apparently to the benefit of the family, wrote that they agreed.

When her first husband, Lord Montgomerie, had died in 1814, she had been given a life interest in a house called Coilsfield, the family seat of Lord Eglinton's grandfather, in which she and her husband had lived after they were married. It was a pleasant modern house in the classical style, small by the standards of those days, with 140 acres of park. She had filled it with her own inherited furniture and pictures and, after her husband's death, had let it furnished to the Earl of Glasgow for £1,000 per year; for when she had married Lamb she had moved to the south and never had any use for it.

She now wrote to the Trustees that, as she was never going to live there again, she would like to give it up. If they would buy all its contents she would, in return, surrender her life interest.

Since the furnishings were entirely hers and, if any disaster had happened to Lord Eglinton, they would all have gone to her children by Lamb, and since they were all of family interest, the Trustees agreed unanimously. They offered her £4,000 for the lot and thanked her for taking the trouble to think of it. They recorded in the Minute Book that they thought this was a 'most advantageous transaction'. For they also considered the annual rent of £1,000 from Lord Glasgow. After saving it for four years to replace the capital, they could use every penny as surplus income towards the payment of the debt.

The moment the money was paid and everything was settled, Lord Eglinton's mother sprang the trap. She had quite forgotten, she said, to mention the fact that Lord Glasgow was giving up his lease. She was most sorry to have been so stupid. She hoped they would find another tenant soon.

The Trustees were fearfully angry at this development and even their calm report in elegant script in the Minute Book shows their frenzy. They could not sell Coilsfield because it was part of the entailed estate and in this year, when bad weather had caused an almost total failure of crops and the whole country was gripped by economic depression, nobody was renting furnished houses in the country. The hopes of finding another tenant were nil. They were forced to manage Coilsfield themselves and when they did so they found it extremely expensive.

Quite certainly because of this transaction, they took an obstructive line shortly afterwards when they met to decide Lord Eglinton's allowance for Eton. He had asked for enough money to take some horses with him. With an instantaneous, firm and quite unanimous voice, they refused it. He was not going to Eton to spend his time and the family money galloping back and forward to Ascot. If he wanted exercise, he could play games and if he needed a horse he could be like everybody else and manage with Shanks' pony.

This rebuttal caused a storm of which there is still an original account and it gives an interesting picture of at least one side of Lord Eglinton's character at this age.

Lord Eglinton was furious and wrote Sir David Hunter Blair a rude letter. Sir David became furious, too, and rode over to Eglinton Castle one Sunday morning from his home nearby, marched him into a dressing room and gave him the sharpest lecture that any earl at the age of 14 had ever endured in his life. Lord Eglinton sat in a chair and glared at Sir David and said nothing. Sir David then went home to Blairquhan but Lord Eglinton continued to sit in the same chair and refused to eat or speak or move for the rest of the day until he went to bed in a rage at nine o'clock. Every half hour Aunt Jane popped in to console him with love and sweetmeats, but he sulked on and would not be comforted.

The next morning Jane wrote to Lord Alloway, now one of the Trustees, a poignant letter on mauve paper. She knew that the Trustees must do what was right, but she begged them to allow Archy just one little horse. He was truly contrite, thoroughly understood the principles of economy and would never spend an extra penny again.

She made Lord Eglinton write him a letter, too, in the same vein which contained the statement that he only wished to be on good terms with his guardians and had no wish to change them. This was a reference to the fact that he was now in a position to do so, having passed his fourteenth birthday. It was a plain lie and he admitted it afterwards. Possibly at that moment he may have meant it, held as he probably was in the consoling arms of Aunt Jane whom he loved genuinely; but as soon as he went south to Sussex and talked to his mother he quickly changed his mind.

At last, now, his mother had reached the moment for which she had waited for more than eleven years. She had no doubt prepared the ground for a long time and no doubt, also, she found it easy enough to persuade a spoilt boy of 14, who only wanted to please the person nearest him, that he ought to make up his mind and live beside her. No doubt, reasonably enough, too, he was more than ready to do so from natural affection.

Yet it was also a decision for which he felt ashamed for the rest of his life, for perhaps no mother in the world can love a boy so much as a spinster aunt, and certainly no aunt ever gave a nephew more love and devotion than Aunt Jane who for twelve years had truly dedicated her life to him.

But having resolved to make a change, he did so at once and whatever pangs he may have suffered when he thought of the pain it would cause his aunt, he certainly must have grinned at the thought of the shock on Sir David Hunter Blair to whom, on the 6th of November, 1826, he addressed the following letter:

My dear Sir David.

As I am now determined to live in future with Mamma, I think it right to inform you of it, and I beg you will make this known to the other guardians, and I hope that none of you will object to it.

Eglinton.

What Sir David wrote in reply is not recorded but the Minutes relate that it pained the guardians considerably. Its abrupt tone was quite unnecessary, and it followed by only four weeks the note which had said exactly the opposite. Since the request was reasonable enough, however, and because they only wished Lord Eglinton well, they decided not to make any difficulty.

Lord Eglinton interpreted this differently and recorded in his diary that they received his letter with consternation and astonishment. The only reason that they ever gave in to it was because they had not the power to do the reverse.

There was nothing more for the Trustees to do now except to arrange his annual maintenance, and his mother wrote that if they would give her 'undisputed care of his person' she would undertake to pay all his school expenses, clothes and servants' wages for the next four years for a round sum of five hundred pounds a year. The Trustees thought this was reasonable and agreed to it. She thanked them and, being always ready to release a parting shot, added that she had not, of course, meant this to include the cost of his journeys to Scotland. If any of them wanted to see him, they must find the money for this journey themselves.

This was a dig at Aunt Jane who had generously offered to stay in the Castle and keep it aired until he should want it. Only a year later, however, she became engaged to a neighbour—John Hamilton, a brother of Alexander West's, the Commissioner—and moved to a pleasant small mansion called Rozelle, somewhat like Coilsfield, which was also part of the family estate. Lord Eglinton offered it to her for life, rent free. This, in turn, was a dig at Alexander West who was then living there. He resigned his lease but also resigned his appointment as Commissioner. He must have felt that to receive notice was really the last straw after all he had done, including foregoing his salary. In fact, there was more to come for he could not even, without the greatest difficulty, get an expense of £862 which was then owing to him. Lord Eglinton travelled up to the Castle and, when he had settled down, sent Sir David Hunter Blair an enormous account for the cost of moving in there. His mother came with him and so did her husband, Sir Charles Montolieu Lamb.

It was only natural from now on that Sir Charles Lamb, by mere proximity if not because of his position as step-father, should help to form Lord Eglinton's character; and this he certainly did. He had succeeded his father in 1824 as 2nd baronet and Knight Marshal and at this time, as he approached forty, had become a fading Regency Buck and a rich, worldly court functionary. His own family had mixed feelings about him. They all agreed that at home in Sussex he was a kind, hospitable and amusing host, but they also agreed that, although he was wealthy and often extremely generous to servants, it never seemed to enter his head to give presents to anybody else, particularly to themselves, his penurious relations.

He liked living with people who agreed with him and, except for an odd fancy for music, for which he had no ability at all, he had no time for the arts or intellect or any of the people who had anything to do with them and in this respect he was even conspicuous amongst his friends who shared the same opinions. He spent much of his time abroad, having villas in France, Italy and Switzerland, and he travelled between them in two huge, four-wheeled mustard coloured carriages, known as Berlins—one for himself and one for his wife—followed by an enormous retinue of servants. He caused Nice to become a popular wintering place, as Lord Brougham had done similarly to Cannes, and he earned the title of 'Le Milord Paysan' by

5. Sir Charles Lamb at Geneva, from an engraving (artist unknown)

riding about the countryside in Byronic *déshabille*, scattering coins in the streets of the villages.

In 1831 he was painted at Geneva by an unknown artist, possibly Danby, by all accounts very characteristically.

Years later Lord Eglinton wrote that 'He was, without exception, the most selfish, arrogant and immoral man I ever met with';* and certainly, seen in this portrait with a wicked, melancholy smile on his lips, the only features which seem to be missing are a pair of satyr's horns on his brow and cloven hoofs splitting the toes of his pumps.

He seduced women wherever he went and encouraged Lord Eglinton to do the same, often passing his mistresses on to him. For a boy of fifteen this was a fresh experience and Lord Eglinton rather enjoyed it. Sir Charles assured him it was quite normal although, of course, better concealed from his mother.

Lord Eglinton's career at Eton, where he now went, was not marked by any kind of distinction either in work or sport. He lived with a tutor of his own—as many students did in those days—and shared lodgings with a boy called James Bruce, son of the Earl of Elgin. These rooms were over a confectioner's in the High Street and, primed in the technique as he was by Sir Charles Lamb, he soon won the confidence of his landlord's daughter, spending the afternoons in her arms, consuming bottles of gin and bowls of quinces. His first tutor was a friend of the family's, to whom he was much attached and who left after a year to marry a cousin, an unidentified Miss Montgomerie. During this time he learnt a certain amount and was kept in control. But his next tutor, although also officially living with him in the same lodgings, actually stayed in Windsor and from then on Lord Eglinton did as he liked.

The headmaster of Eton at that epoch was the famous

* Diary.

E

and terrifying Dr Keate who once publicly flogged eighty boys with a birch in one day, but in spite of Lord Eglinton's easy habits and inattention to work he was only beaten once, having been caught in one of the fields up the river shooting partridges.

Many boys were there with him who took part in the Tournament 12 years later and six of them played a major part in it and became knights—Lords Waterford, Alford and Cranston, Sir F. Johnstone and Sir F. Hopkins, and his half-brother Charlie Lamb, while many others became their Esquires. His future brother-in-law was there, too, Thomas William Newcomen, son of the 2nd and last Viscount of the same name who ought, therefore, to have been an 'Honourable' but in fact was not because he was illegitimate. Lord Eglinton preferred rowing to cricket and won an oar in Britannia in the 4th of June regatta. He was much annoyed from time to time at being called Lord Eddystone Lighthouse. But this feeble joke was also inappropriate, for he was not particularly tall or strong at that time and only achieved his fine slender figure and exceptional ability at games several years later after he left.

He did this at the age of 16 when he went to live with his mother and Sir Charles Lamb in charge of another tutor. This man was no better than the last and his main accomplishment was billiards at which, in consequence, Lord Eglinton acquired an exceptional ability. From now on for the next five years, until he became of age, he simply enjoyed himself, travelling about Europe, falling in love, becoming well known as a crack steeplechaser and learning to drink the extravagant amounts of claret that young men of his set had to be able to consume without becoming incapacitated. Little record of his life during this period exists except his own.

The quantity of claret I imbibed during that winter was fabulous (he wrote of 1832, the year before his majority), the bets and matches of all sorts I made were innumerable, the scenes at night were far from creditable, and the headaches in the mornings were dreadful to think of.

So great a gap exists between his age and ours today that such a life may seem disreputable, especially for a young man who was born to wealth in spite of debts and to great social position and consequent responsibility.

1832 was the year of the Reform Bill, a year of poverty, hunger, cholera and tumult—one of the most critical in England's history when civil war seemed inevitable. But Lord Eglinton never mentioned these things in his diary once. He took a long time to grow up and mature and become the serious and responsible member of the aristocracy for which his family remember him with pride. In his late teens and early twenties he just moved in his own exclusive set of hunting dandies, dressed as they did in the young-exquisite style of amazingly tight buckskin breeches, Hessian boots and sublimely coloured tail coats, and lived, loved and laughed throughout the year from early morning until late at night.

His mother was rich and gave him plenty of money; even so, he was constantly running short of it. The Trustees' Minute Book records this. In the autumn of 1829, after leaving Eton, he asked that the £500 previously allowed to his mother should be given to himself and also be doubled. This was agreed. In 1831 he asked if the sum could be doubled again as £1,000 had proved 'quite inadequate.'

The reason for this appears in the Racing Calendar. He had opened a stud and begun racing seriously with three

49

horses, Paul Pry, Lucifer and a beautiful grey mare called Queen Bathsheba which brought him his first success by winning the Ayr Plate. The Trustees received this request more unwillingly. Eventually they acceded to it but they wrote in their minutes that they thought it was too much. Under all the economic circumstances that still prevailed, and considering all their efforts, they felt that £1,500 ought to have been enough.

In regard to this they were certainly quite correct, having themselves set a fine example of economy. During the last thirteen years, in spite of the steady fall in the value of money and the fall, too, in estate income because of the unavoidable abatements in rents, they had managed every year to put aside seven or eight thousand pounds towards the payment of mortgages. Now, in the last month of their management, when they came to draw a consolidated statement of their activities, they saw they had saved £89,000, of which £20,000 had been put to the redemption of shares in the railway to the harbour and the balance in paying off the debt. They had maintained the Castle and park and gardens, paid all the annuities regularly, reduced the expenses on the harbour to a minimum and had permitted Lord Eglinton a fair allowance. They themselves had taken nothing, even although they were entitled to their expenses, and quite certainly they were more than justified in telling Lord Eglinton not to be extravagant.

Advice and restrictions of this nature were not to Lord Eglinton's taste for under the will of the 12th Earl he acquired an annual allowance of £5,000 when he came of age but he did not gain control of his estates until the Trustees had extinguished the debt. This was going to take them another thirty years at the present rate—so far as he was concerned, more than a lifetime—and they did, in fact, only wipe it out just before his death twenty-four years later. Furthermore, £5,000 a year for a man in his position was no more than pin money. This was not merely by the standards of a spendthrift. As things were by then, it was hardly more than half the amount in real money that it had been fifteen years earlier when settled under his grandfather's will; and even if it had been doubled, it would hardly have maintained him more than adequately. His mother's income alone, for example, was £18,000 per year, so that £5,000 for her son who was head of an ancient and noble family with huge estates and equivalent responsibilities was obviously totally inadequate.

Luckily enough, however, the Trustees agreed about this, too, and a memorandum still exists in the hand of Sir David Hunter Blair proposing to change the will by Act of Parliament. This must have been the first suggestion he had made in twelve years with which each of his colleagues and Sir Charles Lamb, Lady Montgomerie and even Lord Eglinton all concurred instantly.

# Chapter Four

THE ACT of Parliament which changed the will of the
12th Earl received the Royal Assent on the 27th of June,
1834. It was called an 'Act to enable the Trustees of
Hugh Montgomerie of Skelmorlie, Earl of Eglinton . . .
to sell part of the Trust Estates . . .'* and it was back-
dated by eight months to take effect from Lord Eglinton's
birthday. It made him achieve at one stroke the very
dream of every man who has ever felt that he ought to be
rich but found himself chained to five trustees who were
only bent on saving his money.

He acquired complete, free and absolute control of all
his estates and escaped from the grip of Sir David Hunter
Blair for ever. At the same time he left the responsibility
and payment of all the mortgages to the Trustees. By way
of a pinch of salt to flavour the arrangement, he added the
cost of the Act of Parliament, itself £4,805 8s. 10d.

To enable them to meet these obligations, he arranged
for Coilsfield house and park—which was well known to
be a liability—to be sold as quickly as possible and also,
without sentiment for the past, the whole estate at Eagleshame, the original family property which his remote
ancestor, Robert de Mundegumbri, had worked so hard to
obtain from Walter the Steward seven hundred years earlier.

He himself accepted responsibility for the payment of
all his grandfather's annuities—£300 per year to both his
great-aunt Maria and to Aunt Jane;† £20 per year to his

* 4 & 5 Gulielmi IV. Cap. 21.

† Aunt Jane had married by this time and only received £300 per annum,
instead of £1,000 in the will.

52

retired nurse called Jane Wilson; and a few other small amounts to similar faithful retainers. These added up to the fair sum of £820 but, with the exception of Aunt Jane's, they were not likely to need paying for long; for all the other recipients were old and would soon be dead.

From Lord Eglinton's point of view all this was exceptionally satisfactory but it was, too, naturally enough, because of the probity and good sense of Sir David Hunter Blair and the other Trustees, much the best of the many alternatives which might have been adopted. Lord Eglinton probably laughed and thought he had got the better of Sir David but he ought, in fact, to have thanked him sincerely for having forgiven past ingratitudes and for still only truly thinking in terms of the family's benefit. It was certainly an unhappy decision to sell the estate of Eagleshame which had belonged to the Montgomeries since 1157 but the property was much the furthest from Eglinton Castle and therefore the least pleasure to Lord Eglinton personally, and also it was valued at—and in fact fetched—£220,000, almost exactly the amount of the outstanding debt.

As to the settlement of the debt itself, this, too, had become a problem of real urgency. The country was in a state of great turmoil and at any moment a sudden crisis might have caused foreclosure of all the outstanding mortgages. A financial earthquake of this kind would almost certainly have ruined everybody. To get rid of the debt by a sale—and as soon as possible—was therefore by far the wisest course. It was hoped, too, that other parts of the estate which were soon due to be connected to a railway and which already contained profitable coal mines and also —if it were ever finished—Ardrossan harbour, would all in time and with careful management increase in value and make up for the sale of the estate of Eagleshame.

All this would have come into effect if it had not been for Lord Eglinton's extravagance. But at twenty-one, with no debts and the captivating prospect of great income actually available in ready cash—and also having inherited both his grandfather's liberality and his mother's carelessness, to say nothing of having been educated by Sir Charles Lamb, a well known libidinous spendthrift—there was no possible hope of his being either frugal or practical.

The pity was that Sir David Hunter Blair did not have the wisdom or perhaps the means to anticipate this and prevent Lord Eglinton from getting his hands on everything. If he had allowed him, for example, one estate and some of the securities—enough, say, to provide an income of £10,000 per year—and kept the remainder within the Trust, the whole financial history of the family might have been different. For although Lord Eglinton might have been short for a while, he would in the end have inherited his mother's income of £20,000 free of trust, and until that time he might have been reasonably careful.

In the event he did gain control of everything, skilfully countering every argument and refusing every compromise. For the influence of old families like the Montgomeries was still, at that time, enormous, and any desire by a young peer to manage his own estates invariably commanded support in Parliament and general public sympathy.

So, in spite of the loss of £9,000 per year from the sale of Eagleshame, Lord Eglinton still inherited £20,000 per year with the prospect of the same sum again on the death of his mother who was then aged 46—a combined income which would have made him very rich indeed.

Unless a man of his standing and upbringing was born prudent and naturally interested in developing his estates he could not possibly have resisted the temptation to live extravagantly, at least for many years of his early life; and Lord Eglinton was not a man like this.

Shortly after the Act of Parliament had been passed, he discovered a trick he could play on Sir David Hunter Blair which made his mother and Sir Charles Lamb laugh so much that this time they nearly choked for a week. Once again it concerned the furniture at Coilsfield.

By some oversight, this furniture was not included in the agreement which placed the house in the hands of the Trustees for sale and Lord Eglinton tumbled to the fact that everything still belonged to him. He therefore told the Trustees that he wanted it. He well knew, however, that this was impossible, for the house had only recently been let with great difficulty, fully furnished, long after Lord Glasgow had left it in 1826, and the Trustees would be quite unable to break the tenancy and give him the furniture. So they found themselves forced to buy it again for £4,000, the very price they had already given his mother for it seven years previously. This practically finished all their dealings with him. It was, of course, the very line that Lord Eglinton hoped they would follow.

As his 21st birthday approached he travelled up to Scotland with his mother, step-father and half-brother, Charlie Lamb, and spent the last few weeks before the 29th of September supervising the plans for a grand parade and banquet for all the tenants at Eglinton Castle. This month the weather was beautiful and all the riots of the past year connected with the Reform Bill were forgiven and nearly forgotten. All his hundreds of thousands of valuable acres were bathed in peace and warmed in the bright, sunny, soft September air.

A printed list of instructions, with a plan of the procession, surmounted by a coronet, still survives amongst

Aunt Jane's papers at Rozelle and it gives an interesting picture of how such events were arranged at that time and also, so far as the procession was concerned, carries a significant foretaste of the same thing for the Tournament six years later, for which indeed it may have formed a precedent.

At half past nine on the day after his birthday, Monday morning the 30th of September, the whole of Ayrshire was rocked by congratulatory salutes of cannon at Ardrossan harbour and all the tenants assembled at Towerlands, a mansion two miles west of the Castle, and moved off, two by two, in the direction of Eglinton Mains, one of the principal entrances.

They were grouped according to the various estates on which they worked and were led by a Marshal, a band of music, a man on horseback carrying a banner and a Captain Orr, the tenant of Towerlands, who, with a Committee which walked after him, had dealt with the practical arrangements.

After the committee marched the groups of tenants, each preceded by its own band, drums or piper and each symbolised by a man dressed in rustick character such as a sower, or else by a horseman carrying an emblem like a tile, a cheese or a plough, according to the nature and produce of its district.

When they arrived in front of the Castle they were deployed round a prepared space which was roped off. Selected tenants danced a fling, while all the others were told to stand still and not to emulate them. After a reasonable time had been spent in this, as the instructions put it, 'healthful and enlivening exercise', a bugle was blown and the whole party marched off for sports and races at Bogside, Lord Eglinton's private racecourse within the park where he kept his stud.

Finally they returned to Eglinton Castle for the banquet. A number of official toasts and speeches were given, recitations were declaimed, a band struck up and everybody joined in songs and choruses. Some of these were traditional and well known but others were written especially for the occasion and handed round to be sung by those who could read them.

One was composed by a local physician, Dr Gibs, who described Lord Eglinton as a 'gem of the first water.' This lapidary tribute went down so well that it was still remembered six years afterwards and brought him a bit of luck. When the time came to apply for tickets to the Tournament, Dr Gibs wrote to Lord Eglinton, reminding him of this sparkling moment and, as a result, he received a ticket for the grandstand.

Lord Eglinton enjoyed the evening enormously and so did everyone else. No doubt, on this occasion, the Trustees paid for it since the Act did not come into effect until the following morning. But it must have been the last entertainment for which they agreed to provide.

From the next day, the 1st of October, 1833, legally, financially and traditionally, Lord Eglinton pushed off into the world on his own.

As a parting gift the Trustees gave him a bonus of £5,000—a single payment of what would otherwise have been his total annual allowance under his grandfather's will.

But also, in a last brutal measure of financial integrity, they gave away to his creditors all the rest of the money they had in the bank in cash at that moment. It was practically a whole year's gross income, fifteen thousand pounds.

Lord Eglinton's career from now on until he gave the Tournament, and indeed for the next quarter of a century until he turned his attention to politics, can be summed up in a single word of five letters—sport.

He never bothered with social life and, during the next five years, he was only mentioned four times in the national newspapers like *The Times* or the *Court Journal* for doing anything of general interest to Society.

On the 31st of July, 1833, he betted an officer in the Ayrshire Yeomanry that he could race him fifty yards round a post and back again if he were on foot and the officer on horseback. The officer took the bet and Lord Eglinton won it easily.

On the 1st of May, 1834, he took his seat in the House of Lords as Lord Ardrossan, the family's barony of the United Kingdom which had been granted to his grandfather in 1806. He supported the Tories and did so, without wavering, for the rest of his life.

Then, on the 30th of November, 1835, he fell badly while hunting in Leicestershire and broke his collar bone.

He received, on the 16th of July, 1836, an honorary appointment held by both his maternal and paternal grandfathers before him: the Colonelcy of the Ayrshire Militia.

He can be seen as he must have appeared at the age of 21 when he raced the officer in a life-sized portrait by the Edinburgh artist, Blackburn, no doubt commissioned by Aunt Jane, for it still hangs above the stair at Rozelle. His expression appears to be rather peevish but perhaps he was bored by having to be painted, compelled to sit against his will, unable to curb his aunt's adoring insistence.

So far as his own account of his life in these years is concerned there was, according to his own words in his diary, nothing of public interest worth noticing and nothing of private concern that could be decently recorded. He kept women as he kept horses—amongst them possibly Elizabeth Howard who became famous as the Comtesse Beauregard, mistress of Napoleon III. She came to the Tournament rehearsals in St John's Wood, to which Lord Eglinton may have invited her, although at that time she was kept by another. But no woman is identified, even by an initial, except one who cannot be traced, a 'beautiful Fanny B.'

Apart from the outline of these activities which, in spite of the encouragement they received from Sir Charles Lamb, were quite normal for a young man of wealth at that time, there is no mention in his diary of any incident during these years except vague references to playing cricket in Switzerland and hunting stags with the Duke of Orleans in the forests of Compèigne. In other words, even when he was abroad, he spent his time in sport.

Naturally enough, when he was passing through London on his way to or from Sussex or Ayrshire, he went to Court, attended balls, lounged at Crockfords, and left his card on various hostesses of the day, in his case principally Lady Blessington, whose salon happened to contain the group of people he found most interesting.

Benjamin Disraeli was among them, having just then, in 1837 at the age of 33, been elected to Parliament for the first time, and Prince Louis Napoleon, afterwards Emperor of the French, who began his first exile in England in 1838 and attended the Tournament as the principal Visiting Knight.

Lord John Manners was often there, too, with his cousin, Baillie-Cochrane, afterwards Lord Lamington, a neighbour and close friend of Lord Eglinton's in Scotland, and also George Smythe, later Lord Strangford, who became Cochrane's cousin by marriage. These three were as deeply, unconsciously steeped in the current romantic vogue for the Middle Ages as Lord Eglinton himself. They were all elected to Parliament shortly afterwards and, under the nominal and sympathetic leadership of Disraeli, they formed what was known as the Young England Party and preached a return to a more feudal way of life as the only cure for the evils of the industrial revolution.

This proved to be unrealistic but not because they lacked sense or ability. They failed to understand their times economically, although socially they epitomised them. In their admiration of the Middle Ages, in their pride of the part that their ancestors played in its history, in their appreciation of the remains of its splendid architecture and in their devotion to what they believed was its simple, feudal, chivalrous life, they were living symbols of the Gothic spirit, the inescapable, hypnotic essence that dominated their time.

These contacts were rare and casual for beyond his own county of Ayrshire Lord Eglinton did not bother with social life at all and, generally speaking, until he proclaimed the Tournament and became a figure of national interest, he was unknown except in the world of sport.

This exception, however, formed his whole life. During these early years of his twenties every season he became better known and more popular and his colours of blue and green tartan, embroidered with golden thistles and with yellow sleeves and cap, became more widely recognised and acclaimed at every racecourse from his own local one at Ayr to the great courses such as Doncaster and Newmarket.

In 1831, two years before his majority, he had started his stable with three horses and, riding himself at 12 st. 7 lb., had achieved local celebrity by winning three steeplechases in one day. Then, in 1833, he increased his string to five and was noted in the Racing Calendar for winning 100 sovereigns at Edinburgh with a bay gelding, Paul Pry, over two miles in a match against a friend who came to the Tournament as an Unknown Knight, Walter Little Gilmour. In 1834 he added three more horses, bringing his string to eight, and the next year he added a ninth and raced at Newmarket for the first time with a colt called Black Diamond, a name inspired, no doubt, by that of his boyhood pony so fondly immortalised in his 8th birthday ode by Aunt Jane. Finally, in 1838, he doubled the strength of his whole establishment and, with eighteen horses, let himself go on a racing career which became itself part of the great and exciting history of the English turf. His superb victories in the Derby, the St Leger, the Ascot Cup, the Goodwood Cup and the 'immortal' match with The Flying Dutchman against Lord Zetland's Voltigeur did not take place until after the Tournament and were thus still many years ahead of him. But in 1838 he won both the Northumberland Plate and the Liverpool Cup with a brown colt called St Bennett and eleven races out of nineteen with a bay gelding called The Potentate. He was, too, in this year, elected to the Jockey Club which even then with its membership limited, as it still is, to 75, was the most exclusive and coveted club in the country.

From the point of view of finance, however, all this was not done for nothing. Such incomplete personal accounts as still exist show that he lived at once to the full extent of his income and that very soon he began raising extra money by selling various estates which was, so far as the family were concerned, really worse than if he had done so by borrowing.

In 1834 he received as income from his factor and solicitor £13,200 and probably much the same sum in the years following, for which there are no accounts. In 1838, the next period for which there is any record, he received only £11,445, but he supplemented this sum by selling a small estate called Carcluie for £10,000.

This was the first of a series of sales which the whole County of Ayrshire began to enjoy as an annual event and on one particular occasion, 1847, the year before the death of his mother, they raised his income by £57,000.

The year previous to this he had sold the family harbour at Ardrossan to the Glasgow, Kilmarnock and Ardrossan Railway Co. for £74,000, possibly one tenth of the amount his grandfather had spent on it. And in the year before that, 1845, if not many years earlier, he had begun borrowing. A memo for that year shows a loan from the National Bank of Scotland in Edinburgh for £15,000. For he had sold most of his estates by that time although he had not, in every case, received the money, and he clearly began to look round for other sources of revenue.

Under the Act of Parliament he had received £50,000 in cash and securities as well as his estates and as time went on he seems to have spent this also. At all events, by the end of his life, all these sums of money—and doubtless many more that were not accounted for—had vanished without a trace.

But in 1838, the year before the Tournament, and for that matter for many years afterwards, he was still enormously rich and the cost of racing never really worried him. He never failed to win money with his horses and in 1849, when he won the Derby with Flying Dutchman, he netted £19,500 which at that time was a record, while for more than a quarter of a century his average winnings were more than £4,000 per year. He was lucky, too, with his wagers. He collected £30,000 in one day in 1842 when he won the St Leger with Blue Bonnet, and during his racing career, taking all his wins and losses against each other, he gained about £80,000. Of course, in terms of the cost of the whole, this was a trifle but it did at least prove a certain success.

In this year, 1838, with his election to the Jockey Club, and with his colours carried at all the great race meetings in the kingdom, life really began for him.

The great sporting journalist, Henry Hall Dixon, who was known as 'The Druid', wrote in the *Doncaster Gazette* that 'From 1838-40 the Eglinton Stud became a great fact.

For all the rest of the world in England in this year, the social world, the business world and, indeed, the entire community, literate or otherwise, who had ever inhaled the ubiquitous breath of romantic medievalism, ever heard of King Arthur's knights, ever turned a page of *Ivanhoe*, ever admired Gothic architecture or ever watched the sun setting against a crumbling battlement and felt the strange charm of history, the 'great fact' about Lord Eglinton was something entirely different.

It was first a rumour, then confirmed by a small entry on page 538 of the *Court Journal* for the 4th of August, that he planned to give a tournament.

At this moment, romantic interest in the Middle Ages which had appeared first a century earlier in the books and architecture of a few antiquaries was rapidly becoming a national mania.

The Oxford Movement had just developed in order to revive the medieval status, discipline and ritual of the Church, an ambition in its own field that was close to that of the Young England Party in politics. The Gothic Revival in architecture had just received public national approval by the choice of Barry's Gothic plan for the new Houses of Parliament. Tennyson's *Morte d'Arthur*, *Lady Clara Vere de Vere* and many other immortal medieval

63

poems had just been written, were circulating privately and were about to be published to form the first landmark in this popular field of Victorian literature. The Gothic wave was about to break.

Thus, because at this moment Lord Eglinton happened to announce his Tournament, he was acclaimed in a way that at all other times would have been impossible.

He was destined to become known throughout Europe for prowess in the lists as one of his kinsmen had been known before him, Count Montgomerie who killed the King of France in a tournament in 1559. He was due, too, to become the most widely known and popular nobleman in the country.

He was doomed, finally, to make his name a symbol of extravagance, to burden the family with a great debt and to provide history, in the Tournament itself, with the last example of a Gothic folly of the type common in the 18th century—the romantic product of a genuine enthusiasm which a more factual Victorian society was soon to ridicule and sweep away.

# Chapter Five

'When the Eglinton Tournament was first suggested,'
wrote Grantley F. Berkeley, 2nd son of the 5th Earl of
Berkeley, in his memoirs thirty years afterwards,

> I know of nothing that ever seized on the minds of
> the young men of fashion with such force as it did, or
> held out apparently so many romantic attractions. I can
> safely say that, as far as I was concerned, I was seized
> with an extraordinary desire to be one of those who
> would enter the lists, without at first considering the
> consequences which must inevitably attend on such a
> proceeding. Perhaps, assisted by the narratives of the
> *Wizard of the North*, and other illustrators of the olden
> times, all that I thought of for the moment was a
> Queen of Beauty, brave deeds, splendid arms, and
> magnificent horses.

This reaction of Berkeley's was characteristic of almost
all the young men and women of his class. Every one of
them had been steeped in the history of the Middle Ages
since their first efforts to absorb anything. Every girl at
some time or another had dreamed of being acclaimed a
Queen of Beauty by a knight in shining armour, and every
boy had day-dreamed similarly of thundering down the
lists in terrific jousts to deserve the love of a chaste paramour who would then crown him Lord of the Tournament.
To a generation christened Tristram, Launcelot, Isolde
or Guinevere and taught to read from the tales of King
Arthur's Knights, the thought of actually doing any of

these things was intoxicating. From the very first chance of its possibility, the Eglinton Tournament was news.

There is no way of understanding the extraordinary force and hypnotic power with which the image of the Middle Ages obsessed the minds of men and women at this time without studying the history of the movement from its beginning. It is often felt of those days which had no fast, multiple means of communication that no form of mass enthusiasm, no kind of universal craze, could ever have moved entire continents in the way that fashions move them today.

This is not true at all. Long before the reign of Queen Victoria, the romantic charm of the Middle Ages was felt in almost every corner of the globe, and the world sales and influence of a book like *Ivanhoe*, for example, with its famous description of the tournament at Ashby de la Zouch, were just as great, taken over a decade, as those of any successful book today.

The only difference was that ideas took longer to circulate. But when a fashion developed, it went deeper and stayed longer and often lasted for a generation. It sometimes influenced a complete era. And this was the case with the vogue for the Middle Ages. It took nearly a century to arrive, but when it came it dominated an epoch.

The last jousts to be held on English soil, the last friendly tilts between armed knights in the genuine unbroken tradition of the 12th century, took place in the reign of Charles I. They were held at Court for the celebrations at Easter and Whitsun, under the direction of Sir Henry Herberte, Knight, assignee to Sir John Ashley, Knight, Master of the Revelles, and are mentioned in his accounts for 1626.* There may have been others later, for the Easter Revels went on until 1638, but no mention is made of 'tyltinge'. It is quite certain that in this year,

* The Public Record Office, E351/2805, 1623–26.

when civil war broke out in the North, all sports like jousting came to an end.

During the next hundred years, public interest in medieval life declined with each generation until it virtually ceased to exist. This was true of Gothic architecture particularly and also of heraldry, the only aspect of chivalry which still had any practical function. Coats of arms remained fashionable during the Restoration but the heralds themselves became pedantic and expensive, their visitations increasingly unpopular, and after the Revolution of 1688 they were forced to give them up. Once they ceased to record and control coats of arms by calling on families personally, all knowledge and enthusiasm for the subject vanished. Applications for confirmation and grants of arms grew fewer and fewer. According to figures published by the Harleian Society* there were two hundred of these in the first decade of the 18th century, but in the fourth there were only forty. This was only four per year and meant that only one person approached the Herald's College for a coat of arms every three months. It seemed clear that quite soon nobody would bother to apply to them.

In 1732, in a last effort to save themselves from oblivion, the heralds convened the ancient Court of Chivalry, the supreme arbiter of heraldic disputes on the field of the tournament. Many gross breaches of their medieval privileges had been committed in the last fifty years and they felt it was time to assert their authority and put a stop to them. A particularly outrageous case had been that of a Mrs Radburne, a merchant's widow of Mark Lane, London, who, in 1728, had given her husband a heraldic funeral when her local herald, Clarenceaux King of Arms, had told her not to do so. She had designed the hatchment

* Vols lxvi, lxvii, lxviii.

and all the trophies of honour herself instead of having them done by the College of Arms, itself a fearful breach of heraldry, and then, naturally enough, because of ignorance, had mounted them all on the coffin backwards.

Although the Court sat lugubriously for several years, it found there was no means of making Mrs Radburne or anyone else pay any attention to it. The public simply laughed at the heralds and said they were fools with long memories. They were forced to adjourn without achieving anything and their successors did not convene again for two and a quarter centuries, until 1954 when asked to settle a case for the Corporation of Manchester.

After this there was nothing left of all the past magnificence of Chivalry except the presence on a few state occasions of a handful of havering heralds in tarnished tabards who appeared solemnly with rattling parchments and proclaimed announcements which nobody could hear.

'The boast of heraldry, the pomp of pow'r,
And all that beauty, all that wealth e'er gave,
Awaits alike th' inevitable hour,
The paths of glory lead but to the grave.'

Thus wrote the poet, Thomas Gray, in his famous *Elegy* which he began in 1742. He spoke from his own experience for, having lived in London close to the College of Arms where the heralds convened the Court of Chivalry, he himself had witnessed heraldry's extinction.

The mere fact that he wrote about it like this, however, with a certain nostalgia, showed, too, that he sensed the spell that was soon to revive it. He was charmed by its crumbling antiquity and for this reason, as well as lamenting its inevitable death, he preserved its spirit, used it in his work, and thus earned his place as the first major contributor to the medieval revival in literature. For he was, like all creative artists, ahead of the taste of his time; and, in finding emotional expression in the Middle Ages, he perfected an idiom which was not to be widely appreciated for another generation.

In the 1740's, therefore, interest in medieval life reached its lowest point and also started to revive. For in these years a small group of amateur antiquaries like Gray himself—Sanderson Miller, the architect, and Horace Walpole—began to study and appreciate many aspects of medieval life that were then unpopular. In this decade, Sanderson Miller built the first sham castles and ornamental Gothic summer houses. In 1739 Gray, on the Grand Tour with Horace Walpole, first recorded his interest in Gothic architecture. This was exactly a century before the Tournament. In this year, too, Lord Eglinton's grandfather was born.

In nearly every case and in nearly every stage, individually and collectively, the revival of interest in medieval life began with an interest in its architecture. The reason for this was simple. Suits of armour, manuscripts and most other material relics of the time were scarce, but Gothic buildings, decayed or otherwise, were still in use and could easily be studied anywhere.

The best known example of this sequence of development is that of Horace Walpole. First of all, in 1748, he bought his famous villa, Strawberry Hill at Twickenham, and after a few years turned it into a 'little Gothic Castle.' This is generally considered the first landmark in the history of the Gothic Revival in architecture, for although several other people were doing the same thing with their houses at the same time, his position in society, his great circle of acquaintances and his long life gave him a position of leadership.

He held the lead not only in architecture. As everyone

else discovered who took to living in a Gothic house during the next one hundred and fifty years, a new Gothic house needed Gothic furniture to give it authenticity; tapestries and suits of armour to increase its atmosphere; and coats of arms emblazoned here and there to suggest the medieval connections of the family who lived in it. As time went on, Walpole collected all these things, and set an example which many people imitated.

And, like a great number of other people who came after him, amateur as well as professional, many of whom had less ability, he wrote stories about the Middle Ages, too. In 1764, he published a novel called *The Castle of Otranto* which, like the purchase of Strawberry Hill in the field of architecture, is generally considered to mark the beginning of the medieval revival in literature.

It was a tale of the 12th century, filled with knights, castles, ghosts and combats. Walpole wrote it, so he recorded in the preface, after he dreamed of a gigantic hand in armour crashing on to the stair at Strawberry Hill.

As in everything else, he carried away the prize, too, in the field of Gothic dreams.

At this point in the history of the revival—at about the time of the accession of George III in 1760—it becomes necessary to specialise. Every aspect of life began to be affected by it. Not only the great obvious items like literature and architecture, but also the shape of the furniture, the binding of books, the layout of gardens and even the construction of domestic hardware.

A typical example of this was the stove designed by the architect John Soane for Lord Abercorn for the hall at Bentley Priory. It was six feet six inches high and cast in the form of a suit of armour.

Another was a mechanical hermit built for Lord Hill for his garden at Hawkstone in Shropshire. It lived in a

Gothic grotto and whenever anyone opened the door of its cell, it nodded its head.

Other people had real hermits installed in their grottos; but these living beadsmen were not so good, for they developed rheumatism, lost their tempers and failed to nod when visited.

Because all these things developed more or less at the same time, however, it is not so hard to form a complete picture of the movement as it might be otherwise. The history of one aspect was very like the history of all the others, and this is particularly true of the revival of heraldry. It developed hand in hand with architecture and literature. More people in more castles became more enchanted by Gothic literature, built more pediments for coats of arms, took more interest in their own antiquity and had more ambition for heraldic funerals. Thus, side by side with everything else, the interest in heraldry revived.

The first landmark in this particular revival was made in 1764 by a man called Norborne Berkeley, a distant relative of the earls of that family. First of all he followed Walpole's example and converted his house, a Tudor manor called Stoke Gifford in Gloucestershire, into a castellated mansion. It was 'helmèd with a gothic roof'* according to Henry Jones, a local bard, and its great front portico was graced with a huge coat of arms, while its battlements were fretted into the letters of Berkeley's motto: MIHI VOBISQVE.

Next, as soon as the building was finished, he applied to the College of Arms for a pedigree; for during the course of a study of his family's coats of arms and quarterings in the Middle Ages he had found out that he might be heir to a peerage. This was the ancient barony of

* *Clifton* a poem dedicated to Norborne Berkeley in 1768.

71

Botetourt: it had been created in 1305 but for three hundred and fifty-eight years nobody had heard of it because it had lain in abeyance.

A title falls into abeyance if it is claimed equally by more than one heiress, the direct male line having failed. Such an event evolves through the following anomalies: there is no law of primogeniture amongst women to direct it to the eldest; it can not be shared; it can not be deemed extinct so long as there are heirs to it. This happens only to medieval titles known as baronies by writ, and naturally only to those which pass in the female line. It occurs automatically if one of these titles descends to several heiresses.

Once this has taken place, the title rests in abeyance indefinitely. It can only be claimed, unless awarded by the Sovereign personally, by an heiress or one of her descendants who can prove that all the co-heirs and all their descendants are dead.

In the matter of the barony of Botetourt, however, Norborne Berkeley decided that this was the case. He therefore submitted his claim to the House of Lords.

After a number of hearings which caused a good deal of public interest and of which Horace Walpole wrote that 'the town thinks much, and I not at all',* the Committee of Privileges found that Berkeley's claim was substantiated.

The principal evidence had been his new pedigree and for this reason the heralds received a great deal of excellent publicity. For, having composed it from records made at the time of their medieval visitations, they demonstrated that after all—even three hundred and fifty years afterwards —they and their work were not entirely useless.

From their point of view, as well as Norborne Berkeley's, they scored another success which was almost better than

* Walpole to Lord Hertford, 27th Mar. 1764.

the peerage itself and which set them up and established the value of heraldry in the eyes of the public for ever.

In the records of Parliament and on all occasions of ceremony and protocol, Berkeley was given the precedence he would have had if his family had held the title continuously since 1406. And because there was only a handful of barons whose families had actually held their titles longer than this, Berkeley's rank and seniority amongst his peers turned out to be nearly the highest in the House.

The results of this piece of heraldic lifemanship were instantaneous. Every peer who had to walk behind Berkeley was furious. Every commoner of old family who had always known he was heir to a peerage began to study heraldry to see if he could prove it.

Norborne Berkeley died only six years afterwards at the age of fifty-three, a 'cringing, bowing, fawning, sword-bearing'* courtier, according to the bitter pen of 'Junius', and 'totally ruined but quite charmed't, according to Horace Walpole. He went bankrupt because of the cost of his case, gambling, extravagance and investment in a company which tried to convert copper into brass, and he earned the hatred of 'Junius' for having acquired the post of Governor of Virginia through Court influence.

He was an inconspicuous man and, except for his claim to the barony of Botetourt, nobody would ever have heard of him. But in the revival of heraldry, his success formed an important landmark as well as a critical precedent in peerage law. And during the next seventy years it inspired enthusiasm for heraldry enormously.

One of the direct and earliest consequences of Berkeley's case was a great increase in the number of books about the peerage.

* Wade's edition of *Junius;* V.2. p. 212.
† Walpole to H. S. Conway. Aug. 9th, 1768.

Before the accession of George III in 1760, there were few works on this subject available to the ordinary reader—Dugdale's *Baronage* of 1676 and Collins' *Peerage* of 1709 or its later editions being the only two to be found in most private libraries. But it was not long before others began to appear and before the end of the Georgian era at least twenty different peerages could be bought on any bookstall.

Some of these were plagiarised miniatures of existing publications and contained nothing original, while others were works of real scholarship and were so huge that two footmen with stepladders were needed to get them down from a shelf and carry them out of a library. Most of them never appeared again but a few were reprinted with new editions for more than a century and two of them—Debrett's and Burke's, which were first published in 1802 and 1822 respectively—are still standard works in print today.

The proprietors of some of the earlier peerages continued to republish, too, and in 1806 Collins' decided on a new 6th and enlarged edition. They looked round for a suitable person to supervise it and they finally settled on a man who had already published some gothic verses, two novels after the style of *The Castle of Otranto* called *Mary de Clifford* and *Arthur Fitzalbini* and who had, too, established a reputation as a meticulous and fervent heraldic genealogist.

He was called Samuel Egerton Brydges and his mania for pedigree was a byword. It became afterwards, as the years passed, a genuine case of gothic delirium.

Samuel Egerton Bridges—Bruges, Burges or Brydges, as the name had been spelled at different times—was born in 1762, two years before Norborne Berkeley's claim to the barony of Botetourt, the eighth child and second surviving son of a comfortable Kentish family. He lived to believe that his line was of great nobility and antiquity but one of the heralds proved during his lifetime that it sprang from inferior yeoman stock. From the age of eight, he developed a mania for heraldry and genealogy, and he used to pray for tempestuous weather to make all hunting, cricket and other forms of exercise impossible and to allow him to stay indoors by the fire in the library with a good, fat, complicated peerage. He was educated locally and at Cambridge and in 1783 he came to London, took chambers in the Temple and read for the Bar.

By the time he was called, in 1787 at the age of twenty-five, he had already pursued his own pedigree for many years and had pushed it back to the Earl of Comyn who came to England with William the Conqueror. He had shown, too, that more recently it came from the third son of the first Lord Chandos, a peerage created in 1554, and he had reached the conclusion that when the present holder of this barony died his elder brother who was called Tymwell would become the heir to it. Up to this moment he had spelt his name 'Bridges' but, to show his newly discovered kinship with the Baron's family who spelt it 'Brydges', he changed the 'i' to 'y'. He also, naturally, made his brother who was thirteen years older than himself, and in his view 'had no judgment at all', do the same thing. When the Barony became vacant two years later because of the death of its owner the Duke of Chandos, he forced his brother to make a claim for it.

The proceedings which followed were perhaps the most tedious and most farcical that have ever wasted the time of the House of Lords. When the claim was turned down for lack of proof, Brydges produced some more, and when this, too, was pronounced inadequate he began to forge it. As the years went by he conjured up every piece of mysterious evidence that was ever devised by a medieval necromancer.

He found a little black box in an attic which was full of documents, but they vanished when anyone lifted the lid. He quoted entries in parish registers, but these were spirited away when anybody wanted to see them, or else the pages—obviously tampered with—were unexpectedly turned into dust. He actually produced one crinkled parchment but, since there seemed to be nothing on it except a coat of arms and some hyroglyphics, a Mr Robert Lemon, an antiquary from the Tower of London, was called to apply a magic liquid which was said to revive invisible ink. This was done but if any ink had ever been applied it still could not be seen.

At last, in 1803, after thirteen and a half years in which the Committee of Privileges had sat twenty-seven times, they presented their opinion to the House of Lords that Tymwell Brydges 'had not made out his claim to the said Barony.'

If such a verdict were not enough, Egerton and Tymwell —by then on the brink of hysteria—proceeded to urge every peer by circular letter to attend the House to vote against it. This was considered a gross breach of privilege and finally wrecked their case. One of the very few peers who voted in favour of it was the infamous Duke of Cumberland. He did not care for the Barony or Egerton or Tymwell, but his current mistress happened to be Tymwell's wife.

Tymwell died four years later; but for Samuel Egerton this agonising and humiliating public defeat which, as he wrote in his autobiography, 'was received by our enemies with grins of extreme delight', was only a beginning.

During the next six years in which he was compiling the new edition of Collins' *Peerage*, a gigantic work which still serves as the standard reference of its kind for the Georgian era and for which his name will always be remembered, his own supposed rank and family antiquity obsessed his thoughts with the blind force of madness.

Every other consideration of health, sense or duty to his wife and children went down before it. From the date of his brother's death and his own supposed succession, he used the title as if he actually owned it and signed his letters '(*Per legem terrae*) Baron Chandos of Sudely'. When he came to describe the family of Chandos in his peerage, he explained his own claim for thirty-six pages, and once the whole work was finished he threw every other interest aside and wasted the rest of his life and his entire fortune in struggling to prove that his claim was valid.

In one year, 1823, he wrote thirty-three letters to the Prime Minister, almost none of which were answered. He then published at his own expense a thick book called *Lex Terrae* in which he pointed out to the members of the House of Lords that their powers were limited, and explained that in common law he was not bound to pay any attention to them. Finally, he compiled an enormous tome called *Stemmata Illustria* in which with a great shield showing three hundred and sixty quarterings he proved over three hundred pages his descent from the Merovingian kings in the 5th century and showed in more than two hundred and fifty different pedigrees that more blood of Charlemagne flowed in his veins than it did in those of the Royal Family.

In doing all this, he spent more than one hundred thousand pounds and all that he earned was a baronetcy for his work on Collins' *Peerage* and the doubtful honour of being parodied in Disraeli's novel, *Sybil* as a luminous genealogist called Baptist Hatton.

The time described in this novel is exactly that of the Eglinton Tournament and, being a satire of contemporary events, it gives an authentic picture of the extent to which the mania for claiming old peerages had spread. For by that time hundreds of people were chasing them.

'You would like to be a peer, Sir?' Baptist Hatton asks an old baronet, Sir Vavasour Firebrace. 'Well, you are really Lord Vavasour, but there is a difficulty in establishing your undoubted right from a single writ of summons . . . Your claim on the barony of Lovel is good: I could recommend your pursuing it, did not another more inviting still present itself. In a word, if you wish to be Lord Bardolf, I will undertake to make you so . . . It will give you precedence over every other peer on the roll, except three, and I made those.'

'It is wonderful,' exclaimed Sir Vavasour. 'And what do you think our expenses will be in this claim?'

'Bagatelle!' answered Mr Hatton. 'It will not cost you a paltry twenty or thirty thousand pounds.'

In 1837 when Sir Samuel Egerton Brydges died at the age of seventy-five—the last of a line that did not exist—his passion for pedigree and his obsession for composing great heraldic shields of coats of arms and quarterings had already become an accepted part of medieval revivalism. Many people of all literate classes did the same thing, while many others had, in spite of its absurd failure, become impressed by his furious pursuit of his medieval barony.

For slowly but steadily, over the long period since Norborne Berkeley had first successfully claimed his own, the ever widening spread of the medieval revival had made such claims more and more popular.

It was worked out by one enthusiast that since the year 1265 at least one hundred-and-one baronies by writ had fallen into abeyance. There was, for example, the barony of Sampson whose heirs had vanished in 1306 and which

6. Lord Eglinton, aged 24, on Black Diamond
(a painting by Ferneley, 1836)

might, therefore, be claimed by anybody. All that was needed was a nice foolproof pedigree to show that the claimant was a missing heir and a few copies of medieval documents to prove that all the other possible claimants were dead. These were not so hard to find as they might be. All the certificates could be supplied easily by any peerage lawyer or professor of heraldic genealogy.

For these experts were now in good supply. The heralds themselves, many solicitors and a whole group of fraudulent amateurs had appeared conveniently to fill the demand for them. In actual practice, it was almost impossible to prove a unique claim but, for all that, as this particular medieval virus reached the stage of an epidemic, more and more wealthy people determined to have a go at it.

Amongst those who failed were Henry Dymoke, the King's Champion, who claimed the barony of Marmion; Sir Robert Burdett who did not wish to waste his money and claimed five at the same time, Tyes, De Badlesmere, Latymer, Berkeley and Berkeley; Charles Kemys Kemys Tynte whose claim for the barony of Wharton was found to be in abeyance still between himself and four others. One of these was the friend and Ayrshire neighbour of Lord Eglinton's, a keen member of the Young England Party, whose name was long enough as it was: Alexander Dundas Ross Cochrane Wishart Baillie, afterwards Lord Lamington.

Many others succeeded, especially those of old family whose pedigrees were well authenticated already. The peak was reached in the years just before and after the Tournament when five baronies were claimed successfully which had such immense periods of abeyance that even the claimants themselves could hardly remember their origins.

These were Vaux in 1838, Camoys in 1839, Braye in 1839, Beaumont in 1840 and Hastings in 1841. The sum of the lengths of their abeyances came to one thousand seven hundred and fifty-three years.

The longest was Hastings which had lain dormant since 1290 and was claimed by Sir Jacob Astley as the junior co-heir of the junior co-heiress.

Technically, the best was Camoys. This had been held for only forty-three years after its creation in 1383 and had then been forgotten completely. It gave its new owner, the 3rd baron, precedence over the 17th baron Stourton whose family had held his title continuously in male descent for three hundred and eighty-four years.

Lord Stourton was absolutely exasperated by this, and so were many of his colleagues. They decided that it was high time that this particular heraldic dragon was knocked on the head; and since that day, with rare exceptions, only claimants with outstanding pedigrees have been considered for baronies by writ which have lain in abeyance for many centuries.

Although this decision spoilt the game of claiming abeyant peerages, it only encouraged the adoption of other methods of displaying family antiquity and medieval enthusiasm.

A group of baronets under a man called Sir Richard Broun, whom Disraeli caricatured in *Sybil* as Sir Vavasour Firebrace, tried to prove that the medieval status of the baronetcy as a whole had been that of another estate of the realm and, therefore, that all baronets ought to have seats in Parliament. Sir Richard claimed, too, that they ought to be styled 'Honourable' and before he succeeded to his father's baronetcy he demanded for himself the privilege of knighthood which, he said, had been promised by James I in 1616 to all baronets' heirs apparent. When the Lord Chancellor refused to present him to the Queen for this purpose, he assumed the prefix of 'Sir' anyway and signed himself 'Sir Richard Broun, *Eques auratus*'. Finally, in exactly the same manner as Sir Egerton Brydges, he compiled a book, *Broun's Baronetage*, in which he filled the preface with twenty pages of his own arguments and gave his own family three times as much space as anybody else's. He described himself as a 'feudal Baron' and 'chief of his race in North Britain'; for by that time his father had died and at least his rank as a baronet was indisputable.

Another and less elevated section of the community decided not to bother with the House of Lords at all and, taking a different tip from Sir Egerton Bridges or Brydges, took the matter into their own hands and simply changed their names from Smith or Green to what they supposed they had been in the Middle Ages, sometimes adding the particle 'de' in front of them.

De Burghs, De Veres, De Greys and De Beauchamps, all multiplied uncontrollably. A family called Mullins changed their name to De Moleyns. Another in Wales called Wilkins received a royal licence in the same year as the Tournament to assume the surname of De Winton. A few years afterwards, Thackeray's famous character, James Plush, the footman who made a fortune in railway stock, appeared in *Punch* as Jeames de la Pluche, and announced that his direct ancestor, Hugo, had landed in Sussex with William the Conqueror.

It has since been shown by historical research that, except in a few cases like those of Howard de Walden and Willoughby de Broke, the particle 'de' was never used in the Middle Ages except to denote where a person lived, and was never taken in a surname or written in a document except by accident. So that now practically all names of this nature are seen to be concoctions and, instead of proving their medieval origins, reveal themselves as Victorian gothicisms.

But at that time nobody knew or cared about this and several writers besides Thackeray made fun of those who adopted the Gothic particle.

'What can delay De Vaux and De Saye . . .
    And De Nokes and De Styles and Lord Marmaduke
        Grey,
    And De Roe? And De Doe?
    Poynings and Vavasour?'

wrote Richard Barham in his *Ingoldsby Legends*, a popular collection of satires on this and other medieval affectations, published in 1839.\* For the same reason, too, Tennyson wrote the lines:

> 'A simple maiden in her flower
> Is worth a hundred coats of arms'

and also:

> 'From yon blue heavens above us bent
> The Gardener Adam and his wife
> Smile at the claims of long descent.
> Howe'er it be, it seems to me,
> 'Tis only noble to be good.
> Kind hearts are more than coronets,
> And simple faith than Norman blood.'

both in the same poem, pointedly entitled *Lady Clara Vere de Vere*. His uncle who had inherited his father's birthright and whom he disliked had just taken the additional surname and arms of d'Eyncourt; and this had inspired him to write so contemptuously.

However trite Tennyson's remarks might have been, the mania for heraldry was so great by that time that few families amongst the upper classes or aristocracy wholeheartedly believed them. They felt that a maiden with sixteen quarterings had twice as much charm as one with only eight, unless the one with eight—perhaps the

\* *The Lay of St Cuthbert.*

daughter of one of the new, rich manufacturers—had sixteen times as much money.

Even those families who had many titles and quarterings already, like the Montgomeries, were bitten frequently by this form of medievalism and spent fortunes trying to substantiate their rights as heirs to others. Many a dripping interminable Scottish night was spent by Lord Eglinton's grandfather working out his claim to the Earldom of Mount Alexander, an old family honour which had gone to an Irish branch in the Middle Ages and which the Lyon King of Arms in Edinburgh told him was extinct but which he himself believed to be only dormant. He failed to prove it and all his time and effort were brought to nothing.

Lord Eglinton himself was luckier. In 1840 he was served heir male general to the Earls of Winton. This title, granted to the father of 'Greysteel' in 1600, had been attainted after the rebellion of 1715 and had thus automatically fallen dormant. In normal circumstances such an attainder would have caused a bar to any succession, but Lord Eglinton determined to get round it. With careful presentation, plenty of money, good solicitors and expert heraldic advice, he managed to prove his case by 'Speciality'.

Finally, for all those antiquaries, humble or great, professional or amateur, who had no ambition to change their names, to claim peerages or perhaps no money with which to do so, there was always the study of heraldry and genealogy for itself.

They could use heraldic terms as a form of wit in ordinary conversation like the boring herald, Memblazon, in *Kenilworth* who spoke of 'sejeant' instead of 'sitting' and 'reguardant' instead of 'looking', or else they could pass their time alone in their Gothic villas or mansions or chambers, reading peerages and composing enormous shields of coats of arms and pedigrees.

For at this moment in the 19th century when the aristocracy still took a romantic view of medieval life, and the middle classes had not yet spoilt the fun by treating it seriously, there was one thing that everyone wanted—rich, or poor, hoary earl or modern industrialist:—a big bright coat of arms with dozens and dozens and dozens and dozens of quarterings.

This pattern of development of the medieval revival in the field of heraldry—its last use on the field of the tournament in the reign of Charles I; its ultimate decline and apparent extinction in the 1730's; its sole preservation in the hands of a few antiquaries during the following decades; its reappearance and steady return to fashion amongst the upper classes from about the accession of George III in 1760; its final restoration to a state of universal national popularity in the reign of William IV and the early years of Queen Victoria—this cycle over the period of two centuries was the same for all other branches of the Gothic movement and thus for the movement as a whole.

Naturally enough there were variations in time and subject and in this decade or that certain aspects, like jewellery or archery, might be more revived than others, like music or the theatre, but taking the whole movement over the entire period, this was the general graph of its death and renascence.

The history of heraldry illustrates it well for several reasons. The facts are clear, simple and well authenticated by many contemporary documents; the life span and life's work of one man—Sir Egerton Brydges, 1762-1837— precisely covers the whole revival of it and stands as a symbol of all its values—its historical worth, artistic merit and pointless worship of often imaginary ancestors; and heralds and heraldry, being living relics of the days of chivalry in which they developed, were thus, naturally, of particular interest to all those who took part in the Eglinton Tournament.

Moreover, the influence and example of Sir Egerton Brydges' life impinged on the Tournament, too, in another way for, apart from every connection he had or thought he had with everyone else, he did have a genuine link with the family of Lamb of Beauport. It so happened that in 1821, because of inheritance, they had adopted the name of Lamb, but before that they had been called Bruges, Burges, Bridges or Brydges, and they also, like Sir Egerton, claimed kinship with the barons and dukes of Chandos. Furthermore, they were well acquainted with him, for although he lived in Geneva in voluntary exile, Sir Charles Lamb had many maternal relatives and a house in Geneva,* too, and for this reason he and the rest of his family often met him there.

Although most of them laughed at Sir Egerton and his claims and quarterings and ravings about pedigree, yet one of them took him seriously, loved and admired him, to some extent became his pupil and, from his early youth, like Sir Egerton himself, spent his days buried in books on the peerage and passed his sleep dreaming about knights and chivalry.

He gave his toys Gothic names as soon as he was old enough to call them anything; he drew his first heraldic shield with eight quarterings correctly blazoned in gay tinctures for a pet guinea-pig before he reached the age of ten; he began to write his first medieval manuscript on parchment and illuminate it with heraldic signs and knights in combat before he passed the age of puberty;

* The Chateau Banquet.

and he bought his first suit of armour and rescued his first damsel in distress even before he took part in the Tournament.

He was brought up in the same house and at the same schools side by side with a contemporary and half-brother with whom he shared all these dreams and possessions.

This half-brother was Lord Eglinton. The boy himself was the heir to the baronetcy of Lamb of Beauport and to the enchanting, authentic, medieval post of Knight Marshal of the Royal Household—the eldest son of Sir Charles Lamb and Lady Montgomerie: Charles James Saville Montgomerie Lamb.

# Chapter Six

CHARLES LAMB, who was known as Charlie in the family to distinguish him from his father, was born at Beauport on the 7th of October, 1816, four years and one week after Lord Eglinton, and was baptised on the 3rd day of the next month by the Rev. H. Rule Sarel, the local curate of Hollington in whose parish Beauport Park was situated.*

The Lamb family was an old one—Burges, as it was still called at the time of Charlie's birth—and it traced itself back with authenticity to a Giles Burges who was M.P. for Reading at the end of the fifteenth century, while it claimed descent in family legend from a Flemish merchant who came to England in 1230, calling himself Burges or Bruges after the city of his birth.

Whatever its precise origins, the family was one of age and reputable connections and its members had marked the pages of history from time to time in a small but honourable way. Colonel Roger Burges, a direct ancestor of the 17th century, had acquired fame in the Civil War by defying Cromwell successfully and holding the town of Faringdon in Berkshire. A century later, George Burges, another soldier, had taken part in the battle of Culloden and captured the standard of Prince Charles' body-guard, born by the Duke of Atholl.

This man's son, James Burges, the first baronet and Charlie's grandfather, had spent most of his life as an active Member of Parliament and had held the post of

* Hollington Parish Register.

87

Under Secretary of State for Foreign Affairs. He had resigned from politics in 1795 and had then achieved his baronetcy.

At the same time he had received the appointment of Knight Marshal of the Royal Household. He had asked for this because he wanted a position at Court and also because he had fallen under the prevailing spell of the Middle Ages and wished to assume the mantle of a medieval functionary.

Once he had retired from public life, he took to literature and, in 1818, the year before Sir Walter Scott published *Ivanhoe* and brought literary medievalism to a climax, he produced an epic in twelve cantos entitled *The Dragon Knight*.

A mere chance brought him the Lamb estate. This inheritance—which was worth about six thousand pounds per year and included properties in Hertfordshire, Suffolk and Leicestershire as well as a row of houses in Palace Yard, Westminster and a mansion in Golden Square—belonged to a Mr John Lamb, a friend and contemporary of his father's who had made money as an army agent and who, having no relations and being a bachelor, had bequeathed it to him in his father's memory. When Lamb died in 1798, however, he directed it first to another friend called Henry Cock for life and by all normal expectations Cock ought to have outlived Burges by several years. But Cock expired suddenly of a heart attack in 1821. So Burges came into it, and in that year he and his family changed their name by Royal Licence to Lamb.

The house and estate of Beauport where the family had lived for a number of years before they acquired the additional estates of John Lamb had been bought by James Burges in 1794 and was in East Sussex on top of the Downs, facing south towards Hastings, with superb views in all directions. In 1767 it had belonged to General James Murray, one of Wolfe's commanders in Canada, who had rebuilt it in the classical style and changed its name from Beacon Hill to commemorate the Manor House of Beauport near Quebec which had been Montcalm's headquarters before the battle of the Heights of Abraham in which he had taken part. Before him it had been owned by a local family of hop growers and brewers called Rivers. In all probability this was the family who built it.

As a place to live in it was well designed and comfortable and, apart from having an almost perfect situation, it was near the sea, had splendid woods close to it and also, beyond them, the great bare sweep of the open Downs.

It was a plain and pleasant rectangular mansion with sash windows and vaguely symmetrical proportions and was considered, naturally, by all the Gothic enthusiasts of the 19th century as a typical specimen of boring classical architecture.

In compensation, its local village was Battle whose single, straight, ancient street was dominated by the towers and castellated battlements of the great gateway of Battle Abbey. They marked the spot where William the Conqueror had defeated Harold in 1066, and thus they stood as a romantic reminder of the very advent of English chivalry.

Whether or not the existence of such a hoary and picturesque Gothic edifice so close to Beauport inspired the infant mind of Charlie Lamb with medieval ambitions as he walked or rode past it in his early years cannot be calculated.

Certainly it was a fact that almost as soon as he could read and write he began to do so about the Middle Ages and, even before that, to populate the woods and fields around Beauport in his imagination with as many knights and dragons as other children at other times might have filled them with goblins and fairies.

His childhood letters and manuscripts which, strangely enough, have managed to survive although the male line of the family has been extinguished, all the possessions sold or discarded and the house burnt and turned into an hotel, reveal his interests with charming enthusiasm.

In the earliest of the letters, written to his mother on the 16th of October, 1823, one week after his seventh birthday, he announced in the first sentence—without wasting time on preliminary civilities about the weather or anybody's health—that he was going to write the history of his life and adventures, another about the life of Miss Johnson, his governess, and a third concerning Minnikin, Pin and Toby, his guinea pigs.

After stating this, he reverted to everyday matters and said that he had been down to the sea to collect shells, an occupation which, like the study of the Middle Ages, absorbed him constantly throughout his life and which, on this Thursday, made him late for tea.

Then, after tea, Miss Johnson had read to him. She must have done so for several hours, for she got through the whole history of the Wars of the Roses and the reign of Edward IV. Charlie was perfectly entranced by it and told his mother that Edward was 'marvellously handsome but horridly cruel.'

So far as is known he did not, at that time, compile an account of his own life and adventures or of Miss Johnson's, but he did begin and actually finish during his childhood a complete history of the lives of many of his guinea pigs.

These animals, which were favourite pets of the 19th century and which, like shells, were one of the passions of his life, lived in the grounds of Beauport in what became a miniature guinea pig city. It was named Winnipeg and a great castellated hutch called Guinea Pig Castle stood in the middle of it, specially built by the estate carpenter for the King and Queen who were known as Geeny and Cavia.

The manuscript of this chronicle—16,000 words in length, half as long, for example, as the story of Alice in Wonderland—is entitled *The History of Winnipeg from the foundation to the Present time. BY ROYAL COMMAND.* and is written in eight tiny fat volumes which are bound in red and green leather. The style is a comic mixture of biblical phraseology and cockney slang and the narrative is drawn from his imagination, experience and also, according to the first paragraph of the eighth chapter of the third volume, 'from an ancient illumined parchment entitled register of Zeleyor which hath lately been discovered.'

It is illustrated with portraits in water colours of the guinea pigs, drawn from life, with their coats of arms correctly blazoned and tinctured and sometimes described as, for example, those of a warrior called Keelrat, 'a noble Winnipeg who bore for his arms—Arg$^t$ three rats keeled prop$^r$—'.

For, naturally enough, all the guinea pigs were of old Saxon, Norman or even Roman and Greek descent and anxious to prove it, either by displaying their coats of arms or else by assuming the Gothic particle. For 'every lord wished to be a Duke—every Squire a lord.'

The third chapter of the fourth volume which is a good example of the whole work begins as follows:

*The Reign of Albineus*
*the Yellow*
*Earl of Newton*

On the death of Polydorus, the unanimous voice of the people chose Albineus Earl of Ayton and Newton to be Lord Protector of the Kingdom of Winnipeg, with full and regal power. At the time of his accession he was

Warden of the marches, Hyparch of Winnipeg and Viceroy of the Kingdom—mighty offices such as were never before combined in one individual. And he had acquired vast renown in the border wars. Much was expected of him, and much indeed was required. For at this time the state of the Kingdom was seedy indeed. From a commission of enquiry instituted in May year 11 Farai was ruinous, and nearly deserted and the whole country of the border was desolated with war and abandoned by its people. A Census of the whole population including the people of Ermineus shews an amount of three decads and a half. But the spirit of energy, peace being restored, was soon infused into the people. Ino FitsRedais, surnamed the just was appointed bailiff of Peektown, and warden of the gate, bearing the same powers as Hyparch of Winnipeg, he was vigourous but gentle. Altogether perhaps the most perfect character in Winnipeg history. The numbers of the people under the firm rule of these Nobles augmented considerably. It was in August year eleven, that the Earl of Newton, the now a lover lover of peace, yet unwilling that chivalry should languish, inspired, likewise, with the love of Rosabel, Countess of Zelia, instituted the farfamed knightly order of the White Rose, with its well known device '*Sur tous les fleurs la Rose est Belle.*' This high honor was first conferred upon Sir Ino Fitsreds, Knight, Sir Heliodorous, Prince of Rarribun, Sir Alexander Lilli, Kt and Turkwine de Newton, Captain of the guard.

These noble and medieval guinea pigs and their lives and adventures absorbed Charlie for many years, at least until he was past the age of eleven, for he wrote to his mother from Eton on the 6th of February, 1828, and commanded her, as his Agent, to supervise the erection of a tombstone to Cavy, the first chatelaine of Guinea Pig Castle. Cavy seems to have died in the Christmas holidays and, since guinea pigs live for about six or seven years, her birth can be guessed at the early 1820's; and these years must roughly date the beginning of the Beauport dynasty.

As a piece of literature and an example of nursery Georgian gothicism, his work must be unique and, unlike most childish compositions which are soon forgotten, it lay in his mind and inspired him years later to go to the Tournament as a representative of its noblest Order of Chivalry.

In this way, in the best tradition of all fairy stories, the guinea pigs slept in their tiny graves for twenty years and then awoke as shining knights.

For although it was thought to be Charlie who galloped down the lists inside the armour of the Knight of the White Rose, in fact it was nothing of the sort, but the incarnation of one of the four original members of this Order who took it in turns to embody him. The Prince of Rarribun, Sir Ino FitsRedais, Sir Alexander Lilli or Turkwine de Newton, the finest flowers of the Chivalry of the city of Winnipeg.

There are two portraits of Charlie during his childhood, one painted by Kinson in Paris in 1821 and the other by Ferneley at Melton Mowbray in 1822. Kinson's was burnt at Beauport a century later and a poor copy of it, done by an old gentleman called Brooke which hung at Eglinton Castle was sold when the place was demolished in 1925 to an unidentified Mr Fraser for six guineas and has since completely vanished. A faded photograph of it exists, however, and also a lithograph. Ferneley's portrait, with all the charm and excellence for which that artist remains admired today, escaped the fire at Beauport because it was small enough to be snatched up and rescued, which

Kinson's was not, and it still belongs to one of Charlie's descendants.

Of the two, Kinson's is easily the worse, but it has more value from the biographer's point of view because it includes the only known portrait of Charlie's mother. It shows Charlie in life size, standing beside her in a smock against the marbled entrance of an Italianate room, looking past the head of a gigantic St Bernard which is lounging near her feet and staring up at her moodily. The family always considered that Kinson had made a good likeness of Charlie but had drawn Lady Montgomerie two inches too short, and the apparent magnitude of the dog which looks enormous seems to justify this criticism.

Ferneley's portrait shows Charlie in a grey top hat and pink riding costume, trotting across a field on a black horse with a collie running ahead of him, a hoary oak in the right foreground and the great classical portico of an unidentified mansion in the far distance beyond a lake. In this work all the subjects retain their expected sizes.

As might be expected from Charlie's manuscripts and letters, he appears in both pictures—and also the lithograph which has slight differences from the original—as a dreamy boy with a look of intelligence and sensitivity. His face is small, delicate and pointed and his head covered with jet black curls like those of his father. His hair and brows and eyes are so black and his skin so dark that he might indeed have inherited Moorish blood, as was often said of both of them. But no trace of such a mixture exists in their pedigrees unless it crept in with Anne Montolieu, his French grandmother.

Kinson's portrait gives this impression of foreignness particularly and in after years, with a black and curly beard and sidewhiskers, Charlie's aspect in armour was truly Saracenic. As a child, however, it made him in-

MARY LADY MONTGOMERIE & Mᴿ CHARLES LAMB.

7. Lady Montgomerie and Charlie Lamb (by Kinson, 1821) from an engraving in *The Memorials of the Montgomeries* by Sir Wm. Fraser

teresting and attractive. With his white gown-like smock touching his feet and his head of curls, he resembles the boy in the much loved picture of a later period who is seen in a desert in a nightie with various wild animals.* It illustrates the sixth verse of the 11th chapter of Isiah 'The wolf also shall dwell with the lamb, and the leopard shall lie down with the kid; and the calf and the young lion and the fatling together; and a little child shall lead them.' And certainly, if Charlie had modelled for this infant, he would have done so to perfection.

As often happens in such cases with children of radiantly angelic countenances, although Charlie had a way with animals and might easily have managed to make lions and leopards and lambs and kids lie down together by personal magnetism, he could not have done so by the assertion of holy innocence. For inside he was thoroughly wicked, or at least according to the opinion of the few adults who described him a quarter of a century later and who judged him then by the standards of orthodox Victorian morality. For no account of his childish character written at the time has come down to us.

While he was truly a born naturalist and loved shells, birds, insects and guinea-pigs, and much preferred to spend his time with them, even at that age, instead of with other children, he soon began to make seriously impious observations about them. It was not long before he decided that fundamentally there was little difference between beasts and men at all except, of course, that human beings could talk and were highly developed. Therefore, he concluded, the whole concept of the immortal soul was ridiculous.

In this, as in many other subjects, his ideas were ahead of his time; and if he reported his early life to his children

* By William Strutt, 1896, Brecon Cathedral.

95

H

accurately, and if they, in their turn, writing many years later still, recorded them correctly, he reached them all entirely by himself at a very early age.

He became an agnostic, a socialist, opposed to capital punishment and in favour of homeopathy and birth control, not knowing the predelictions of Sir Charles and the temptations he was likely to inherit in connection with this last doctrine.

The fact that upset his descendants the most was the early age at which he adopted all these practices. For, according to his first and practically illegitimate daughter who became the well known authoress 'Violet Fane' and who recorded these details about him in a biographical novel called *Sophy* in 1881, he was still only a child when he did so. He was hardly ten when he first began to think about them and in two years time had come round to them all, including an absolute refusal to pray and an open denouncement of religion. She could not refrain from adding in the novel that a judgment fell upon him because of it and that, like Saul, he lost his eyesight—which in actual fact he did before he was middle-aged.

At this point, it was generally felt by the family after-wards, his mother ought to have taken a firm line with him and led him back to the meadows of virtue. But as it happened, Lady Montgomerie herself had long since given up any idea of praying to God or supposing He took any interest in her although she was born, presumably, with His benevolence, into a coveted *milieu* and one of the richest heiresses in Scotland.

But when her first father-in-law, the 12th Earl of Eglinton, had assumed the custody of her sons against her will at the time when she married Lamb, and when she had prayed to be given them back and only suffered the death of her eldest child instead, she had quite lost faith in

God's justice or prayer's efficacy. If religion opened the gates of Paradise in after life, she was glad to hear it and she hoped her little Hugh was there already, but she herself decided to worry about this at a later date and for the time being to enjoy the world as she knew it. Naturally enough, she permitted Charlie to do the same thing.

In this respect, as well as in every other, Lady Montgomerie was a complacent mother and the perfect wife to Charlie's father who thought, too, that the only thing to do was to live in the present and to drink, travel and amuse himself so long as he had the inclination. If God existed at all, He clearly favoured the aristocracy, and as they were both born in the highest social scale—Lady Montgomerie especially—there was obviously nothing to worry about.

This particular aspect of both their philosophies—their aristocratic outlook and their belief that only Kings, Princes, Dukes (and not many of them, either) were better than the Earls of Eglinton—was one of Lady Montgomerie's dominant characteristics, and for her the world was divided simply into two social strata, the upper—containing Sir Charles Lamb, herself and their families, known privately as 'Ourselves'—and the other—embracing everybody else who were vaguely called 'The Others'.

She was two years younger than her husband, being born in 1787, and was thus twenty-nine at the time of Charlie's birth. How she met Lamb has not been established, but she seems to have known him well before the death of Lord Montgomerie for she planned to marry him only eight months afterwards and would have done so but for illness. Possibly she met him in Sicily, for the secretary to Lord William Bentinck was called Lamb and he may have been a connection of the Henry Lamb who bequeathed the fortune to the Burges family, and he may have brought them together. If this happened, and if she met Sir Charles at Palermo, she might well in such a restricted community have got to know him intimately. Otherwise, in spite of his Arabian good looks, of the Knight Marshalship and the family baronetcy, she might, in a larger city, have classed him as one of 'The Others'.

She herself was not particularly handsome, having a rather heavy face in her portrait photograph, with a low forehead overhung by coils of dark hair, lidded eyes, full nose and lips and the same pointed chin that is seen in Charlie. She was not considered beautiful by the Lamb family and, in fact, to speak the truth, she looks rather goat-like. But in the lithograph she is depicted much more delicately, and perhaps the lithographer drew from Kinson's original while the photographer worked from Brooke's copy. As both are missing it is now impossible to say. Her presence and carriage made up for her looks, however, for she was above middle height and had an imposing and gentle manner which, in the best sense of the word, was thoroughly aristocratic.

By temperament she was yielding, lazy and affectionate, loving animals like her son, Charlie, proud of her wealth and the comforts it brought her family but too lethargic ever to attend to its management or even to dictate its succession after her death. So she died intestate and caused an appalling struggle between the Lambs and the Montgomeries for, although her estates were entailed and went to Lord Eglinton, her marriage settlement, drawn up by the old 12th Earl, was, in the view of both parties concerned, such a 'triumph of Scottish Law' that no one from that day to this has ever been able to untangle it.

She had much money, plate, furniture and many family pictures and jewels which had not been left in tail male by her grandfather, the 9th Earl, in his new Will in 1729, but left in tail general and had therefore descended to her absolutely. Nevertheless, the Montgomeries claimed them as family heirlooms and the Lambs held on to them and said they were nothing of the sort.

So it was that if anyone asked her to see about anything, to make a Will or come to a decision about the future, she nodded and promised to do so but never got round to it.

The same process occurred over Charlie's atheism. She meant to tell him to try to be a Christian but she quite forgot and only smiled when she said good night to him, and constantly omitted to insist that he said his prayers.

Probably the last time that he went on his knees for any purpose except for a maiden's love was when he attended mattins on his last morning at Eton in the autumn of 1828. There, where daily worship was compulsory, he must have knelt on the hard floor beside Lord Eglinton, secretly raced mice and beetles up and down the long bench seats of the hard stalls beneath their faces or sat and admired the chapel's Gothic sublimity while he listened to the Scriptures.

A year or two before that he had probably worshipped beside Lord Eglinton at Mitcham, for although it is not certain that he went with him to the academy there, it is likely that he did so. There, in terms of early Gothic experience, he was lucky, too, for Mitcham's ancient parish church had just tumbled down and been rebuilt in a style that was 'strictly Gothic'. It was one of the earliest examples of the more 'correct' Gothic work which preceded the Gothic Revival in church architecture and it was, according to Pigot's Directory of 1824, 'perhaps as beautiful a structure as is to be met with in any village in the Kingdom.'

Whether he went to Mitcham or not, it is certain that he stayed with Aunt Jane at Wimbledon at times between

1825-1827, for several letters written from there to his mother are among those that she treasured. They reveal him, in these last years of his childhood, as a very normal, genial little fellow, except for his special interest in shells, butterflies and insects. Every letter contains references to them, either pleas to his mother to be sure to collect some from where she happened to be staying, or else reports of having written to those family friends who were going abroad to do the same thing, or else details—already too technical for normal understanding—of those he had found locally. They are often sketched, too, for Charlie knew how to draw charmingly.

It is clear that he ought to have been a naturalist and in this respect he took after his grandfather's sister, Mary Anne Burges, who was born in 1763 and was known in the family as Maria. In her circle she was recognised as a woman of outstanding intelligence and ability, reading Latin, Greek, German and Swedish, speaking French, Italian and Spanish, drawing and painting excellently and being also a keen botanist and leaving among her MS a beautifully illustrated account of the lepidoptera of the British Isles.

She was also, it would seem inevitably, an absorbed student and composer of Gothic literature and, although she never published in this field, she left to the family a MS novel in twenty-four books entitled *Aracynthus*. It is faultlessly written in a clear hand, and superbly illustrated in water colours with almost as many pictures of knights in combat, maidens and bleeding dragons as there were of dragonflies and moths in her catalogues of lepidoptera.

It is evident from Charlie's letters that he loved staying at Wimbledon with Aunt Jane and his half-brother and was much happier there than he was at Eton. He was not miserable at school but all forms of work beyond his specialised interests bored him. He seems to have suffered from cold and chills frequently which he welcomed in a way for they forced him to stay indoors out of class. They allowed him, in writing to his mother, to enjoy the contradiction in terms of being 'out' because he was 'in' and enabled him also to stop wasting his time with scripture or mathematics and to concentrate on insects and medieval history. He often wrote to his mother for books on these subjects and she sent them to him conscientiously, including Mawe's *Conchology*, Nicholson's *Encyclopaedia*, *The Cunynghame Tales* and *Melmoth*. This last, a grisly Gothik Tale, he enjoyed particularly.

There is an account of him in his half-brother's diary during this time, written many years afterwards but still probably describing him as he appeared to many people at that age as his personality developed.

I have seldom met with a more extraordinary character than his (Lord Eglinton wrote). He was gifted with talents of a very high order, a wonderful memory, and a power of argument that I have never seen surpassed, but there was no discretion, no judgment, no system, and I do not believe that under any circumstances he would ever have made a practical or brilliant use of his advantages. As he was, he was utterly thrown away. He was spoilt by both parents, by kindness on the one side and indifference or worse, on the other. He left school at the early age of 12 and had no teaching, except what he picked up for himself afterwards. Biassed at first by the base and irreligeous principles of his father, under the influence of a bad course of reading and an unfortunate choice of friends, he became I fear almost an infidel, he never went into society, and spent his time entirely in the country among his shells, insects and guinea pigs, of which latter collection he had several hundred. Of his unfortunate marriage and miserable end* I shall speak afterwards. With all his faults he was a fine, honourable, warmhearted fellow, and I was very fond of him.

There is an account of Charlie's departure from Eton in one of his letters, or rather a prayer that he may be allowed to leave at the same time as Lord Eglinton which, in fact, he did. It is the last of the series, the last indeed of any of his letters which have survived, and parts of it are worth quoting for they give a picture of the cheerful, whimsical, likeable characteristics which Lord Eglinton attributed to him. He begs his mother to be allowed to leave, if only because of the cold to his toes in the coming winter, especially during the lessons before breakfast under the terrifying Dr Keate whose very shadow could chill the bones of anybody.

Money is scarce, what beautiful things there are at Eton to desire! We have scarcely got as much as we might want, even with next allowance.

I hope the guinea pigs are all well, you should put them into some warm place, now the cold weather has come on, or they will all die! every man jack of them; would not that be a pity?     Yours     C. Lamb

Now lastly! if you have any humanity or natural affection you will make us leave, or you will have your son's toes drop off one by one and the apalling sight would [word missing] terribly I know!!!

This fearful prospect obviously weakened Lady Montgomerie's resolution for she gave in to him and he left in

* Disowned by his father and deserted by his wife he died blind and alone at the age of forty in a cottage near Eglinton Castle.

the Christmas holidays of 1828, having only just passed his twelfth birthday. He had hardly been at Eton for three halves and by the standards of the day he ought to have stayed there for another two or three years at least. But his mother and father both agreed that scholastic education was unnecessary. So he made his *vale* and returned to Beauport, saving his toes and ensuring also the precious lives of his guinea pigs.

There is absolutely no record of his life and activities during the next few years but, according to his half-brother's diary, his mother, father and Lord Eglinton himself spent the next few years travelling about Europe, and presumably he did also. Until Lord Eglinton reached his majority in 1833 and took up residence at Eglinton Castle on his own, which caused the family to split to some extent and to live more independently of each other, they all seem to have followed the same pleasant circuit together, spending the summers in Geneva, the winters in Nice and the intervening months at Eglinton or Beauport.

The boating portrait of Sir Charles Lamb was done at this time, in 1831 at Geneva, and since Sir Charles failed to attend the coronation of William IV, which took place that September, perhaps his interests or family in Switzerland prevented him. It was the first of the now, economical coronations without the banquet in Westminster Hall and the ceremony of the Champion in which, as the wits said, the Government half crowned a half-wit for half-a-crown— and perhaps Sir Charles was so disgusted by this parsimony that he refused to take part in it. At all events, he was absent and his place was filled by the Deputy Knight Marshal, his cousin George Head.

Lord Eglinton speaks of these four years between leaving Eton and gaining his majority as being the happiest in his life, and the same was probably true for Charlie.

On one occasion, however, they—or, at least, Lord Eglinton—nearly found himself in prison. They began playing cricket on the Plaine de Plainpalais, then an open space outside the city walls, when one of the Genevans walked into the middle of the pitch and asked them to stop. The park was a public place, he said, and the game was a nuisance. Lord Eglinton refused to listen to him and one of the batsmen drove a ball at the citizen's head with such force that it almost cracked his skull. The police arrived, Lord Eglinton had to appear in Court and only escaped a term of imprisonment by paying a large fine.

It must have been during this period that Charlie came to know Sir Egerton Brydges, for one fact is certain about his interests and development after he left Eton—that once he escaped from the chains of scholasticism and was left to himself to study as he liked, he spent more and more time working on heraldry, genealogy and medieval history. His next manuscript proves this conclusively. After the completion of the History of Winnipeg, he set about a full scale family history and autobiography, the same history of his life and adventures which he had promised his mother to write in his first letter to her from Beauport, now so many years ago.

This work, entitled *The Red Book of Beauport, by C. Burges*, 1832, is of no interest as a book in itself for it is not finished and, unlike the history of the guinea pigs which stands on its own as an enthralling childish work, is also very dull. But as a guide to the way in which Charlie was growing up, it is truly fascinating. For it shows him ripening into an exceptional product of romantic gothicism and more and more living in what he imagined to be the atmosphere of the 12th century, if not yet as a knight errant rescuing captive maidens, then at least as a monkish chronicler, recording dynasties and wars.

It is not revealed why he chose this particular title but perhaps he possessed and enjoyed a collection of stories about King Arthur and his knights entitled *The Red Book of Hergest*, a book that contained, as well, a group of tales from Welsh mythology known as the *Mabinogion*, meaning, appropriately enough, 'The instruction of young bards.'

And if the bardic profession included the ability to write Gothic script, to illuminate capital letters, to compose family histories and to illustrate them in the margins by colourful pictures of great events and coats of arms, then Charlie did not waste his apprenticeship.

For the Red Book, written naturally on parchment, had all these items in profusion, including the coat of arms of Ludovici de Burges suspended by a choleric cherub with scarlet wings; a dramatic representation of Colonel Burges snatching the standard of Bonnie Prince Charlie's body-guard at the Battle of Culloden; and a superscription over the preface of two knights fighting on horseback, their lances just at the point of impact, one red and the other blue, chased by a tiny squire in a Roman legionnaire's skirt waving a miniature sword.

I, Charles James Saville Montgomeric Burges of Beauport in the year of our Lord one thousand eight hundred and thirty three, in the second year of the reign of our most gracious sovereign William, and the six-teenth year of my age have begun this writing, meaning it to contain an account of the period I live in, adding thereunto anecdotes of individuals of my acquaintance such as may prove interesting to those living hereafter, perhaps two or three hundred years, as illustrating the more minute particulars of the manner of life of their ancestors.

To this I shall add all I know concerning my family

estate, &c., and other things which might prove curious to my immediate descendants (if I should have any). And should this book not be brought to light till some far distant far distant period when British men and laws and manners may have passed away, it may still be looked into with curiosity by those who have heard that such a nation was. Great events too may happen in my days which may lend it a double interest. Affairs seem to be taking serious aspects which may end in wars, rebellions and what not—there is only one who knows.

Now, more than one hundred years later, when we, too, beside the God that Charlie refused to believe in, are blessed with the knowledge that the Reform Riots to which he referred never developed seriously, that the British nation still survives, and that his Red Book has certainly proved curious to his immediate descendants, are burdened also with the depressing knowledge that he never managed to finish it.

The Gothic script which begins so boldly with the words 'De Familia' at the head of the first chapter, recording the lives of remote ancestors in the early Middle Ages, dwindles away by the time it reaches Charlie himself to a spidery running hand and finally, after unexplained blanks and missing paragraphs, peters out in wispy pencil memoranda. The illuminations suffer the same decline. At the beginning, as in the case of Charlie's own complete armorial achievement, they cover entire pages. But after this the or, argent, sable and azure tints give way to bare outlines of ink and at last, as the MS comes to an end, they are only sketched in pencil.

It is clear that the whole effort became a bit of a bore and, seeing the work that must have gone into it, for a boy of sixteen, this is not surprising. For it is one thing to dream of the leisure and tranquillity of a medieval scribe but quite another, given the chance of trying it out, to sustain the purpose and inner composure to enjoy it.

Perhaps he came back to Beauport from the Continent one day in the early spring, sensed the primeval urge of rising sap, once again looked at his MS and suddenly felt that there was no point in going on with it and that he had been a monk long enough. At any rate, he gave it up and turned his thoughts to chivalry. If he had lived in the Middle Ages he would then have been a Squire or shield bearer; so he bought a razor, stroked his chin and began to think of ways of proving his manhood.

It is well known that no knight is worth the smallest rivet in his harness unless and until he can find an exquisite, young and virginal maiden in the clutches of a dragon and carry her off with perfect chivalry far away to his own impregnable demesne. It is well known, too, that no manly indignation at lascivious conduct can equal that of a Casanova who has sinned like a dragon himself, and if the next recorded step in Charlie's medieval apprenticeship is any guide to the way in which he passed the next few years, it is safe to assume that he spent them in practising seduction.

He could hardly have failed to do anything else, given a father like Sir Charles Lamb whose only pleasure in life was wenching and whose only paternal instruction—so far as Lord Eglinton was concerned, according to the diary, and presumably so far as Charlie was concerned, too—was the practical step of handing down to his children a series of cast off mistresses. But a gap exists in the history of Charlie's life after 1833, and every detail of his day to day occupations, his education, travel, hunting, shooting and fishing, breeding of guinea pigs and chasing butterflies and women must all remain surmised.

Being only the son of a baronet, having only an allowance of £500 per year which, by contemporary standards was small, not bothering to race or hunt beyond his own county of Sussex or his half-brother's of Ayrshire, he left no public record of any of his doings in the *Court Journal* or any of the national or even local newspapers. The family archives, such as they are, have left this period undocumented.

But after five years his life suddenly comes back into focus again with authenticity. And what appears fully makes up for the blank in the missing years.

At the end of July, directly after the coronation of Queen Victoria, he went over to West Sussex for a week's racing at Goodwood. On the whole, this pastime bored him, but he thought of Goodwood as his local course and always went there, and he liked it particularly because of the sublime new Gothic grandstand which had just been built in the Perpendicular manner. He rented lodgings at Bersted, near Bognor, a few miles east of Chichester, an area which at that time was just becoming a fashionable seaside resort and which liked to describe itself as the 'Montpellier of England'; and in all likelihood he shared them with his half-brother although it was still some years before the latter raced at Goodwood. He did not bring a damsel with him hoping, as usual, to find one near the course.

One morning, as he went for an early ride along the shore, he found instead, to his perfect astonishment, a young maiden, alive but wilting, quite alone and clearly in terrible distress. She was weeping bitterly and wading into the waves towards the Witterings. She was so upset that for half an hour she could hardly bring herself to speak.

At length, as Charlie sprang from his horse and led her to dry sand by a breakwater, she explained her predicament which, to a man of Charlie's experience, was perfectly familiar. She worked as a maid in one of the villas at Bersted and during the previous night the owner had tried to seduce her. She was only fourteen and even Charlie could see that she spoke the truth when she said she was inexperienced. The man had sworn at her through her bedroom keyhole and promised that the coming night he would make a woman of her. This in itself was frightening enough but the type of man that he was made it worse: he came from India, said he was a Raja, appeared to be an infidel and certainly was black.

It is quite unnecessary, knowing Charlie's obsession with knights and chivalry and also his amorous temperament, to recount what happened next. Research has failed to authenticate a great deal of what became a family legend but a few facts exist to confirm it sufficiently. The girl, who was called Charlotte Gray, was aged fourteen, the eldest daughter of a draper, Arthur Gray, who conducted his business in North Street, Chichester. The date of her birth is not recorded but she was baptised on the 14th of March, 1824, in the parish church of St Andrew, her mother's name being Maria, according to the Baptismal Register, and her father describing himself as a mercer. She was the second child of several brothers and sisters.

The Raja, if this part of the story is true at all, may possibly have been Raja Ram Roy, the son of the late Ram Mohun Roy, the distinguished religious reformer, for he was the only eminent and educated Indian who moved in English social circles at that time and a friend of Lord William Bentinck, Lord Eglinton's god-father. This is mere speculation, however. In spite of her youth, Charlotte was a strapping girl, as Charlie found out later to his disadvantage.

At this moment he did not waste time testing her

biceps, identifying her enemies or meeting her family. Incensed at the idea of such a young and beautiful girl—as indeed she was—being placed in such circumstances, he swore by the bones of Sir Walter Scott that he would rescue her.

She had hardly dried her tears, put up her hair—which was raven black and literally reached to her feet, according to Little Gilmour, the Black Knight at the Tournament, who met her afterwards—before Charlie had made a plan and explained it to her. She was to go home and watch for a series of daring, romantic and complicated signals, which were quite unnecessary, and come back that evening to the same barnacle-encrusted breakwater and wait for him.

Twelve hours later, cloaked and hooded, with all her possessions in a small black hair trunk which survived to become a sacred family relic, she returned to the *rendezvous*. And before the last beams of the day's sun had set on the Bognor briny, Charlie had met her with a darkened coach, lifted her into it and carried her away.

As time went by and the news of his knightly deed leaked out amongst his friends, it was thought by some, including Lord Eglinton, that he had behaved rather foolishly. But it only seemed to Charlie himself that under the circumstances no gentleman with a grain of chivalry could have acted otherwise and that, so long as he wished to be true to them, all the principles on which he had based his life in the last eighteen years absolutely demanded this course of action.

For now he had become, at the age of twenty-two, an exceptional product of the 19th century romantic gothicism. Byronic, artistic, intelligent, sensitive, claiming to be born with almost as many coats of arms as Lady Clara Vere de Vere and ready, too, to protect and admire the flower of a simple maiden.

He was not a snob but all the same he preferred people to be noble if they could be, and as he and Charlotte arrived in sight of the new portcullis of Arundel Castle, shining in the moonlight, he whispered in her ear that he proposed to give her the courtesy title of 'Lady'.

When it came to dialectics of this kind, Charlotte was no fool herself and she whispered back that it was hardly necessary for, as it happened, her maternal grandmother had been sired by the Duke of Norfolk.

Only one thing was now missing in Charlie's imaginary world and that was the actual experience of wearing mail, tying his paramour's favour to the point of his lance, and challenging other fearful opponents to mortal combat in the lists. For this purpose he began to collect armour and to build a tilt yard in the garden at Beauport, the existence of which is still remembered by many of the older inhabitants.

In a few weeks all these preparations became unnecessary. For unexpectedly, the half dozen casual words by his half-brother about having a Champion at the next race meeting at Eglinton Park flashed up and down the country with the speed of the newly developed electric telegraph and became in a week the germ and promise of a genuine medieval tournament.

The latent Gothic emotions of half the people in the Kingdom were set alight, and the romantic longing to see a joust which had stirred so many for a hundred years and had grown so great since the publication of *Ivanhoe* were brought to the point of dramatic hysteria.

Thus, with veritably magic speed and unexpectedness, in the summer of 1838, in the twenty-third year of his age, Charlie Lamb found himself summoned to a tourney.

Every knightly ambition seemed to be coming true and every youthful dream of chivalry brought to the point of fulfilment.

I

## PART TWO

## The Event

A gentle Knight was pricking on the plaine,
Ycladd in mightie armes and silver shielde,
Wherein old dints of deepe woundes did remaine,
The cruel markes of many 'a bloody fielde;
Yet armes till that time did he never wield:
His angry steede did chide his foming bitt,
As much disdayning to the curbe to yield:
Full iolly knight he seemd, and faire did sitt,
As one for knightly giusts and fierce encounters fitt.

Spenser
*The Faerie Queen*
(Canto I. 1589)


Now Eglinton, let minstrels praise
Who, spurning cold formality,
Restores 'the light of other days'
And, eke, their hospitality.

*Bell's New Weekly Messenger**
21st July, 1839

* Later, the *News of the World* 1855

# Chapter Seven

DURING THE year which began in the summer of 1837, the first in the reign of Queen Victoria, many events took place throughout the realm of exceptional interest to everybody.

A number of these, like the maiden speech in Parliament of Benjamin Disraeli, the legendary heroism of Grace Darling, the publication of the *Pickwick Papers* or the tragic decease of Lady Flora Hastings, are still remembered today.

Many others, now forgotten, enthralled everyone at the time, too, and none more so than a handful of items which were symptomatic of the prevailing Gothicism.

On the 8th of July, 1837, two weeks after the Queen's accession, the *Court Journal*, a gossipy newspaper of no official standing, revealed the news that the Queen was planning a tournament. The heralds were setting off to all parts of Europe to announce it, after the fashion of the Middle Ages, and one hundred Knights of England, picked from the ranks of the nobility, would be called to defend her name against the challengers. It would be held in the autumn at Windsor and run for four days on the lines of a knock-out competition. On the final day the last six combatants would fight to a finish with sharp lances. The Queen herself would crown the victor and shortly afterwards make him her Prince.

Such was the state of public opinion at that time, so great the pleasure of having a young and virgin queen and so wide the enthusiasm for medieval life that many people believed it.

'We already behold the "Mad Marquess" biting the dust . . .' continued the *Journal* in the next issue, referring to Lord Waterford who was well known as a dashing blade and spirited practical joker. Warming to his task as letters poured in asking for confirmation, the editor wound up by saying that Lady Seymour and other fashionable beauties planned to attend in medieval costumes and that, to conform to the habit of pledging a quaint vow to enhance a feat of chivalry, Lord William Beresford, Lord Waterford's brother, had sworn to ride night and day through the streets of London until he had captured the glazed hats of one hundred policemen with which to adorn his tent.

The *Court Journal's* rival, the *Court Gazette*, poured scorn on all these fairy tales and said they were ridiculous. But the author proved himself a gifted journalist with this piece of nonsense, for two years afterwards the Eglinton Tournament brought his fantasy to life. He had sensed the spirit of his times perfectly and had even predicted the behaviour of individuals. Lord Waterford did tumble off his steed and bite the dust, and Lady Seymour and the rest of society's beauty did come to the lists in medieval dresses.

He had only failed to mention Lord Eglinton, and for this he must have kicked himself. But the moment he heard the rumour of the Tournament, he seized his chance to make up for it. In one, short, unchivalrous article, he squashed the *Court Gazette* with the obvious claim, if not the truth, that the whole idea had been his. This was simply not the case, in spite of the coincidence, and there is no evidence of any kind that Lord Eglinton had ever heard of the Windsor tournament, or ever perused the *Court Journal*. When he announced his own Tournament, however, it must have helped him. Then everyone must have remembered it, and transferred to him their frustrated enthusiasm.

Another item of a similar nature which beguiled the fashionable world in the first year of Victoria's sovereignty was an opera written by Lord Burghersh, the eldest son of the 10th Earl of Westmorland. To the joy of the editor of the *Court Journal* and of all the other addicts of medieval life, it was called 'THE TOURNAMENT'. Lord Burghersh, a professional soldier and diplomatist, the founder of the Royal Academy of Music and an excellent amateur musician, had written it twelve years earlier in Italy but for some reason had never produced it in England. He did so now, in the summer of 1838, and the whole *ton* of London's society flocked to the St James's Theatre to listen to it.

The scene was set in the 12th century, and the plot hinged on the love of Helen and Albert, two members of the court of the King of England. Their hopes of marriage were crushed when Albert's father was found dead and Helen's father was thought to have murdered him.

In the second act, Helen's father was thrown to the ground by an unknown knight at a tournament. This knight proved to be Albert, and Helen, who was the Queen of Beauty, was caught between honour, love and duty. For when the victor approached her throne she ought to have crowned him Lord of the Lists.

Suddenly Albert's father was found to have died by accident, so all came well in the end. The two lovers plighted their troth, and the curtain fell on a note of happy revelry.

The *Court Journal* and other fashionable newspapers received this opera well, but the *Musical World* did not think quite so much of it. Mrs Bishop, the wife of the immortal composer of 'Home Sweet Home', and Miss Windham, a star member of the Italian Opera Buffa Company, who took the parts of Helen and Albert respectively, were in excellent voice. But the man who played Helen's father—Ivanoff, the 'Nightingale of Russia'—was hoarse and Mr Stretton, the bass, who assumed the role of the king, growled at the audience 'most vilely' and was asked by the critics never to appear again.

It is not recorded whether Lord Burghersh was satisfied with this performance or whether he tried to have it improved at another production with other artistes, but he never appears to have done so. Lord Eglinton did not go to it and nor did he subscribe to its publication which took place a year afterwards. But he knew Lord Burghersh well and asked him to his Tournament, and perhaps then he was given a copy of it. Possibly, too, as several other people were staying at Eglinton Castle at the same moment whose names appear in the list of subscribers—notably Lord Saltoun, another well known musical enthusiast who was at the Tournament as Judge of Peace—he was also favoured with some of its arias and melodies.

For those people who failed to hear this opera and perhaps, also, missed the joke of the Windsor Tournament in the *Court Journal*, there was much to be seen of Gothic interest at the exhibition in the Royal Academy which had just moved from Somerset House to the present National Gallery in Trafalgar Square.

As had been the case for many seasons, narrative compositions of medieval life had drawn the crowds increasingly, and they were now, without argument, acclaimed the cream of the exhibits.

There was a great triumph for Daniel Maclise, the R.A. who had passed the previous winter in composing a huge tableau, 'Merry Christmas in the Baron's Hall'. During these months the Thames had frozen throughout its length, the snow had lain in drifts fifty feet deep, the poor had perished in the workhouses in flocks, and Charles Dickens, torn by their condition, had written *Oliver Twist.* 'This is an admirable work,' reported the editor of the *Brighton Guardian*, one of the many provincial papers that kept abreast of art. 'The various groups offer enough for half a dozen pictures.'*

There were, also, many illustrations from the books of Sir Walter Scott. For of all the sources of inspiration available to artists of that period, from history itself to Shakespeare and Byron, none charmed the painters so much as the 'Great Enchanter's' romantic masterpieces.

It is hardly possible to realise today the immense influence of this author on contemporary drama, literature and art. His early poems like the *Lay of the Last Minstrel* and *Marmion*, which were first published in 1805 and 1808 respectively, and his great series of tales in prose which began with *Waverley* in 1814 and reached its peak, according to many critics, with *Ivanhoe* in 1819, the year Lord Eglinton succeeded his grandfather, truly hypnotised all who read them.

The proof of this may be seen at a glance in the catalogues of the major exhibitions throughout the country. In the twenty-five years between the first appearance of the Waverley Novels in 1814 and the Eglinton Tournament in 1839, two hundred and sixty-six different pictures inspired by the pen of the 'Wizard of the North' appeared in public galleries; every summer without a break, a scene from *Ivanhoe* was the subject of two of them.

This year they were shown in the Royal Academy. The first, which depicted the knight 'Ivanhoe' himself, was painted by 'I.S.B.'; the other, 'The Tournament at Ashby de la Zouch' was presented by Thomas Allom.

Many other canvasses besides these delighted all who came to see them. There was 'Marmion' by J. Waylen;

* July 25th, 1838

119

'Tales of the Crusaders' by G. P. Jenner; two illustrations for *Talisman* by Charles Landseer; and two by his famous brother, Edwin, not perhaps inspired by Scott but at least tainted with genuine medievalism. Their titles were as follows: 'The life's in the old dog yet' and 'None but the brave deserve the fair'. The first depicted a hound in a crevasse and the other two stags preparing for a tournament.

There were, finally, three others of particular interest to Lord Eglinton: a portrait by J. Wood of John Fairlie, a friend and neighbour in Ayrshire whose son, James, was the Knight of the Golden Lion at the Tournament; 'Earl Percy and Earl Douglas meeting at the battle of Chevy Chase' by G. Morley, the famous encounter of 1388 at which Lord Eglinton's ancestor, Sir Hugh Montgomerie, had smitten Lord Percy with a spear which had gone through his body and come out the other side 'A long cloth yard and more'; a fine composition by Joseph Severn, the well known artist and friend of Keats, who had married Lord Eglinton's natural, paternal, half-sister, Elizabeth, the ward of Lady Westmorland, step-mother to Lord Burghersh.

Severn had won the Royal Academy Gold Medal in 1819 with his 'Una and the Red Cross Knight in the Cave of Despair' and he now exhibited an inspiring work, 'The first Crusaders in sight of Jerusalem'. Here, in truth, was a subject to uplift the imagination: Godfrey of Bouillon, Raymund of Provence, Tancred, nephew of Bohemund of Otranto, and ten thousand knights standing before the walls of the Holy City on the 15th of July, 1099; then, 'sobbing for excess of joy' as, after an appalling combat, they reached the Sepulchre through rivers of blood.

Any members of the public who were bored by art and never went to the Royal Academy had another way to uplift their imagination during the first year of the reign of Queen Victoria. They could go to Astley's Amphitheatre at Westminster Bridge, opposite the Houses of Parliament, and reserve a seat at one of its fabulous tournaments.

Astley's Royal National Amphitheatre of the Arts, as it was called in full, the Mecca of circus lovers throughout the world, had been founded seventy years earlier by Philip Astley, the modern father of this form of entertainment, a retired sergeant major in General Elliott's Light Horse. It had started life as a riding school and, having been burnt down and rebuilt several times, it was now the finest covered arena in London, one hundred and forty feet in length and sixty-five in width, and owned by Andrew Ducrow, the foremost ringmaster in Europe.

As well as being a circus it was used as a glorified music hall and from time to time it transfixed its audiences with *Love, Jealousy and Revenge—a Day of Strife*, or with *Jack o' Lantern in the Dismal Swamp with an Extensive Frozen Landscape*. As a real people's theatre in the classic tradition, reflecting the taste of the times, it also presented dramatic historical pageants. Many of these were set in the Middle Ages and their dazzling panoplies of medieval life were superb examples of popular romantic Gothicism.

These stupendous peeps at the past were just as famous as Ducrow's feats of dressage and acrobatics. Vast, glittering, equestrian spectacles, they were one of the rare treats of the metropolis, with emperors, queens, knights, princesses, ferocious bands of antagonists who frequently lost their tempers and had to be torn apart at the end of the performances, and colossal fortresses which were actually burnt to the ground in front of the audience.

Their titles still read excitingly on the old playbills, now to be seen in the Victoria and Albert Museum. *The*

*Storming of Seringapatam and the death of Tippoo Saib*;
*The Conflagration of Moscow*; *The Victory of Waterloo*; *The
Seige of Jerusalem*; *The last days of Napoleon*; *The Conquest
of Mexico*; *The Battle of Agincourt and the Field of the Cloth
of Gold*.

One of the best was Byron's *Mazeppa* in which, at the
end of a terrific battle, the hero, Ivan Stephanovich, Polish
nobleman and Hetman of the Dnieper Cossaks, was
strapped naked to a wild horse which was lashed round and
round the arena until it was nearly demented. Many others
were based on popular mythology. Others, again, were
drawn from the works of Scott. For here, once more, at
Astley's Amphitheatre, almost as many romantic tours de
force were inspired by the 'Great Northern Bard' as they
were in the Royal Academy.

Andrew Ducrow was completely uneducated and can
never have read a word of the Waverley Novels or anything
else, but their fame was such, even amongst his illiterate
colleagues, that he knew their plots and dramatised many
of them.

He staged the magnificent revels in *Kenilworth*; the
dramatic elopement of Lochinvar in *Marmion*; the savage
battle in *Rob Roy* in which he galloped about the ring on
tip-toe, clad in a kilt and sporran; and, best of all, the
prodigious tournament in *Ivanhoe*.

But as time went by and the Gothic mania increased and
spread downwards, even to simple audiences, the success
of the tale of the Disinherited Knight completely eclipsed
the rest.

This same triumph was repeated on many other stages
besides Ducrow's. For when *Ivanhoe* first came out as a
play in 1820, having been published the year before, it
created a record. It carried London by storm in five
different interpretations running concurrently in separate

theatres, while before the end of the year it appeared in a sixth.

Ever since it has kept ahead of all the other dramas based on the books of the same author. Several fresh texts have been written in every decade, and nearly fifty original scripts in many languages for stage, screen, ballet, opera, radio and television are now recorded on the shelves of the world's libraries.

In spite of the moves which were going on at this time in the House of Commons to extend the laws of copyright and preserve an example of everything published— sponsored by Thomas Talfourd, the famous Sergeant at Law to whom Dickens inscribed *Pickwick Papers*— Ducrow's *Ivanhoe* has vanished. There were probably never many copies at all, for nobody spoke much at these performances, according to the theatrical chat of the day, and if they did so they soon shut up.

'Cut the cackle and come to the 'osses', Ducrow used to bellow at them, helping them up with a smart flick from his long ringmaster's whip which often surprised them frightfully.

This year, at least, they could not be touched, for all were clad in armour from head to foot.

The scarlet words on the bills which proclaimed *Ivanhoe* in huge dimensions throughout the city promised a thrill that was hardly exaggerated—a Jew, a Prince and a Queen of Beauty; a maiden carried away on a Spanish steed by a black Saracen; a raving Saxon hag and a burning fortress; four divisions of champing cavalry; twenty armed knights in a fearsome tournament.

The show ran throughout the summer to packed houses for more than fifty performances; and after this it remained a standard part of the repertory for the next fifty years until, at last, in 1895, many old buildings south of West-

minster Bridge were taken down to widen the road and
Astley's, too, was demolished.

Lord Eglinton never visited Astley's Amphitheatre, or
if he did so he never left any record of it. Although he
loved horses, he disliked circuses and was thoroughly
bored by theatricals.

It was often said that if he had watched a Ducrow
tournament he might never have held his own, seeing the
obvious cost and immense difficulties of such a production.

Yet these things never troubled him at all and, on the
contrary, the sight of so many knights—possibly even a
representation of his own ancestor, Sir Hugh Montgomerie, in *The Battle of Chevy Chase*, or Ducrow as the
King's Champion in *The Coronation*, actually casting a
glove—would more than likely have made him keener
than ever.

For one of the deepest yearnings of all people with
romantic temperaments in the 19th century was the urge
to experience every emotion personally; and the great
ambition of every Gothic revivalist was to taste the drama
of medieval life in as many ways as possible—in hawking,
archery, in a Merry Xmas in the Baron's Hall with a yule
log, malmsey wine and a boar's head; and also, naturally
enough if given the opportunity, in wearing armour and
taking part in a tournament.

Another spectacle of great interest to which Lord
Eglinton never went in this first year of the reign of
Queen Victoria but to which the public swarmed excitedly
was Queen Elizabeth's Armoury. This was a splendid
hoard of suits of armour, long preserved as works of art,
that had once been used at various royal tournaments.
Since it was housed in the Tower of London and guarded
by Yeomen in antique dress, it was, to any Gothic
enthusiast, trebly worth the cost of a special visit.

The person to whom it owed its gleaming state and magnificent presentation at this particular moment was the leading expert on medieval weapons, Sir Samuel Rush Meyrick. Born in 1783, the son of Hannah and John Meyrick—the former an heiress, *née* Rush, the latter an agent who worked in Westminster—he began his life as an attorney. But finding himself more and more absorbed in the Middle Ages, he decided to leave the Courts and become an antiquary.

At the age of twenty he married against his family's advice and was disinherited although in some unexplained way when his father died he managed to gain control of the money which legally passed to his son. Using his son's name, he formed a collection of arms and armour for which he became famous and which, by a twist of fate, in spite of his parents' wishes, he finally came to possess. For his son, dying as a young man without children, he became the next to succeed to it.

Long before this, however—which only happened in 1837—he found, as many other collectors had done before him, that he needed a house equipped with a proper armoury. For his own in London at 20 Upper Cadogan Place had become like a medieval battlefield. The whole area was strewn with weapons, and every approach was barred by knights who fell upon his guests with frightening suddenness.

So, having for many years coveted Goodrich Castle—a perfect ruin near Tintern Abbey where Wordsworth had met the child of *We are seven*—he approached the owner, hoping to buy and restore it.

When she refused—luckily enough for us since the castle is one of the finest in Herefordshire—he bought the hill on the other side of the river which overlooked it across a deep dingle. Retaining Edward Blore, Sir Walter Scott's architect at Abbotsford, he constructed a house in the style of Edward II.

Approached by a drawbridge, through a groined gateway, between two round towers which led to a Gothic porch above which were turrets, pinnacles and battlements, it was put together with hunks of local red masonry and embraced a Grand Armoury eighty-six feet in length and twenty-five in width. Here he installed his collection— forty-six figures in full armour, ten of which were mounted on barbed stallions; many others from India, Asia and the Pacific and, in a special 'hastilude chamber' an enormous tableau of a tournament.

As the house completely wrecked the prospect from Goodrich Castle, Wordsworth, to whom the whole district was sacred because of its many poetic associations, wanted to 'blow away Sir Samuel's impertinent structure and all the possessions it contained.'* So, too, did the person to whom the ruins belonged, a Miss Catherine Griffin. Now, perhaps, their ghosts may smile for, like many buildings of the same period, good of their kind but extremely large, it has recently been demolished.

Meyrick, however, who looked in the other direction, was naturally very pleased with the view while Blore, the architect, was perfectly delighted with it and capped his triumph by having his plans hung up at the Royal Academy.

At about the same time as he started to build his house, Meyrick was asked to report on Queen Elizabeth's Armoury because he had written a book in which he criticised it. Much of the contents needed repair and, after a series of talks with the Master General of Ordnance in charge of military stores which still, technically, included suits of armour, he recommended a number of changes

* Quoted by Arthur Mee in *The King's England—Herefordshire*. p. 76.

including a different form of display, and offered to do the work at his own expense.

As a result, a new museum was built at the Tower of London, shaped like a capital 'E' of a typical Tudor manor, lit by eight sash windows of Georgian type and topped by a fringe of battlements.

Inside it was a beautiful Gothic cloister, one hundred and forty-nine feet in length, which framed the figures of twenty gleaming knights arranged historically from Henry VI in 1450 to James II in 1685, interspersed by dashing noblemen like the Duke of Suffolk in 1520 and the Earl of Strafford in 1635. Each sat on an armed horse beneath an arch from the point of which hung a crimson banner on which was written his name and the date of his armour in golden Gothic lettering. All around them were shining weapons and dazzling suits of armour of different types.

This had been finished in 1828 but because, under an ancient precedent, the price of admission had been kept at three shillings, one of which went to the Beefeater who showed the visitor round and the other two to the principal storekeeper's pocket—large sums in those days—it had not been often or easily seen by the ordinary members of the public.

By the year of the coronation of Queen Victoria, however, under the vexatious pressure of Joseph Hume, a champion of public rights for thirty years who, according to the Dictionary of National Biography, 'spoke longer, oftener and probably worse' than any other private member of the House of Commons but who usually got what he wanted in the end, the fee was lowered to one shilling.

As soon as this reduction was announced the place was literally beseiged. A special contingent of eighteen extra Beefeaters had to be massed to protect the ticket office

K

which happened to be in a former lion's den of the old menagerie, and more than one of them lost their tempers and compared the mob to a pride of wild beasts, all of them being perfectly enraged at having their perquisites diminished.

The files record that one, Thomas Kinnak, called a tourist a 'drunken vagabond' twice—right in front of a figure of Henry VIII.*

Forty-two thousand people entered the armoury during the following months, and twice as many did so again when the fee was cut to sixpence.

All fell into a Gothic trance as, pushed along by sullen Beefeaters, they gazed at the treasures within it.

There was, finally, in this first year of the Queen's reign, another vision of medieval life which entranced the coronation visitors as well and inspired Lord Eglinton personally. This was a display of arms and armour staged by Samuel Luke Pratt, a young but already well known dealer in Bond Street. Although it did not compare in size or quality with Queen Elizabeth's Armoury, it possessed a glorious advantage: that, apart from being easy to reach, its entire contents was actually for sale; so that any school-boy wanting a battle-axe, any artist seeking a model or any antiquary forming a collection had only to go there and buy whatever he required.

Many great and rich families collected armour during the early part of the 19th century, and more and more as the years passed and the Gothic mania attacked them. Involved, naturally enough, in other Gothic endeavours as well, nearly all of them dabbled in architecture and quite a number in the struggle for ancient peerages. One family enthused another and often enough they were either married or related.

* Public Record Office—WO/44/304.

An interesting case is that of the Russells of Brancepeth Castle in Co. Durham, and the famous family of Tennyson. Matthew Russell, the richest commoner in England, married Elizabeth Tennyson, the poet laureate's aunt. His collection of arms and armour was renowned and he lived in fabulous baronial state in a palace restored for £120,000 by John Paterson, the architect of Eglinton Castle.

Elizabeth's brother, George, who was head of the family, changed his name to Tennyson d'Eyncourt to enjoy the Gothic particle. He amassed enough arms and armour to equip a small crusade and so fortified his home, Bayons Manor in Lincolnshire, with moats, walls, drawbridges and keeps that even his sister could hardly hack her way into it.

Two of the others who were not related were Lord Brougham and Vaux, the extraordinary Lord Chancellor who incorrectly claimed descent from the Barons of Vaulx and the ancient Lords of Brougham Castle in Westmorland, and Lord Zouch, better known as Robert Curzon the distinguished author and traveller whose title, recently prized from abeyance, dated from 1308. Both these accumulated splendid collections.

All four, and everyone else, visited Samuel Pratt. So, too, did Charlie Lamb whose great collection, when it was sold, comprised, according to a note by an expert* 'all varieties of arms and armour of the choicest and rarest kinds.'

In spite of the fact that Pratt traded at the same premises in Bond Street for forty years—No. 47, on the corner of Maddox Street—practically nothing is known about him. Any record, if there ever was one, of his looks, character or private life, whether written in a diary by himself or by

* Cripps-Day, *Armour Sales*, p. 249.

anyone else who ever dealt with him, seems to have vanished completely. Apart from the armour he bought and sold, much of which is still recorded, nothing else has survived. He died in 1878 at the age of seventy three; his Will may be seen in Somerset House*; but any descendants have proved impossible to find.

One thing is certain about him, however, that arms and armour were the whole passion of his life. And at least in 1838, as well as providing a comfortable income, their direct contact with the Middle Ages, their authentic connection with famous princes and their very damage in forgotten combats really appealed to him personally.

One of his claims to fame today is the valuable manner in which he compiled his catalogues, being the first in the Gothic Revival of arms and armour to describe the various pieces properly and also the first to illustrate them. This has enabled collectors to trace them since.

The way he wrote also revealed his enthusiasm.

'To gaze on the plumed casque of the Mailed Knight equipped for the Tournament, and to grasp the ponderous mace, yet encrusted with the accumulated rust of centuries, cannot fail to inspire admiration for the chivalrous deeds of our ancestors,' he declared in the preface of his first catalogue, the one for the year 1838.

As the Tower Armouries were inconveniently far away, he continued, he hoped his galleries would please the public generally, while since the exhibits might also be bought he aspired as well to help collectors revive 'the splendour of our ancient Baronial Halls.'†

This, indeed, he certainly did; and not, as experts discovered afterwards, entirely with genuine pieces.

But in this first year of the reign of Queen Victoria, his

---

* No. 808 of 1878. Personal estate under £10,000.
† V & A Library, Fine Art Pamphlets, 1838, H.8.

own opening year in Bond Street, probably few of his wares were fakes and most of his efforts were put to showing them off.

'This splendid pile of steel . . .' he proclaimed of one particularly massive suit of knight's *cap-à-pie* armour, 'is replete with all the additional defences worn at the JOUST, consisting of *Passegardes and Garde de bras of grand character.*' 'THE GEM OF THE COLLECTION' he pronounced of the costly, engraved and inlaid harness of Alphonso II, the last reigning Duke of Ferrara, the home of the finest swords in the world, which was shown complete on a stuffed horse, itself encased in armour of violet and gold; 'A noble Suit of *Cap-à-pie* Tilting Fluted Armour . . . of collossal size'; 'A suit of Engraved and Gilt German Armour for a Knight . . . of peculiar grandeur and beauty'; 'A Massive Polished Steel Shield, 60 lbs in weight'; so on and so forth, throughout the catalogue which had six hundred and seventy items, many of which referred to knights who were shown on horseback, locked in combat, as though engaged at tournaments. There was even 'A very singular suit of bright steel armour evidently made for a *Female* . . .' Although its history was actually unknown, he could not resist the obvious temptation of alluding to Joan of Arc to whom, he said, it might have belonged and whom he quaintly termed the 'Virgin Combatant'.

His own shop being too small to contain such a huge collection, he leased another across the road in 3 Lower Grosvenor Street and fitted it up with the help of the architect Lewis Nockalls Cottingham who had worked for Lord Brougham and Vaux at Brougham Castle and had won a reputation for medieval work by restoring Magdalen College Chapel at Oxford and for building Snelston Hall in Derbyshire in a style that was 'richly Gothic'.

He designed for Pratt 'a truly Gothic Apartment'*; and the *Gentleman's Magazine*, which both had led and reflected aristocratic taste for more than a hundred years, thought the exhibition was 'one of the most brilliant and interesting ever seen in London.'†

So, too, did Charlie Lamb who rushed Lord Eglinton to see it.

And when, towards the end of the summer, the latter decided to hold a tournament, he naturally turned to Pratt for help and advice.

So that Pratt, as well as Charlie Lamb, was given the chance of a lifetime. For never, in all his grandest dreams, can he possibly have thought of selling armour to the very cream of Britain's nobility for the very purpose for which it had once been made.

In the same dramatic and unlooked for manner, by the same strange assembly of events, all his hopes of wealth and success and every conceivable romantic ambition were suddenly placed on the brink of reality and brought within his grasp.

* *The Times*, Apr. 16th 3.b.
† May, p. 532.

# Chapter Eight

TOWARDS THE end of the autumn of 1838 when, after the usual summer holidays, the fashionable world had returned to London, Lord Eglinton compiled a roll of competing knights and called a meeting to discuss the preliminary arrangements. According to Grantley F. Berkeley whose *Recollections* have been quoted earlier— one of the many dashing youths whose pulse had surged at the news of the Tournament—this took place at Pratt's showroom in Bond Street. One hundred and fifty competitors came to it and, by a strange and ominous coincidence, this was just the number of knights that once met at King Arthur's Court and swore to honour the vows of the Round Table.

To stage a pageant of any past event, let alone to attempt to revive it, requires a knowledge of all the basic facts. Before Lord Eglinton held the conference he ought to have tried to master them, either by reading Strutt's *Sports and Pastimes of the People of England* or Samuel Meyrick's *Antient Armour*, both of which are known to have been in his library. But being in no sense an antiquary and accustomed to leave the details of life to somebody else, he never bothered to do so; and he soon discovered that Pratt's specialised knowledge of arms and armour did not wholly cover the running of tournaments.

All sorts of problems quickly presented themselves. How were tourneys proclaimed, for example; ought one to ask the Queen's permission; should the College of Heralds be approached; what were the proper dimensions for the lists?

Each of these and many others about costs, scoring, forfeits, challenges, *gages d'amour* and the Queen of Beauty were all debated interminably, every knight having his own ideas, right or wrong, sensible or otherwise, according to his strength, wealth and temperament, and each insisting that he alone was right. Towards the evening, most of them lost their tempers and, but for Pratt's agonised entreaties, the Eglinton Tournament might have begun that night.

Before any question could be answered, a decision had to be taken on styles and dates, for during the time that tournaments were held—a period of more than six hundred years—they changed their form completely. What kind did Lord Eglinton want—a simple, brutal, medieval struggle; a colourful, chivalrous passage of arms; or a mere parade with dainty jousts of the time of Charles I?

Invented, so it is said, by a French seigneur, Geoffroi de Preulli, who died tourneying in 1066, they started out as baronial gang fights or private battles. Groups of knights met by arrangement in an open space, armed with swords, lances or battle axes, and fought either on foot or horse-back, trying, in certain types of combat, to cut off the crests of each other's helmets.

Hence the use of the word 'crestfallen', for the ones who lost forfeited their horses and armour although they could always buy them back. By such ransoms many tough knights like the famous 1st Earl of Pembroke in the 12th century, who is said to have conquered five hundred opponents, earned a cheerful living, while those who paid them, by going from one tourney to another, often lost their whole family's inheritance.

They were likely, too, to suffer terrific casualties, for only men of huge strength and in perfect training had any chance of ending the day on their feet.

'A youth must have seen his blood flow and felt his teeth crack under the blow of his adversary and been thrown to the ground twenty times . . .'* before he could hope to be worthy of manhood, wrote the old chronicler, Roger de Hoveden, one of Pembroke's contemporaries.

Sir William Montague, a knight founder of the Order of the Garter, killed his own son in a tournament in 1383 and his father, the 1st Earl of Salisbury, died of wounds in another. History is filled with tales of similar losses; in one simple engagement at Cologne in 1240, more than sixty knights are said to have perished.

Of these, many died of asphixia, for lack of air and excessive heat were always hazards to a man in armour, and how the Crusaders, dressed in thick quilted tunics under their mail shirts and similar garments under their helmets—much of which they never took off for months—survived the burning sun of Palestine remains an historical mystery.

At tournaments, too, there was always a danger of dust, for the ground was strewn with sand or other soft material to break the falls of the combatants which, although usually watered beforehand, often rose in choking clouds; while any knight who unstrapped his helmet to take a breather literally chanced his neck.

Those who survived had to eat, drink and dance all night and be ready at dawn for a final test of prowess. For although the ladies whose favours they wore in the lists were always supposedly virgins or married women of perfect virtue—known as paramours because, according to the rules of chivalry, the champions fought for them 'par amour'—the knights also frequently became their lovers.

Those who did not and were self-controlled had to be beware of prostitutes. These rampaging professional

* *The Tournament*, p. 2. F. H. Cripps-Day.

paramours came to the tournaments in hordes; and fierce groups led by Amazons who were sometimes clad in suits of armour challenged the knights as they clanked homewards and, with threats or taunts of weakness, dared them to come to bed.

Understandably, the Church tried to prevent these pointless struggles, saying that all who fought would be excommunicated, and by making clear that the ones who fell, being denied a Christian burial, would be carried away by the Devil.

But most of the knights decided to take pot luck and in the end, as in the case of actual warfare, the Popes were forced to capitulate.

William the Conqueror forbade tournaments in Britain altogether—it is thought to avoid unnecessary incidents between the French and Saxons; for, like any form of thrilling public contest, as for example football matches today, they brought together large numbers of supporters who frequently stormed the field and took part in the fight.

And so, although tournaments may have been held earlier, they are not recorded in England before the 1130's. They did not receive official sanction until Richard Coeur de Lion signed an edict at Lewes in 1195 allowing them at five specified places—Salisbury, Warwick, Stamford, Brackley and Tickhill—to which, by custom, was added Smithfield in London. The Archbishop of Canterbury was obliged to supervise them, and the knights were taxed according to their wealth and status.

Clearly this species of tournament—a free-for-all by teams of knights, called a *mêlée* by those who invented it and a pelly melly by the Saxon underdogs who could never master the Norman language and were much laughed at by the French in consequence—was not the kind for Lord Eglinton.

His idea was for individual knights to fight on horse-back with lances, watched by the others—a form of combat only used in the early days to settle a private feud or limber up before the actual *mêlée*. This kind of engage-ment, known as a Joust of War or Joust of Peace, de-pending on whether the weapons were sharp or blunted, superseded the *mêlée* as time went by and attained its greatest vogue in the 14th century.

If the jousts were held for fun between small gatherings of knights to pass the time, then the meeting was known as a Round Table—what, in fact, was actually given by Lord Eglinton; and if they were staged before the King with all the trappings and procedure of chivalry, then the occasion merited the title of a tournament.

This was the time, now thought of as the legendary age of chivalry, when knights were given peacock pie at fabulous banquets and issued poetic vows to prove their valour, sometimes adding strange conditions to make their tasks more difficult.

An authentic case is that of Michel d'Oris, an esquire from Arragon who sent a challenge to the English knights at Calais in 1400, swearing to wear a piece of leg armour until he had jousted twenty times and earned the right to remove it. He must have hobbled about for life since the tournament never came off.

Such engagements, when they were met, were full of excitement and pageantry. At one such in London in 1386 before King Richard II, the proceedings began with 'three score Ladyes of honour mounted on fayre palfreys, ryding on the one syde, richely apparelled; and every ladye ledde a knight with a cheyne of sylver, which knights were apparelled to just.'*

Not so hard as the earlier *mêlées*, these colourful battles

* *The Tournament*, p. 60. F. H. Cripps-Day.

were still ferocious; and as time passed and the fire of chivalry began to wane, a fence was installed in the middle of the lists, five or six feet high, running lengthwise halfway down, to prevent the risk of collision.

The knights charged on either side of it, keeping it on their left and not the other way round as one might expect, and since, under the rules, they had to hold the lance in the right hand, they could only aim at an angle of 30° over their horse's necks and merely strike the hardest blow obliquely.

This restriction lessened the perils enormously and, although there were sometimes serious accidents—the King of France, Henry II, was actually killed by one of Lord Eglinton's forebears, a Count Montgomery, in 1559, jousting across a barrier—the use of a fence or 'tilt', first mentioned in 1429, brought an end to the days of excessive casualties.

It also altered the whole tenor of the joust which became a trial of skill instead of force. Those men who were born bullies and who, in the past, had challenged others just for exercise and often killed them, were forced to look for other forms of amusement. For if the knights were using 'arms of courtesy'—blunted lances with spiked iron rings on their tips, known as coronels, or wooden discs, known as rochets—and if they were wearing the enormous helmets and huge shields that were made specially for such contests, they were half blind, half deaf, half stifled and half cooked, and if they struck their opponents at all, they only gave them a buffet.

Doomed to be drawn like this for ever afterwards by caricaturists, by the end of the reign of Queen Elizabeth they were nearly as helpless as tortoises; they could hardly mount their steeds without assistance and they fell as heavily as ripe coconuts the moment they lost their balance.

Such encounters were known as 'triumphs'; and in these twilight years of chivalry, interminable complaints by hoary knights of the abominable decadence of modern youth compared to the strength and prowess of their grandfathers were heard in every country in Europe.

They inspired the story of Don Quixote which was published in Spain in 1605 and translated into English seven years afterwards. As Byron said: 'Cervantes smiled Spain's chivalry away.'*

It is interesting to compare an authentic challenge of the 14th century with another from a triumph of 1612, the one an invitation in clear, cordial terms to a trial of manly skill and courage, the other a perfect example, almost meaningless, of the rhetoric of decadent chivalry.

In 1389, three famous French knights, de Boucicaut, de Sampi and de Roye, wishing to avenge a technical insult to one of their friends and also to impress some 'frisky ladies', obtained the royal consent to the following announcement:†

From the great desire we have to become acquainted with the nobles, gentlemen, knights and squires bordering on the kingdom of France, as well as with those in the more distant countries, we propose being at St Ingelvere‡ the twentieth day of May next ensuing, and to remain there for thirty days complete; and on each of these thirty days, excepting the Fridays, we will deliver from their vows all knights, squires and gentlemen, from whatever countries they may come, with five courses with a sharp or blunt lance, according to their pleasure, or with both lances if more agreeable.

* *Don Juan* xxxvi.
† Froissart, Johnes Edn. Vol. 4, p. 99.
‡ A village in Picardy near Calais.

On the outside of our tents will be hung our shields, blazoned with our arms; that is to say, with our targets of war and our shields of peace. Whoever may choose to tilt with us has only to come, or send any one, the preceding day, to touch with a rod either of these shields, according to his courage. If he touch the target, he shall find an opponent ready on the morrow to engage him in a mortal combat with three courses with a lance: if the shield, he shall be tilted with a blunted lance; and if both shields are touched, he shall be accommodated with both sorts of combat. Every one who may come, or send to touch our shields, must give his name to the persons who shall be appointed to the care of them. And all such foreign knights and squires as shall be desirous of tilting with us, shall bring with them some noble friend, and we will do the same on our parts, who will order what may be proper to be done on either side. We particularly entreat, such noble knights or squires as may accept our challenge, to believe that we do not make it through presumption, pride or any ill will, but solely with a view of having their honourable company, and making acquaintance with them, which we desire from the bottom of our hearts. None of our targets shall be covered with steel or iron, any more than those who may tilt with us; nor shall there be any fraud, deceit or trick made use of, but what shall be deemed honourable by the judges of the tournament. And that all gentlemen, knights, and squires, to whom these presents shall come, may depend on their authenticity, we have set to them our seals, with our arms, this twentieth day of November, at Montpellier, in the year of grace 1389.

Three hundred years later in England, the Duke of

Lenox and the Earls of Southampton, Pembroke and Montgomery\* issued the annexed terms for a joust, the MS of which may be read in the British Museum.†

To all honourable men at Arms and Knight adventurers of hereditary note and exemplary nobless that for most memorable actions do wield either sword or lance in quest of glory:

Right brave and Chivalrous wheresoever through the world we four knights errant denominated of the fortunate Island, servants of the destinies awaking your sleeping courages with Martial greetings.

Know ye our sovereign lady and Mistress, mother of the fates, Empress of high achievements, revolving of late the Adamantine leaves of her eternal volumes, and finding that the triumphal times were now at hand, wherein the marvellous adventures of the Lucent Pillar should now be revealed to the wonder of time and men (As Merlin, secretary to her most inward design did long time since prophesy) hath therefore most deeply weighing with herself how necessary it is that some opinion should prepare the way to worthy celebration of so unheard of matter, been pleased to command us, her voluntary but ever most humble votaries, solemnly to publish and maintain by all allowed ways of knightly arguing these undisputable propositions following:

1. That in service of ladies knights have no free will.
2. That it is Beauty maintains the world in valour.
3. That no fair lady was ever false.
4. That none can be perfectly wise but lovers.

The St Inglevere tournament, held on the 21st of the

---

\* No relation to the Eglinton family.
† Harl. MS. 4888.

'charming month of May' in a place that was 'smooth and green with grass', was a great success, and more than sixty English knights and squires sent their armour to Calais and jousted there for a week.

The challenge of 1612, if it ever was met, was probably held on the Whitehall tiltyard, the present Horseguards Parade, part of a triumph that was organised annually to mark the King's accession.

It is strange to reflect, when thinking about these latter-day attempts at knightly endeavour, so often inspired by the myths of King Arthur's Court, that none of the great legendary heroes of the British Isles—like Lancelot or Tristram—ever took part in tournaments at all or ever consciously observed the canons of chivalry.

King Arthur was probably a Welsh chieftain, lightly armed with a mail shirt and a bronze shield and helmet, who rode a pony and, if he ever lived—which has never been proved—he did so during the 5th or 6th centuries, hundreds of years before the age of the joust.

He became a knight in the Middle Ages when scribes, living in a feudal society, wrote about him as one of themselves in terms of their own environment. The invention of printing caused their texts to be fixed, the standard version in the English language, published by Caxton in 1485, being Sir Thomas Malory's. But for this, the tales might have gone on changing, each generation portraying Arthur in the form they admired the most and, if such a thing were possible, in two or three millennia to come, he might have been said to have been a knight of space.

The fact, however, that the sagas became settled in the Middle Ages had this important consequence. That the deeds described, the jousts and tournaments, and the way the knights prepared and fought in them, allowing only for poetic exaggeration, are quite correct and perfectly feasible in terms of the age of chivalry; for Sir Thomas Malory, a knight himself, wrote from his own experience. This gives the tales an authenticity and accounts for their great appeal to Gothic revivalists.

*So when King Arthur was come they blew unto the field; and then there began a great party, then was there hurling and rushing. Then Sir Tristram came in and began so roughly and so bigly that there was none might withstand him, and thus Sir Tristram dured long. And then Sir Tristram saw ... forty knights together ... and he fared among those knights like a greyhound among conies; and at every stroke Sir Tristram well-nigh smote down a knight. Then King Arthur with a great eager heart he gat a spear in his hand, and there upon the one side he smote Sir Tristram over his horse. Then foot-hot Sir Palomides came upon Sir Tristram, as he was upon foot, to have over-ridden him. Then Sir Tristram was ware of him, and there he stooped aside, and with great ire he gat him by the arm, and pulled him down from his horse.

Then Sir Palomides lightly arose, and then they dashed together mightily with their swords; and many kings, queens, and lords stood and beheld them. And at the last Sir Tristram smote Sir Palomides upon the helm three mighty strokes, and at every stroke that he gave he said, Have this for Sir Tristram's sake. With that Sir Palomides fell to the earth grovelling. And then Sir Tristram ... rode to an old knight's place to lodge them. And that old knight had five sons at the tournament, for whom he prayed God heartily for their coming home. And so, as the French book saith, they came home all five well beaten. And to make short tale

* Book Nine—the tournament at the Castle of Maidens.

L

in conclusion . . . by cause Sir Launcelot abode and was
the last in the field the prize was given him. But Sir
Launcelot would neither for king, queen, nor knight
have the prize, but where the cry was cried through the
field, Sir Launcelot, Sir Launcelot hath won the field
this day, Sir Launcelot let make another cry contrary,
Sir Tristram hath won the field, for he began first, and
last he hath endured, and so hath he done the first day,
the second, and the third day.'

To what extent, if any, all these various facts were
finally unearthed by the Eglinton knights before they left
the meeting at Pratt's workshop is not precisely recorded.
But when they parted, one point at least was clear to
everyone—that if they were going to fight at all they would
have to do so over a tilt, and the very most they could hope
to revive was something after the style of the 16th century.
Anything else in modern times, any form of open joust, or
any attempt at a general *mêlée* would be obviously quite
impossible. So in the end they decided to settle for a
'Triumph'.

At this more than half of them resigned, especially
those who were young and tough, who had looked forward
to a rollicking fight with the hope of winning a ransom.
For only a few were as rich as Lord Eglinton, and none of
the others could agree to the rule that, if they lost a joust,
they would forfeit their equipment.

About forty determined to go on, for the more they
talked of the deeds of old—even the tilts of Henry VIII—
the more they longed to attempt them.

So it was decided to meet again; and those who had not
got armour at home and had no friends from whom they
could borrow it, gave provisional orders for suits to Pratt.

During the months that followed, the winter of 1838,

nothing special occurred of any interest. Lord Eglinton spent the season hunting, taking a lodge at Melton Mowbray to follow Lord Suffield's hounds; the Lamb family went to Nice; Pratt visited Portugal, Spain, Italy and Germany and purchased quantities of armour.

Little happened either in the country generally. The various sources of contemporary history, like the *Annual Register* and the *British Almanack*, merely record a number of petty events which were strange then because they were new, are quaint now because they are old, but had no intrinsic significance.

The famous astronaut, John Hampton, ascended 9,000 feet in a balloon, jumped out of it over Cheltenham and floated safely back to earth by parachute. A man who was aptly surnamed Hopper ran half a mile in less than two minutes. He actually did it in one hundred and twelve seconds by leaping down a hill, but at the bottom he nearly died of exhaustion. An equinoctial gale of amazing velocity blew a pair of locked, empty railway carriages $24\frac{1}{2}$ miles in the middle of the night on a new unopened line from London to Maidenhead.

It was, if anything, a winter of plans and projects and, although many of them are seen now as important bricks in the constitutional fabric, they were unappreciated at the time and completed later. This was true of the scheme for a penny postage. The idea of a flat rate, paid in advance by way of a sticky stamp for all letters up to half an ounce to be carried to any place in the British Isles embraced a new principle. It was then in the hands of a Select Committee of the House of Commons and quite inevitably many people, especially all the officials of the Post Office, swore it would never work.

Another important change was urged by the Chartists. Called thus because they supported a 'People's Charter', recently devised by the famous Feargus O'Connor, they demanded the following reforms: annual parliaments, manhood suffrage, votes by ballot, and payment of Members of Parliament who should not be required to be owners of property. Drawn from the new industrial working classes whose already pitiful state was doomed to be worse as sodden harvests raised the price of bread and old restrictive laws forbade its import, they stole weapons, drilled secretly and went at night to wild heaths for mysterious torchlight meetings. As yet they were only a nuisance to local authorities although, before the end of the coming decade, they forced the Government to prepare for a civil war.

In the late spring the Whig Government, which had lost ground steadily for several years, failed to get a majority and the Prime Minister tendered his resignation. Queen Victoria sent for Sir Robert Peel, the leader of the Tories, but when, contrary to normal practice, she refused to dismiss her Ladies in Waiting and appoint others with different sympathies, Sir Robert declined to co-operate. This was a stroke of luck for the Ladies in Waiting, as well as a tactical triumph for the Whigs. So Lord Melbourne had to be asked to return, and as the Queen particularly liked him—to such an extent, in fact, that people had started to comment—she, too, felt in luck and there was, to use an Arthurian expression, 'great joy and great nobley' in the hearts of all who lived at Buckingham Palace.

For one of these ladies, however, there was only misery and death and on her account the first stain fell on the record of the Court. Lady Flora, the daughter of the Marquess of Hastings, who attended the Duchess of Kent, the Queen's mother, and had held her train at the coronation, was a quiet woman of thirty-three who had never chosen to get married. Quite suddenly, she appeared to be having a baby. And because she held such a prominent position it was felt that she ought to be questioned. When accused she proclaimed her innocence and, in the end, to quell the rumours, permitted a doctor to make an examination. A few months later she died of cancer of the liver. So there was a scandal of another sort and some unjustly blamed the Queen for ever allowing such doubts on a lady's honour.

As the months passed and the summer approached, the Eglinton Tournament came more and more into prominence. What had been planned as a private garden party had developed into a rout for practically everybody. Each week in all the newspapers there were more notes about the arrangements, more gossip about the knights, more details about their armour and more stories about Lord Eglinton himself. For the Tournament, now, had made him a national figure and, within the limits of those days when important people still had privacy, everything he said and did was published in the press.

When the hunting season was over, he went to Ayrshire for his annual spring race meeting and Easter house party. At this time, when he had first thought of it, he had hoped to hold the Tournament but, even after the opening meeting at Pratt's in the previous autumn, he had seen clearly that, with so many difficult matters to organise, such an early date would prove impossible. So he had put it off to the end of the summer.

Among his guests at Eglinton Castle were both the Londonderrys, the Marquess soon to be King of the Tournament and his wife, so the papers hinted, the one for whom the jousts were really to be given. For no one could believe that there was not a woman in the background. In fact, nothing was further from the truth for, although Lord Eglinton and she were friends and a generation younger than her husband, there was never the slightest trace of an affair between them.

When news is scarce trifles are recorded. The *Glasgow Courrier* announced that his guests had presented £30 as an Easter offering to his local kirk at Fullarton; *The Times* confirmed his arrival in London; the *Court Journal* revealed that he went to a ball at Buckingham Palace; the *Morning Post* reported his presence at a dinner at Holderness House.

This banquet, held by the Londonderry's, was given in honour of the official visit of the eldest son of the Emperor of Russia, traditionally known as the Czarevitch. He was making his first tour of Europe on coming of age and, to mark the occasion, he founded the famous Czarevitch stakes at Newmarket. He had been at Turin during the previous February and there his host, the King of Sardinia, a noted collector of arms and armour, had welcomed his presence with a tournament. Although it had not really been anything more than a military review with knights in groups, every detail, if he spoke about it, must have interested Lord Eglinton.

For now, at the height of the summer season, the latter's own attempt was drawing close. And because, like any budding knight he and his horse required experience, he decided the moment had come to arrange some practices. So after the races at Ascot, at which the unfortunate Queen was hissed because of the demise of Lady Flora, he and the rest of the Eglinton knights—now reduced to thirty-five—agreed to arm and stage a series of rehearsals.

Pratt having been badgered almost beyond his wits by the press in the previous months—being a mere tradesman in a shop without the protection of class or money—knew the public would like to watch and managed to persuade the champing knights to agree to it.

So the dates of the rehearsals were announced and, in the words of a contemporary journalist, 'all persons of good taste and rank and fashion were on the *qui vive*.'\*

\* Richardson, p. 1. intro. to *The Eglinton Tournament*.

# Chapter Nine

To WALK about in a suit of armour is a strange and interesting experience.

When the knights went round to Pratt's and saw their harness hanging in lifeless shapes on dummies—the correct term for which is a dobble—they must have expected like everyone else who has ever tried one on in present times that, apart from the apparently obvious limitation on ordinary movement, the weight alone would be crippling.

But that all suits of armour weighed an enormous amount is a modern popular fallacy. The average field suit for wear in battle during the 15th century, when armour was still in normal use, tipped the scales at five or six stones or eighty pounds, and this included the clothes that were worn underneath it. (see plate 8.)

These garments certainly—the stiff, quilted, sleeved bodice of leather or fustian, known as the arming doublet, and the heavy iron shirt of mail, the hauberk, reaching almost down to the knees to protect the fork—constricted the wearer seriously—but the armour itself, so long as it fitted—and this was a matter of the greatest consequence—felt extraordinarily light.

The reason for this was the distribution of its weight which, as all soldiers knew, was achieved best when the cut of the suit was correct. Every wealthy knight kept his own armourer and dobble and, if he commissioned a suit from abroad, from one of the great smiths in Germany or Italy, he had to send his precise measurements, very often a suit of clothes, and sometimes even a wax model of his legs.

For these limbs had to be fitted perfectly. The shoe, naturally, had to snug the foot; it was called a sabaton and was really a sole-less overshoe. The gaiter above it was properly called the greave. Here, both the length and diameter were critical; it had to be fashioned to enclose the calf and it had to bridge the exact distance between the heel and the kneecap. Over the knee was a 'U' shaped piece called the poleyn and connected to it, over the thigh, a wide, flattish, curved plate, the cuisse. The length was the point to watch with this. If it was too short, it exposed the groin and, if it was too long, it fouled the tasset, the over-lapping plate which hung down from the cuirass.

The cuirass itself, which comprised the back and breast-plates together and enclosed the trunk, weighed about a third of the whole and was also particularly important. It had, of course, to box the chest comfortably and it had to rest on the hips and shoulders exactly. If it did not it could cause the greatest discomfort, either by hanging too much on the neck or by bearing down too hard on the pelvis. It might even choke the wearer to death, the collar, or gorget, pressing against his Adam's apple and the chin guard, or bevor, supposedly called thus from the French 'to dribble', grinding against his jawbone. He would then not be able to open his mouth, draw a breath or even gulp to his squire that he wanted his help.

The need for the right pieces for the hands, the correct size in gloves or gauntlets, and the proper sheaths for the shoulders and the arms—called respectively the pauldrons and the vambraces—is basically the same as that for the feet and legs and is clear and perfectly obvious.

With the helmet, the requirements were rather more complicated. Weighing six pounds at least, which is three times more than the modern military equivalent, it had to sit on the head correctly because of the level of the sight.

This was the slot through which the knight peeped and, with the type of helmet known as the sallet which swept away at the back and was used for ordinary fighting, this line had to be even with the eyes.

As a result, apart from having to fit, it had to be firmly fixed for, although it provided excellent forward vision when it was adjusted, it blinded the wearer at once the moment it slipped. Lined with leather and worn on a specially padded cap, it was held in place by a sometimes painful chinstrap.

Most of the armour supplied by Pratt was sold afterwards and has since vanished, but the suit worn by the 3rd Marquess of Waterford was bought at a sale the following year by the Tower of London for exhibition in Queen Elizabeth's Armoury. It can be seen now at Windsor Castle and, although in fact a fake, it is such a good one that Pratt himself undoubtedly thought it genuine.

Of a type generally described as 'Gothic'—that is to say, of the 15th century—of thin, light hard steel that even now refuses to be welded, it was probably made in Germany. With long detachable points to the toes, shapely sabatons, elegant greaves, winged poleyns, fluted cuisses, laminated vambraces, massive pauldrons, pouting breast-plate and sweeping sallet, all shining with a grey light like old, smooth, burnished silver, it is indeed a work of beauty and craftsmanship. To stride about in such a suit is to sip the cup of vanity. No wonder that a 'shining knight' has remained a popular image!

Lord Waterford certainly looked superb in it and, once the others had joined him at Pratt's and assumed their own as well, they were all suddenly touched by a medieval spell. They strode about, couched lances, admired their figures like a group of actors and banged each other cheerfully on the head.

Pratt was completely enchanted, too; and thus, in June, 1839, the final steps were taken to launch the Tournament.

The place at which the knights decided to rehearse was a large garden behind the Eyre Arms, a popular tavern close to Regent's Park. Now a block of flats called Eyre Court, on the Finchley Road, it stood on a hill on the route to Golders Green, a traditional, spacious, comfortable, Georgian hostelry. Its roof, from which the view was magnificent, was furnished with tables and chairs for the summer evenings, and its green and shady grounds were used for sports like cricket and archery, as well as for launching balloonists. It contained, too, a small theatre and ballroom in which there were cheerful plays and other amusements; for St John's Wood was the haunt of many charmers. One of the sweetest, Elizabeth Howard, was soon to become the mistress of Louis Napoleon. Known earlier by the name of Haryett, and then protected by a Major Martin, she is said to have first seen the Prince during the Tournament rehearsals.

If the knights supposed, like the crowds who came to see them, that having to practise wearing armour and generally limbering up for a tournament was a shameful necessity, enforced by modern conditions, they were very greatly mistaken. The only cause they had for shame, in terms of genuine knightly habit, was the age at which they were doing it.

In the days of chivalry, a potential knight, having left his mother to become a page or varlet at the age of seven, advanced to the state of esquire at the time of puberty and from that moment rode in armour and embarked on a course of the strictest military training.

If he were tough he might have started earlier like the great French knight, de Boucicaut, one of the three challengers of the tournament at Calais in 1389, who beat his tiny friends to jelly almost before he could talk and in later youth, according to the *Livre des faits de Boucicaut*, hardened himself by wearing armour for every conceivable exercise—for running, jumping, turning somersaults and even for swimming and dancing.

Most of the Eglinton knights were tough, some even had left their homes at the age of seven but none, naturally, had ever done anything like this.

The ground on which they assembled behind the Eyre Arms was railed off against the public to prevent accidents, just as it would have been during the Middle Ages, and contained a tilt or barrier down the centre as well as a piece of equipment known as a quintain. This gadget for training mounted spearmen—one of the oldest methods there is and still employed by cavalry today—resembles a man's torso with arms outstretched and was so fixed to an upright pole that it twirled freely like a weathervane. If it was struck on the chest exactly square by the charging knight, it caused his lance to shiver; if it was hit on the right or left breast it spun about and whacked his head as he passed it.

As well as this there was a dummy knight perched on a wooden horse on wheels which rocketed down a pair of grooves towards the barrier and which, therefore, might be used as an opponent. Everyone called it the Railway Knight and thought it a real piece of contemporary ingenuity; in fact, they were three hundred years behind the times, for just such rolling dummies were used in the 16th century.

If the knights discovered that nothing new could be said about learning to joust, so when they tried it they encountered all the difficulties known to their medieval ancestors. The greatest of these was teaching the horses to gallop close to the barrier, not so near that the rider's leg was crushed, and not so far that a blow became impossible. Some of the mettled hunters on which they were mounted simply refused to do it while others only finally complied after weeks and weeks of exhausting and tedious training.

Eventually most of them managed to succeed, including Lord Waterford, riding, according to the *Morning Post*, 'a handsome bay horse with a plain smooth bit in his mouth, with which no other man could possibly control him.'* But this was only after repeated tumbles, made the worse in Lord Waterford's case on one occasion by being locked in his armour, face downwards on a heap of dung and sawdust for twenty minutes while his baffled squires struggled to wrench him out of it.

Even this was an old experience. Jousting armour was held together with nuts and bolts which required a spanner to take them apart and if they were damaged they often jammed. In Arthurian legend, the young Sir Percivale who, like the Eglinton knights, had never been trained as a page or esquire and had reached manhood without a knight's experience, having killed the Red Knight in his first joust, could not unfasten the latter's suit of armour. So he decided to build a bonfire and consume the body inside it; but, as he began, Sir Owain arrived and showed him the proper way to take it to pieces.

A knight who failed to school his horse completely was the Hon. Edward Jerningham, 2nd son of Lord Stafford of Costessy Hall in Norfolk, an old house recently modernised in the latest Gothic manner. He appeared as the Knight of the Swan, his family emblem, and so perfectly copied the flight of this marvellous bird that, darting down the lists at the Railway Knight, he lost his balance and flew

* July 8th 3.c.

into the sunshine while his horse, suddenly relieved of his control, trampled over an innocent nearby varlet.

Everyone laughed but, had they known it, many an ancestor had done the same before him. One is even specifically recorded doing so—Henry Jerningham, the first of Costessy, who fell off his horse outside Calais in 1547 as he, too, rehearsed for a coming tournament.*

Oddly enough, however, apart from a few sprains and bruises, there were no serious accidents except in the case of one Scottish laird, John Campbell of Saddell, who allowed himself to be charged at the first rehearsal to test the force of the impact. Sitting motionless on his horse and wearing only a breastplate, he received a direct hit from a lance which slipped to the side, pierced his elbow and snapped off, dragging him out of the saddle. This could never have happened had he been properly armed. He was said by a wit—reputedly Theodore Hook—to have lost his family seat; and many weeks passed before he recovered.

From other points of view beside his own, it was just as well that he survived since, when the news of his accident reached the Sheriff of Ayr in whose shrievalty Eglinton Castle stood, it caused the latter, very sensibly, to threaten to ban the jousting altogether. For according to 'No Tilter' in a letter to *The Times* on the 11th of July, who quoted Blackstone, any knight who caused the death of another would be guilty of manslaughter, while anyone present, even, for example, the Queen of Beauty, could be charged with aiding and abetting him.

This was assuming, quite correctly, that Lord Eglinton held the tournament without the Queen's permission; at least no trace of an application has survived in the Royal

* *The Encyclopaedia of Sport*, V. II.—article on tournaments by Viscount Dillon.

Archives; for which, under the edicts of Henry III, he ought to have lost his honours and been disinherited.

If, however, he failed in this respect, in all others he took the greatest precautions. He assured the Sheriff that no knight would engage in combat without being wholly and properly equipped and that all the spears would be arms of courtesy which, to make them snap cleanly and not splinter, would be cut from light pine on the cross grain. As the ground would be deep with sawdust and as the knights would be clad in armour, they would suffer far less danger in a fall than they would if they fell out hunting.

Furthermore, at the rest of the rehearsals, he issued the following instruction:

It is expressly ordered by the Earl of Eglinton, and must be distinctly understood by each knight upon engaging to run a course, that he is to strike his opponent on no other part than the shield; and that an atteint made elsewhere will be adjudged foul, and the match forfeited.

Particular attention is most earnestly requested to be paid to this injunction for the general good and credit of the proposed tournament, as any untoward accident might throw discredit upon it, or even prevent its ever taking place, by force of law or public opinion.*

All these efforts had their effect; no further accidents occurred and after a while the Sheriff withdrew his objections.

One of the points about which the press wrote much and everyone talked for hours was the probable cost which was obviously going to be stupendous.

* *The Standard*, July 15th, 4.b.

When the knights had met at Pratt's showroom the previous autumn, they had worked out, with the latter's help, that they ought to have managed for £40 each— perhaps £150 in the 1960's.

But before the summer, the figure per head had risen to £400 while even this, for any knight who wished to make a display with a fine retinue of men at arms and tents, banners and heraldic trappings, was clearly going to be inadequate.

One of the knights for whom this was the case was Lord Glenlyon, aged 25, nephew and heir of the 5th Duke of Atholl. Both Pratt's estimate before the rehearsals and the receipted final account, which was settled two years afterwards, as well as the very armour itself, are still to be seen at the family's ancestral home, Blair Castle in Perthshire; and so, from them, we can note the actual facts.

Although Lord Glenlyon bought his armour, the printed estimate, headed 'THE EGLINTON TOURNAMENT' in Gothic letters, for the 'ARMOUR, HORSE CAPARISONS, &c., of a KNIGHT, with the COSTUME, &c., for the ESQUIRE and PAGES,' reveals that he might have hired it.

'A plain Suit of KNIGHT'S *Cap-à-pie* Armour, fitted and lined with leather, &c., &c., with Tilting pieces complete', could be bought for 150 gns or hired for 60 gns, the 'Modelled Crest and emblazoned Banner' which went with it being for purchase only at 8 gns. The *richest emblazoned* Housings, Saddle, Bridle, and Horse Armour, as equipped for the Tilt to the Plain Suit,' could be bought or hired for 50 gns or 20 gns respectively; a 'KNIGHT'S Encampment, two Pavilions, Camp Bed, &c.,' could be borrowed for 40 gns.

If this was a lot, it was only the beginning. Lord Glenlyon's account came out as follows:

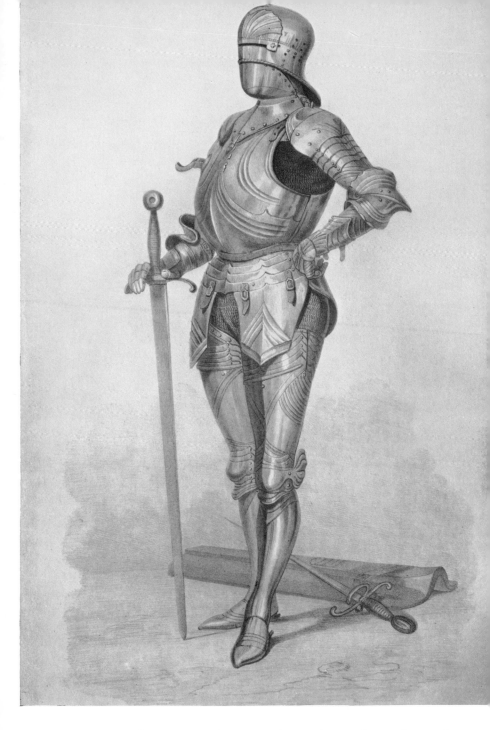

8. A suit of armour, in the Musée de Tsarskoye-Selo, similar to the
one worn by the Marquess of Waterford (a lithograph by Asselineau
of a drawing by A. Rockstuhl)

| | £ | s | d |
|---|---|---|---|
| A suit of Knight's polished steel *Cap-à-pie* Tilting Armour with steel Manteau d'arme and Mentonière, &c. | £105 | 0 | 0 |
| A Modelled Crest and emblazoned Banner | 8 | 8 | 0 |
| A set of Horse caparisons with tilting saddle and Horse Armour complete | 42 | 0 | 0 |
| Loan of encampment consisting of large tent & two pavilions in own colours with Bed, &c. | 42 | 10 | 0 |
| A buff Leather Dress to wear under Armour | 5 | 5 | 0 |
| Extra, for a finely fluted and engraved helmet instead of plainer one for suit | 7 | 7 | 0 |
| Emblazonments of armorial bearings on Horse caparison—extra | 4 | 4 | 0 |
| An Emblazoned Shield with Armorial bearings highly finished* A rich silk Gonfalon Banner edged with rich fringe with Armorial bearings & staff complete | 11 | 11 | 0 |
| Additional crests made from mould and finished in proper colours | 2 | 18 | 0 |
| Emblazoning Manteau d'arme with Armorial bearings—at the point of attaint | 1 | 11 | 6 |
| Expense of cleaning and repairs of Armour after practice at St John's Wood, cartage to ground and attendance, &c., Gauntlets, &c. | 12 | 14 | 0 |
| A rich velvet Mortière cap for practice | 1 | 12 | 0 |
| A rich silk velvet hood for procession | 2 | 12 | 6 |
| A chain mail hauberk shirt, to order | 12 | 12 | 0 |

* The cost of a shield like this in 1278, made specially for a tournament at Windsor, was 5d. R. C. Clephan *Armour* p. 81.

M

| | | | |
|---|---|---|---|
| A strong mêlée sword made after ancient model with Buff Belt, Mêlée scarf, etc. | 4 | 4 | 0 |
| Loan of a coronet for Helmet | 1 | 5 | 0 |
| Making up a rich evening costume out of tartan velvet supplied by Lord G. with cap & plume and a pair of superior scarlet silk hose pantaloons | 17 | 0 | 0 |
| An extra pair of elastic silk hose pantaloons | 3 | 3 | 0 |
| A rich velvet mantle made to order lined with satin edged with rich lace, &c. | 8 | 8 | 0 |
| Embroidering Ancle Boots | | 15 | 6 |
| A short silk shirt | | 16 | 6 |
| A polished steel demi suit of Armour for practice in Scotland, with buff coat, gloves, &c. | 9 | 9 | 0 |
| Case for ditto and packing | | 3 | 6 |
| Loan of 15 additional lances painted in own colours (3 splintered) | 10 | 10 | 0 |
| A pair of gilt Knight's spurs | 3 | 3 | 0 |
| Case for Armour and packing up ditto, & encampment costume &c., & expense of carriage of ditto to Eglinton Castle and part back | 14 | 15 | 0 |
| A beautiful model of *cap-à-pie* suit of armour on jointed figure | 12 | 12 | 0 |
| | £346 | 9 | 6 |

In addition to this, Lord Glenlyon spent £1,000 in equipping, clothing and feeding a grand retinue of 78 officers and men from the private regiment, raised in 1777, which is still maintained by the Dukes of Atholl today, known as the Atholl Highlanders.

No final total is available but, including the usual,

unforseen expenses which are paid in cash and never recorded, it must have been little short of £1,500.

For the other knights who had not inherited feudal, ancestral retainers in highland garb, Pratt ordered four hundred authentic uniforms from Messrs Haigh, Theatrical Costumers, of Covent Garden, every one of which was exactly copied from a portrait or medieval manuscript.

Such a desire to have everything perfect, characteristic of the whole tournament as well as the Gothic Revival itself, was a real proof of Pratt's enthusiasm and also, perhaps, of the folly of those who paid him; for the work and time involved in this alone must have been quite prodigious. At least he was praised as well as being remunerated. Every reporter from every newspaper proclaimed that what he had done was truly marvellous.

The particular day about which the press wrote with such enthusiasm was Saturday afternoon, July 13th, the last and dress rehearsal. The first really huge crowd, 2,690 of 'the very *élite* of the most *élite*,' in the words of the *Court Journal*, drove out to see it in brilliant sunshine, each bearing a personal card of admission, specially printed and signed by Pratt, the mere labour of doing which must again have been enormous. Every road and street within half a mile of the Eyre Arms was jammed with carriages three and four abreast and by 2.30 the block was complete, in spite of the efforts of a strong contingent of Division 'S' of the Marylebone Police under Inspector Furlong. Late arrivals had to walk, and some very peculiar medieval words were said to have passed between them.

Inside the grounds things were better. The lists, a long rectangle of four acres, had tiered benches along the sides with plenty of room for everybody, and groups of tents at either end, some for use of the competing knights and others for distinguished visitors.

The guest of honour was the Duchess of Cambridge, Princess Augusta Wilhelmina Louise of Hesse-Cassel, the wife of the 7th son of George III, to whom Lord Burghersh had dedicated his opera *The Tournament*. His absorbing work, now a year old but still remembered, had just appeared in print and, according to current rumour, was soon to be followed by another. This was more than some could bear and Barnard Gregory who, as editor of the *Satirist*, was always in trouble for spreading impertinent scandals about the aristocracy, implored his Lordship to have the courage to destroy it.

The knights, first 150 strong, then diminished to 35 and now reduced to 19, were announced in the papers as follows: The Duke of Beaufort; the Earls of Eglinton, Cassillis, Craven; The Marquess of Waterford; the Viscounts Alford, Glenlyon; the Lord Cranstoun; the Hon. E. Jerningham; the Baronets F. Bathurst, F. Johnstone, F. Hopkins; the Captains Gage, Maynard, Beresford, Fairlie; the Esquires J. Campbell, C. Boothby, and Charlie Lamb.

The Marshal of the Lists who acted as umpire was not, for some reason that is not explained, the official already appointed, Charlie's father, Sir Charles Lamb, but Lord Gage, his neighbour, of Firle near Lewes.

Apart from the fact that the jousts did not begin until nearly four o'clock—although they were due to start at three—everything went off perfectly. All the knights were bright with armour, all their steeds were gay with caparisons, all their tents were adorned with banners, all the heralds were tricked in tabards, while men at arms in appropriate costumes kept the crowds at bay with gleaming halberds. The combatants charged the Railway Knight, attacked the quintain, and then, after a pause to adjust their harness, bowed to the Duchess of Cambridge and ran their courses.

No scores were kept but although several knights, notably Lord Glenlyon and Captain Gage, were still unable to control their horses which swerved away from the barrier, most of the others, including Lord Eglinton, struck each other's shields with a bang and broke their lances splendidly. Captain Maynard—a knight who did not appear at the real Tournament a month later, perhaps through illness—performed various modern lance exercises on a 'very beautiful charger' and leapt back and forward over the barrier in full armour. Throughout the day the weather was hot and brilliant; not a cloud crossed the sky and not a breeze stirred a hair or ruffled the hem of a petticoat.

Even those who, up until then, had condemned the affair as silly were forced to admit that, after all, perhaps it was fairly effective and, setting aside the already much debated social question of whether or not a man might do what he liked with his own, agreed that the Tournament looked like being a success.

For in every respect the knights were jousting properly; and no amount of reading *Ivanhoe*, staring at pictures in the Royal Academy or watching a fight at Astley's Amphitheatre could give so good an idea as the actual thing.

Nothing remained now but the Tournament itself which the papers announced for the 28th of August. All the knights went off to the races at Goodwood—Lord Eglinton staying with the Duke of Richmond and running St Bennett, one of the best horses he ever possessed—while most of the others reposed at Bersted, the very place from which Charlie Lamb had ridden forth the year before to meet his fate in Charlotte. After the meeting, on Saturday

August 3rd, they went to Firle Place. Here, the Gage family home since the 15th century, where Captain Gage's Eglinton Tournament armour may still be seen, his father, Lord Gage, whose very title derived from the glove that was flung by knights for a challenge, gave them a farewell banquet. Then, in a state of gay excitement, they galloped away to their own ancestral homes.

'My dear Rush,' Lord Eglinton wrote at the last minute to his personal chaplain, Henry John Rush—possibly a cousin to Sir Samuel Meyrick and the local vicar at Beauport—the only invitation in his own hand that research has brought to light.

> If you have any idea of ever coming so far north, and you think a Tournament a sufficient temptation to undertake so long a journey, I hope my Chaplain will give me the pleasure of his company on that occasion. Pray excuse the lateness of this invitation, and believe me,
> very sincerely yours,
> Eglinton

Newcastle, Tuesday.
 I am so far on my way to Eglinton.

For those intent on every development and not blessed with intimate notes like Henry Rush, the newspapers kept them posted.

Every day every editor released a revealing titbit. Even the sober readers of *The Times* were kept informed to the minute. They were told that everything was going splendidly; the final work at Eglinton Castle was progressing with 'railway speed'.

# Chapter Ten

THE COUNTY of Ayrshire, towards which so many people began to turn their thoughts as the month of August progressed, lies on the west coast of Scotland to the south of Glasgow and forms the eastern shore of the Firth of Clyde.

Although it is in the Lowlands and only fifty miles from the English border, its moors and hills, if not so grand, are as wild and beautiful as any to be found in the north, while towards the sea, towards the capital of Ayr itself and towards Lord Eglinton's castle and estates its farms and meadows are rich and lush and justly cause its cheese and cattle to be famous.

The air is sweet in this part of the country, soft, enchanting and filled with the promise of the sea. Gulls mew in the wake of the plough, the sparkling bays are splashed with tumbling gannetts and the grey cliffs and beaten rocks echo the piping cry of the paddling oyster-catchers. After rain on a sunny morning, the view of the mountains over the shining white rippling sands and green water— the isles of Bute and Arran and the Mull of Kintyre— casts a spell on the heart and memory of all who have ever seen it.

The only great snag is the changeable weather. The prevailing, warm, Atlantic wind causes persistent rainfall. If the hills can be seen clearly, then it is likely to be wet soon and if they cannot be seen at all, then it is certain to be raining already. The sun shines, the sea evaporates, clouds form and are wafted to Ayrshire. There they begin to lift and precipitate, finally to burst with the force of a Biblical deluge.

By a stroke of exciting luck for all who wished to go there from the south—those who wanted to attend the Tournament and the usual sportsmen who were after grouse—a large part of the journey could be made in a train. A new railway stretched as far as Liverpool and, although the fare was double that by coach—roughly 3d per mile instead of $1\frac{1}{2}$d—the time taken was exactly half and the extra comfort and convenience almost incalculable.

A first class, single, day ticket for one of the four places in a 'car' cost fifty-three shillings. This was a beautiful black and Post-Office red carriage which bore the mails, the seats upholstered in drab cloth with a silk fringe and a padded headrest, facing each other in pairs as they did in a stage-coach. Second class carriages were roofed but open at the sides and third class were simply uncovered trucks. Ten trains left Euston daily; the 8.45 in the morning, for example, permitted time for refreshments in Birmingham and reached Liverpool at 6.15 that night.

By a second stroke of exciting luck, the rest of the journey could then be made by steamer. The Glasgow and Liverpool Royal Steam Packet Co. had just purchased two splendid and powerful ships, the *Royal Sovereign* and the *Royal George*, the first iron steamers to be taken into service.

Both had about the same displacement of 290 tons; carried sails, fore and aft, and one tall black and white funnel between the paddles. The promenade deck of the *Royal George* was two hundred feet in length and her engines at 21 r.p.m., at full pressure, developed 'the muscular strength of two hundred and fifty horses.'* A passenger could travel inside or out at a fare, respectively, of twenty or seven shillings.

* *Liverpool Courier*, 7th August, 1839, 255, e.

Both these steamers made connections with some of the trains from London and, as the end of the month approached and huge crowds began to travel, the owners scheduled an extra call at Ardrossan. Anyone sailing from Liverpool in the evening sighted Ayrshire as the sun rose and stepped ashore in time for a Scottish breakfast.

After this, if no train or carriage were available, a man could easily finish the journey on foot. It was only eight more miles to Eglinton Castle; and already the visitor stood on Eglinton property; already he cast his eyes on heroic ground.

During the course of the month the press had announced that, while the knights would be seen perfectly from the rising, wooded slopes which enclosed the lists, admission to which would be free to all, the best view would be had from the open, tiered stands on either side of the Queen of Beauty's Pavilion, tickets for which could be had from the Eglinton Office. One of the factors, Stewart Blair, had been seconded from his normal duties and given the special appointment of 'Clerk to the Tournament'; and these tickets could be had gratis by all who chose to apply for them.

It was only after this announcement that most of the staff on the Eglinton Estate and even, perhaps, Lord Eglinton himself had any idea of the scale of coming events.

Of course they had reckoned on a large turnout; all the people from round about, probably a sizeable contingent from Glasgow, and possibly one or two coaches with parties from Edinburgh; and in preparation for a crowd like this, such as they got at the Eglinton race meeting of a thousand or fifteen hundred at the most, they had made arrangements for all to be comfortably seated.

For although they had thought to hear from the well-to-do who subscribed to *The Times*, the *Morning Post*, the

*Court Gazette* and the other important or popular journals in which the offer of tickets had appeared, they had never expected that thousands of others who only perused the local newspapers like the *Bath Figaro*, the *Cornish Guardian*, the *Sheffield Iris* or the *Wisbech Star in the East* would also immediately write to them. But such papers took their national news from the national press and, as well as having relayed an account of the rehearsals, they had also, later, repeated the offer of tickets.

These readers wrote to Lord Eglinton in scores. From every county in the British Isles, ten thousand visitors, at least, seemed to be heading for Ardrossan. Their letters spoke in terms of numbers—parties of twenty, fifty and a hundred—which left his staff aghast.

Nearly a thousand of these epistles—nine hundred and forty, to be exact—are still to be read in the family archives, bound with leather into hefty books, the largest quantity of surviving Tournament documents.

They reveal in many charming ways how terribly badly people wanted to be present.

Since the word had spread about that Lord Eglinton hoped that as many people as possible would come in costume, uniform or fancy dress, a large number of aspirants promised to do so.

'We would be happy to appear in our Knight Templars dresses,' wrote J. W. Dunlop of himself and three friends from Edinburgh. 'I intend to appear in a Red Hunting Coat,' announced James Edington from Glasgow. 'I beg to solicit the information whether I will be admitted in the Walking Summer Costume de Campagne of a French Gent. of La Manche, Normandy, viz: a large straw hat and Blous of Checked Cotton' enquired Jas. Tertius Momsen who lived in Avranches. 'I will appear with the Livery of His Majesty of Sweden whose Consular Representative in

this city I have the honour to be,' undertook Mr J. Brook,
a Director of the Ayrshire Railway. 'As to fancy costume,
I doubt not every gentleman will comply as far as possible,'
assured James Dalglish who proposed to make up a party
of fifty and charter a steamer from Glasgow.

I find on a hurried enquiry today that some of my
friends have such dresses as they wore at Fancy Dress
Balls at different festivals in England—these can be
used if wished and upon receipt of a reply I can call a
meeting of all our party who are here and request that
those who have no such dresses may appear in sailors
dresses with Tartan Scarves.

'If costume be necessary, I for one, will come in that of
the Royal Archers of Scotland,' promised Robert Monteith.
'Two of us will appear in full Highland Costume, and the
other in the dress of an old Farmer in ancient times,'
engaged a Mr Wish. 'Being a Proprietor in the Highlands
and as Member of Direction of the Celtic Society it is my
intention to wear the Garb of the Celt,' said a Mr Patrick
Forbes.

Will you be kind enough to secure a ticket for myself
and wife—she expresses so great an inclination to be
present that I cannot refrain from troubling you in this
matter (wrote Andrew Maclure who was printing the
tickets—founder of the firm of Maclure and Macdonald
which is still in business in Glasgow today).

I sent a variety of Costumes to Mr Moffat—male
and female—of the 14th and 15th centuries—for him
to choose upon—he seems divided between a plain
Citizenie garb and that of a Scottish Peasant (early)
which will become him much, and be easily got up.
If like I will send you a few sketches of costumes I have
them from good authority.

I shall send a proof of the admission ticket, I expect, tomorrow evening.

A letter from Messrs Dale and Lockhart in Glasgow bears the following endorsement by Lady Montgomerie:

Mr Dale is of Ayrshire and much interested— Mr Lockhart is the brother of John Gibson Lockhart* and with his partner is likely to appear in some peculiarly fanciful and becoming garb for which Mr L has a great taste and fancy.

Many others based their claims on feudal connections, a common ancestry or a mutual love of the past. They confessed that, like Lord Eglinton himself, (or rather, if they had known it, Charlie Lamb), they had always dreamed of the days of chivalry, had always doted on the tales of Froissart, had always admired the works of Scott and had always, more than anything else, longed to witness a tournament. Amongst these was Lieutenant Sydney Gore of the U.S. Navy, a Dr W. F. Montgomerie from Dublin, and a Mr Douglas of Glasgow who described himself with a Gothic touch 'as one of loyal vassalage.' Another stated, 'I am a vassal of the Earl of Eglinton and Lady Mary Montgomerie—I served under the late Earl as an officer in the Ayrshire Volunteers 35 years ago, and was repeatedly employed by his Lordship on business.'

Others, again, presented their requests politically. Lord Eglinton was known to detest the Whigs and so dozens of applicants played on this and affirmed or implied they supported him.

'I have the honour to be
    A staunch Conservative—and
        Your Lordship's
        Most obedient Servant,'

* The biographer of Scott.

170

wrote a Mr W. B. Coates in a strange, backward sloping hand, in bright blue Tory ink.

'Give a ticket' minuted Lord Eglinton.

'The *only Conservative* in Stevenstone,' Lady Montgomerie scribbled at the foot of a letter from a Mr Allen.

Other tacticians were not so lucky. A Mr Paxton, writing from Kilmarnock, was just about to be sent a ticket when somebody checked him up. His letter bears the following evidence:

'Granted' (heavily scratched out)
'Enquire if a Conservative'
'NO'
'Refused' (fiercely underlined)

Robert Owen, the 'Founder of Socialism' also wrote to Lord Eglinton. In a curious document entitled *A Challenge—To the most learned and experienced in all countries . . .* he outlined his co-operative theories in twelve paragraphs and sent it off with the annexed personal note:

It may be added that it is the highest interest of each guest at your Tournament to promote the fair and full examination of these subjects, not only in the British Empire but over the World.

In consequence the Queen of Beauty and the Hero of the Tournament are requested to recommend to all Foreign Knights and their Esquires to urge the learned and most experienced in their several nations to accept this *Challenge* which is given solely to promote the happiness of all the human race.'*

Owen did not receive a ticket.

'Sir,' wrote a Mr W. F. Blair in a covering note to his namesake, the Clerk to the Tournament,

* The Eglinton papers, No. 2841. Register House, Edinburgh.

I am afraid I am taxing you too much, but as this application comes from one whom we are very anxious to be friendly too Mr MacDonald who has taken our Iron Works and who is to make us all rich, of course I am anxious to favour him.

Sir (wrote a Mr William Aitcheson) I have taken the liberty of soliciting the favour of three tickets for the Tournament to my wife, my daughter and myself. I intended to have made this application in person but could not get away. If political conduct is any inducement to grant such a great favour, it is well known that my wife with a Candlestick and I with my sword as a Leve Lieut of the Sharpshooters nearly killed a Radical at the rising in 1819 and on that occasion it was the public opinion my wife ought to have had a pension. I have suffered unendurably by adhering to the Tory party for fifty years. My daughter will be in costume and my wife very well and for myself I shall wear my cocked hat as Town Clerk of Anderston (the western suburb of the city) the most steady adherents of the Conservatives.

Glasgow, 23 Aug. 1839

By the 21st of August, however, two days before Mr Aitcheson wrote, all hope of getting a ticket had gone; for a letter of that date from a Mr Murdoch who acknowledged a couple and asked for others is minuted, 'To be written to that no more could be procured, and that it was with difficulty that these two were.'

So unless the Town Clerk was given a special seat in Lord Eglinton's private enclosure which, from his record, he certainly deserved, he must have been disappointed.

In certain cases letters were exchanged which combine to form a series:

S. F. Blair, Esq. Redburn, Irvine.

Dear Sir: Observing in the Glasgow paper of this morning a notice that application for seats at the Tournament at Eglinton Castle is to be made to you, and being anxious with a few lady friends from the United States to witness the sports, I will feel much indebted, if agreeable to the Right Honourable Earl of Eglinton and yourself if you will reserve and forward me by mail four tickets.

Being myself from the United States, and somewhat a stranger, I beg you will excuse me if my application be ill timed; and with many apologies for troubling you,

Believe me, Your very obdt Servt

B. F. Babcock

Glasgow, Aug 13, 1839

My address is Care of W. B. Huggins and Co. Glasgow.

*Paid* Glasgow 21 Aug 1839

Dear Sir: I have the pleasure to acknowledge your esteemed favour of yesterday, and am very much indebted for your kindness and politeness in proferring your services to procure lodgings etc for myself, Mr Ricards, and the two ladies. I accept with much pleasure and many thanks your good offices so courteously tendered, and will feel obliged by your engaging for me two bedrooms with parlour if practicable and Co. from the afternoon of the 27th to the morning of the 30th. I shall be quite satisfied with neat plain accommodation, and not disposed to grumble at some inconveniences on such an occasion. The names of the Ladies who are much indebted to you for your attention are

Miss Maria E. Babcock ⎱ of New York
Miss Harriet P. Swan ⎰

who with Mr Ricards and myself make up the proposed party.

Again acknowledging my obligation for your courteous attention, with many wishes that I could reciprocate the favor, and many thanks,

I am Your mo. obd. Servt.

B. F. Babcock

S. F. Blair, Esq
Irvine

Glasgow, 19th Aug 1839

Sir: I am favored with your note of yesterday. Since I had the pleasure of writing to you soliciting tickets for the Tournament for myself and ladies from the United States, the difficulty or rather impossibility of securing accommodation at or near Irvine has compelled the ladies with much reluctance to abandon their intention of accompanying me. I will feel much obliged if tickets be granted to myself and my friend Mr Jms R. Ricards of Baltimore, U.S.

With many thanks for your attention

I am Sir

Your obd. Servt.

etc., etc., etc.

B. F. Babcock

S. F. Blair, Esq.
Redburn
by Irvine

Glasgow, 22nd Aug., 1839

Dear Sir: It is with a sad heart I address you today. The Physicians have pronounced my dear and only child, now very ill, past hope of recovery. Myself and

9. Charlotte Lamb
(by Grant, c. 1843)

10. Charlie Lamb
(by Grant, c. 1843)

11. The Marquess of Waterford
(by Thorburn)

12. Louisa Waterford
(by W. Ross, R.A.)

sisters therefore on whose behalf I addressed you
yesterday will not visit the Tournament.

I cannot, my dear Sir, express my thanks for your
kindness and consideration, nor sufficiently deplore the
sad cause which blasts many, very many, of my hopes
and plans.

I hope you will hand me note of any expenses incurred
on my acct. through disappointment in lodgings you
may have engaged for me or otherwise which I will
cheerfully repay you—and believe me

> Your much obligd and humble Svt
> In haste
> B. F. Babcock

S. F. Blair, Esq.
Irvine

This last group of letters which, by their sudden, pitiful
climax, wring the heart for the unknown Babcock and, by
the answers they obviously received, throw such a warm
light on Blair, reveal, too, one of the latter's almost in-
superable difficulties. This was the finding of places for
people to sleep.

In those days even the humblest professional and business people travelled with servants—every woman, at
least, took a personal maid—and this factor doubled the
problem for a start. More than two weeks before the event
every single available space had already been bespoken
and yet, by then, only half the potential visitors had so
much as asked for tickets.

When they did so in all innocence, with no idea of the
struggle ahead and never dreaming that others were doing
the same, they were even quite peremptory.

'Dear Sir,' wrote one to a friend, the proprietor of the

Head Inn, close to Blair's office, marking the letter 'Deliver Instantly';

> By return of coach I will thank you to procure and send to me three tickets of admission to the Tournament agreeable to the enclosed note and the cash what ever it is shall be immediately returned. Do not forget this and say if you have any spare beds if good and their price. No Wines Rum, Brandy, or Ginger Cordial required on the present occasion (but?) Champaigne or claret. I am in haste
>
> Yrs truly
> James Alexander Jr

This friend lived in Irvine, the nearest so-called town, $2\frac{1}{2}$ miles from Eglinton Castle, a typical, ancient, Lowland burgh with one long wide street, 'Not only beautiful but very salubrious',* and five thousand inhabitants. Its only decent hotel was the Eglinton Arms, and here in normal times he might, if his own house had been full, have arranged the accommodation. But on this occasion its every room from attic to cellar had been booked in advance by Lord Waterford.

There was nothing else but the homes of the local inhabitants. Rooms which were let casually sometimes during the summer at four or five shillings for bed and breakfast were offered and seized at a pound and, as more and more people poured into the vicinity, every house and cottage became crammed, and even the Presbyterian Minister thanked God for a heaven-sent opportunity to practise Christian hospitality and rented his manse to a party for 30 guineas.

A similar boom in accommodation was soon enjoyed in all the towns and villages round about, and especially so

* *The New Statistical Account of Scotland*, Parish of Irvine, 1841, p. 624.

at Ardrossan. An American author, Nathaniel Parker Willis, 'a fine, tall, handsome man with an intellectual face and refined manners,' an essayist now entirely forgotten but one whose works, after his death were said to have 'floated triumphantly down the literary Ganges with their burning lamps rendering the air bright and odorous to their many admirers,'* described the scene in his *Loiterings of Travel*.

He boarded the *Royal Sovereign* at Liverpool on the 26th and disembarked at Ardrossan the following morning after a very rough passage of seventeen hours. On the trip he had shared a cabin with an English businessman who was also bound for the Tournament and, having been told that the best hotel in the place—in fact the only one—was the Eglinton Arms, they got hold of a porter together to carry their bags and trudged after him towards it down the slipway.

This hotel, like everything else in the town, had been built by the 12th Earl and was a fine, commodious Georgian edifice with eighteen bedrooms, well equipped for a normal volume of traffic which, as the harbour had never been finished, was yet extremely small. Twice a day for the last few days, however, the *Royal Sovereign* and the *Royal George* had landed people by the hundred. The weakest members of the previous contingent were still fighting at the front portico as Willis and his friend arrived.

One hundred and fifty years ago, before the Americans were rich, they were hardy travellers and Willis, who seems to have stood the uncomfortable journey better than most of the two hundred others who staggered after him down the quay, punched his way through the entrance and called for the landlord. He asked for a place in which to wash and shave, and when he was told that this was out

* *Poems of N.P.W.* with a Memoir, Routledge and Sons, 1891.

of the question and that even rooms reserved for weeks had all been stormed and occupied by others, he went upstairs to take a look for himself.

Finding an open door on an attic landing through which he observed a number of beds and wash stands, he pushed into it, took some water and made a start to his ablutions. From time to time some youthful maids whose room he supposed it to be, rushed in, squeaked and rushed out again; but he took no notice of them. He washed thoroughly in the largest basin and, since he lacked a towel, he used their sheets.

After a meagre breakfast of tea and toast—all there was to be had for love or money—he went out to look for a billet. For most people at this time—only a day before the Tournament—the task would have proved impossible, but Willis had not, at the age of thirty-two, travelled across the Atlantic and about Europe without discovering how to look after himself, and by nine o'clock he had fixed his arrangements perfectly. He and his Liverpudlian friend had cajoled a cottar, at what price can only be guessed, to provide them with bunk or 'press' beds, let into the wall, each with clean linen and a copy of the Bible. They were in a garret whose skylight overlooked the horsedrawn railway which led to Irvine and, seeing a carriage about to start, they ran downstairs, determined to take a ride in it.

Within an hour they arrived at Eglinton Castle. 'The day was heavenly;' Willis wrote with excitement, 'the sun-flecks lay bright as 'patines of gold' on the close shaven grass beneath the trees.'

He spent the morning lounging happily around the Park admiring the Lists and then, as nobody seemed to object and the doors were open, he even went into the Castle. Here all was frantic hustle and bustle. The great octagonal hall—which was hung with weapons and trophies of the chase and furnished with a frightening antique chair, made from the rafters of 'Alloways' auld haunted kirk', the work of a tiresome local antiquary—was bright with the blazoned banners of the visiting knights. Beyond, in what was normally the library, were crates of pink costumes for the servants, embroidered with a huge 'E' and a coronet, and staggering quantities of halberds and armour for the men-at-arms and retainers. The place was packed with members of the staff waiting to be given appropriate suits and Pratt himself with thirty assistants was busy taking their measurements.

As well as various people like Willis who were merely idle and curious spectators, another group who were not so innocent passed the day before the event in apparently casual reconnaissance.

Ever since the first announcement, all stratas of the kingdom's underworld had looked forward to attending the Tournament with the keenest professional enthusiasm. Now they descended on Eglinton like locusts; the Swell Mob, the aristocracy, terrifying characters like Elephant Smith who travelled north in their own carriages; gangs of others who came by rail; and a huge rabble who made the journey on foot.

Hardly able to believe their luck, they found, in the guise of harmless tourists, they could ask as many questions as they chose and go wherever they pleased to reconnoitre.

As nobody at Eglinton had given security a thought, they had every reason to expect a perfect field-day. There were no police in Ayrshire at all and the nearest regular corps was in Glasgow, thirty miles away to the north, with no prerogative to act beyond the metropolis. Apart from two sleuths from the latter force who wore plain clothes and could be hired privately who were sensibly retained by the

Irvine authorities and two of the famous Bow Street Runners, urgently engaged in London by Pratt, there was no one to prevent them stealing whatever they liked. Two hundred special constables had been sworn for the occasion by the local authorities but these were merely ordinary civilians who had never even so much as arrested a tramp.

The only experienced detective present, the Chief Criminal Officer for Stirlingshire, was solely there, as his letter shows, because he proposed himself.

Lennoxtown, 17th Augt, 1839

My Lord

May the Subscriber who has been a Criminal Officer in the west of Scotland for a number of years and has a knowledge of the greater part of notorious Bad Characters that are in the habit of frequenting Public Places of Resort state to your lordship that he intends to be Present at the grand Tournament to be held under your lordship's Special Patronage. I therefore Most Respectfully solecites that your lordship will give such instructions as your lordship deem proper, to furnish me with a *Ticket of Admission* to the said Tournament that I in my official Capacity may have a Sharp Look out after Bad Characters who invariably attend all places of Public amusement, and of which at this Place and time there is every Reason to Expect a great number.

I have the honour
to be your lordship's Most
Obedient Servant
James McDougall

It is strange to record that Captain Miller, the Superintendent of the Glasgow Police, by far the nearest and most important official, who ought to have been consulted first,

was only approached at the last minute when he wrote to
Blair for a ticket.

He was naturally rather piqued by this.

Police Chambers

Glasgow 26th August 1839

Sir:

I received your favour this morning and feel obliged
for your kind offer to keep a couple of tickets for the
approaching Tournament.

I have already complied with the Town Clerk's
request to send two of our Criminal Officers to Irvine
tomorrow or on Wednesday at farthest, and am still
willing to send a few additional men, if necessary.

With reference, however, to your request that I
should myself go to Irvine by the Coach on *Tuesday
night* and that I should 'superintend on Wednesday and
Thursday', I beg to say that this being the first notice
I have received of a wish that I should attend, and being
in total ignorance of the arrangements made, it is
impossible that I could, with any degree of satisfaction
to myself, undertake such Superintendence in a matter
of so much difficulty and responsability. I would have
most cheerfully, tendered to the Noble Earl the benefit
of the experience I have acquired in Police matters, if
an opportunity had been afforded me of previously
inspecting the ground and making myself acquainted
with the intended arrangements on this great occasion.
But, while I am not even yet aware of these, or of the
regulations to be observed by the spectators, I do not
see, I could now render available and creditable assistance in the way of Superintendence.

At the same time, I shall be happy to offer any
suggestions that may occur to me in reference to the

arrangements, on hearing from you, and of a proper conveyance by which I can travel—the stage coaches being all already engaged.

If Elephant Smith and his friends had been able to read and if they had managed to see this letter, they would surely have laughed like anything. For well before the time it arrived, the penultimate day before the event, they could all have briefed the Superintendent perfectly.

Another, smaller, professional group who spent the day before the event in getting to know the lie of the land were the people who had to report it.

From all over the British Isles they arrived at the Castle in scores, for although Lord Eglinton seemed a reactionary —he could hardly pretend to be anything else considering what he was doing—he had, with a curious, incongruous and modern touch, promised the newspapers a special stand with two places for each of their representatives.

In the ordinary way newspaper correspondents remain anonymous, especially those who relate the doings of Society, and this is particularly so of another age; so, for a change, it is nice to salute their ghosts and turn the tables; for, since they had to write for tickets, they left a record of their names.

Glasgow Herald Office

19 Aug 1839

Sir: The bearer is Mr Pagan, our Reporter, for whom Mr Johnstone, Redburn, was kind enough on being applied to, before your name appeared officially to promise every necessary accommodation at the Lists at the approaching Essay of Arms.

Well aware of the annoyance, both yourself and Mr Johnstone are likely to encounter in applications for Tickets, we should be sorry to add thereto, but as

The Queen of Beauty, Lady Seymour, surrounded by her escor
James Henry Nix

-of-honour and Atholl Highlanders (an engraving of a drawing by
;hed 1843)

the 'Press' is usually privileged to claim somewhat of a preference in such exhibitions, on *public* grounds, we hope you will so far extend your indulgence as to allow one or two tickets in addition to Mr Pagan's one, as Mr Dun, at least, one of the acting partners of the *Herald* is very desirous of witnessing the assault of the Knights.

John Richardson corresponded for *The Times*, James Hedderwick wrote for the *Scotsman*, Charles Mackay for the *Morning Chronicle*, James Paterson for the *Ayr Observer*, all of whom were successful literary figures; for the editors took the Tournament seriously, and either sent their ablest journalists or, like W. P. Brynem of the *Morning Post*, actually reported it themselves. Some of them wondered what to wear and *The Times* advised the *Ayr Observer* to accoutre its scribes in foolscap.

As remains the case in Society today, newspaper men were considered dangerous and were hardly classified as gentlemen. They were, therefore, placed in a stand by themselves as far away from the nobility and gentry as possible. In the Castle they were offered refreshments but told to eat them in the servants' hall and, although they were reasonably democratic, they felt that such treatment was unnecessary.

John Richardson who, perhaps because he represented *The Times* or because he was in the Church and a Doctor of Literature, seems to have been the doyen of the corps, was deputed to make a complaint. He sent a message to the Majordomo that unless they were treated with greater respect not one word about the Tournament would appear in a single newspaper. As a result they were given a room to themselves.

A fourth group which arrived on Tuesday, the 27th of

August, and spent the day reconnoitring the grounds was a company of the Atholl Highlanders.

During the summer, Lord Glenlyon, who was due to appear as the Knight of the Gael, had called for volunteers from amongst his clansmen to form his official bodyguard or, as they say in Scotland, to make his tail; and having returned to his home in Perthshire after the rehearsals, he had chosen seventy-three of the fiercest applicants.

These men—four officers, three sergeants, four corporals, four pipers, two orderlies and fifty-six privates—whose names, addresses, occupations and heights may now be read in the published family *Chronicles**  were led by his brother, James Plantagenet Murray.

Each was equipped in a new and specially made uniform of a blue jacket with short tails without facings, green kilt and plaid of hard Athole tartan, red and white diced stockings, black brogues and blue Glengarry bonnet with a silver badge, and each carried his kit in a knapsack lettered ATHOLE and defended himself with a light target and a broadsword.

They had left Perth the previous Thursday, floated down the river to Dundee, shipped around the coast to Edinburgh, barged along the canal to Glasgow and, finally, on Tuesday morning, had arrived by steamer at Ardrossan.

There Lord Glenlyon had inspected them and, to the noble measure of the pipes, had marched them up to the Castle.

The kilt is never worn in Ayrshire and the sight of so many hairy mountaineers from the heathery north made the hearts of the natives hesitate; and, in a picture painted two years afterwards, they certainly looked extremely grand and ferocious.

* *The Atholl Chronicles*, by the 7th Duke of Atholl. Printed privately, Edinburgh, 1908.

In the evening after dinner they entertained Lord Eglinton's guests with a stirring exhibition of piping and reels.

Lord Glenlyon was the last of the Knights to arrive and if there was little hope of a bed in the district for all who were merely casual spectators, the same, by now, was equally true in the Castle. Lord Glenlyon himself had shelter for, as one of the Knights, he was naturally given a suite, but his brother had to put up with a tent, while a host of minor relatives and friends had to make do in the stables.

A list of the Castle guests would be tedious—of which, according to Dr Richardson, there were all together ninety-one—but the Knights must be enumerated. In alphabetical order they were:

Viscount Alford, aged 27
                    Knight of the Black Lion.
Capt. Beresford, aged 32
                    Knight of the Stag's Head.
Earl of Cassillis, aged 23
                    Knight of the Dolphin.
Earl of Craven, aged 30
                    Knight of the Griffin.
Capt. Fairlie, aged 30
                    Knight of the Golden Lion.
The Hon. H. Gage, aged 25
                    Knight of the Ram.
Viscount Glenlyon, aged 25
                    Knight of the Gael.
Sir F. Hopkins, aged 26
                    Knight of the Burning Tower.
The Hon. E. Jerningham, aged 35
                    Knight of the Swan.

C. Lamb, Esq, aged 23
>                         Knight of the White Rose.

R. Lechmere, Esq, aged 40
>                         Knight of the Red Rose.

W. Little Gilmour, Esq, aged 32
>                         The Black Knight.

Marquess of Waterford, aged 28
>                         Knight of the Dragon.

In all, in spite of hopes to the contrary, and not including Lord Eglinton himself, there were, in the end, only thirteen combatants.

But such by then was the final excitement that nobody thought to lament their absent friends, and what with pages, esquires, varlets, a troup of 'pilgrims' who followed Lord Waterford, an escort of archers for Charlie Lamb, to say nothing of Lord Glenlyon's highlanders, the scarcity of actual knights was hardly noticed.

There were, too, the other noble participants: Lord Eglinton himself, the Lord of the Tournament; the Marquess of Londonderry, the King of the Tournament; Lord Saltoun, the Judge of Peace; Sir Charles Lamb, the Knight Marshal; each of whom had a corps of attendants; also their wives with ladies in waiting; Lady Seymour, the Queen of Beauty, with sixteen graceful handmaidens; and the principal, official guest of honour, Louis Napoleon, the Knight Visitor, with a suitable retinue headed by the faithful Persigny.

When at last they sat down to dinner, all was laughter and gaiety. The knights were obliged to call each other by their crests, so that Waterford, for example, could only be addressed as Dragon. This gave rise to a certain amount of nonsense. Burning Tower went out into the garden because, he said, he was overheated; Swan began to talk too much and was told that he ought to be mute; and White Rose, deeply flushed with goblets of claret, was warned that unless he drank some water he would soon be taken for a hybrid.

There was, naturally, talk of an all-night medieval vigil to prepare the spirit for the morrow's struggles, but this idea was defeated. They all felt they had done enough as it was and by twelve o'clock they were more than ready for bed. In spite of the usual, inevitable rush at the last minute and the times when it had seemed that nothing would be ready, all, in fact, appeared to have been completed. Even the weather had remained perfect; and now, in the warm summer night, a huge, golden moon hung over the trees.

It is hard to guess what they may have thought as they climbed the great wrought iron staircase which encircled the central hall to the height of the upper turrets and took their candles to bed. No record of the night survives and although they must, in a way, have felt a certain natural anxiety, they probably hardly gave the morning a thought. Too many days had been spent preparing for it, too many nights had been passed discussing it.

Charlie Lamb possibly dreamed of his guinea pigs; for at last his childish dreams were about to be consummated. Lord Eglinton probably dreamed of nothing at all, slipping away into fathomless sleep, content, amused and tired.

# Chapter Eleven

As ALL could see who arrived the following morning and bought the special 'Guide to the Tournament' with 'MAP, (see front endpapers) shewing Eglinton Castle, Grounds, & Tilt Yard, with the approaches thereto', on sale by touts at every entrance and produced by Messrs Maclure and Macdonald who printed the tickets, the Castle stood to the east of a road that is now the A78, between the little towns of Irvine and Kilwinning.

For many years it has been demolished although the ruins can still be seen, but it rose then on a small bluff, built of blocks of brown freestone, a vast, rambling, impregnable pile, if not exactly hoar with age, at least impressively Gothic.

It was only Gothic in the literary sense, however, for in actual fact it was really a square Georgian mansion with a great embattled, octagonal central tower and four smaller embrasured turrets at the corners in a style that is known as castellated.

Yet, with the ancient family name, it had somehow acquired a medieval air and, as the home of the Lord of the Tournament, it suitably inspired the spirits of all who saw it.

At the foot of the bluff ran a small river, the Lugton, which flowed through the park in a wide horse-shoe loop, in the 'U' of which, a quarter of a mile to the east, was the field assigned to the Lists. The land rose on all sides, making a shallow amphitheatre, and the river was spanned by a newly constructed cast-iron Gothic bridge. Now the

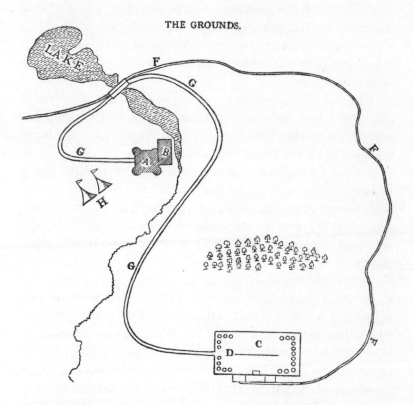

A. Eglinton Castle
B. Temporary Banqueting Hall
C. The Lists
D. The Barrier
F. Route taken by the company on their way to the Stands

G. Enclosed space by which the Knights, etc., approached the Lists
H. Purple Pavilion

A drawing in *Tait's Edinburgh Magazine*
November 1839

site is nothing but a marsh, but it was then, especially in summer, a beautiful, springy meadow. On the rising slopes there were marvellous groups of old umbrageous trees, and deer and sheep had nibbled the grass to a nap as fine as velvet.

To erect the spectators' stands at the Lists required a competent team of men and, as well as several hundred joiners from the Eglinton estates, Pratt had mustered eighty carpenters from London.

All the stands except the one for the press were along the east side which faced the Castle, the tower of which, with banner waving, could be seen beyond the trees and, extending for nearly six hundred feet—almost the whole length of the Lists—seats were provided for four thousand people.

In the middle, soaring up to a height of fifty feet, was a covered grandstand in the Gothic manner—fretted, pinnacled, arched and castellated—which might, indeed, have come from the desk of Sir Walter Scott although it was probably conceived by the architect Cottingham. A royal box for the Queen of Beauty, approached by stairs on either side, jutted forward under a canopy and the columns, sides and even the roof were hung with cloth of gold and crimson damask.

The Lists themselves were a long rectangle, six hundred and fifty feet in length and two hundred and fifty feet across, running approximately north and south which was not, in fact, the medieval practice because the sun would have dazzled the eyes of the knight who stood at the northern end. Down the centre ran the barrier, three hundred feet in length and five and a half feet in height, with a deep layer of sawdust strewn beside it to break the falls of the combatants. Round the edge was a double post and rail fence to keep off the crowd, while at both the ends were

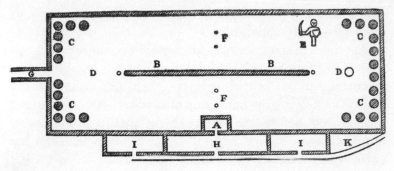

| | | | |
|---|---|---|---|
| A. | Loge of the Queen of Beauty | †G. | Enclosed space by which the Knights entered the Lists |
| B. | The Barrier | H. | The Queen's Gallery |
| *C. | Knights' Pavilions | I. | Open Galleries |
| D. | Piles of Lances | K. | Route taken by the company on their way to the Stands |
| E. | The Quintain | | |
| F. | Ring Posts | | |

gates to admit the knights whose martial tents were pitched on either side of them. In the south-west corner nearest the river was a small uncomfortable pen for artists and the press.

At an early hour people began to converge from all directions and those like Willis who had come in advance and had managed to find some form of accommodation were soon repaid for their efforts. Once again he mounted the horse-drawn railway and arrived at the Castle by nine o'clock, but even by then the roads were packed, both by a huge company on foot and a vast number in various types of vehicles.

It is usually not realised today that the complex problem of controlling transport did not begin with the motor car. Long before the 20th century, in the narrow thoroughfares of many cities, the queues of traffic were often streets in

* In actual fact these were outside the Lists.

† There were in fact two entrances — one at either end.

o

length and at any public event like a race meeting the jams were frequently appalling.

As time passed and noon drew near, everything on wheels heading for the Park became completely stationary. According to one reliable witness, the thirty mile highway from Ayr to Glasgow had a line of coaches almost from end to end and before the Tournament finally began every approach was blocked by carriages whose owners had left them where they stood to finish the journey on foot.

People who came by sea were hardly luckier, for although they reached Ardrossan in comfort and prepared for the day with a piping nautical breakfast, they had still, somehow, to cover the remaining distance. Many had hoped for a seat on the railway but a party of eighty Campbells from Dunoon, with the canny foresight for which that clan is famous, had chartered a special steamer of their own and skillfully managed to reach the quay and get to the station before them.

Camouflaged in tartan from head to foot, they captured all the available trucks and trundled off towards the Lists, led by a band of fearsome pipers playing 'The Campbells are coming.'

This was all very fine for them but, as the journey took over an hour and as there was only a single track, it was not so stirring for everyone else who had nothing to do but wait for the wagons to return.

In the interval, vessels berthed from as far away as Dublin and ships from the Royal Northern Yacht Club tacked their way across the Clyde and docked in a perfect flotilla.

It was fully eight miles to the Lists and the thought of hiking there and back daunted the spirits of many of the passengers, half of whom decided to stay in Ardrossan.

But the Royal Yachtsmen had been given tickets and

had promised Lord Eglinton to parade in uniform; so they determined to step it out; and they marched off to the cheers of the natives, forming up behind their Commodore, James Smith, Esq., of Jordanhill.

The people who really fared the best were those who travelled in a proper train to Irvine. A new line had just been finished from Ayr, and as it had only been opened a week, they were almost the first members of the general public to use it. Traffic figures for the day are not available but the company, the Glasgow and Ayrshire Railway, must have enjoyed a splendid profit for, as well as the eight scheduled services—four one way and four the other, the line having only a single track—four Tournament Specials were announced, and the price of the tickets was trebled.

Even so, the passengers fought to buy them for at least they knew they would arrive safely and then have only a couple of miles to walk. To go to a medieval tournament by train was thought an amusing anomaly, and especially when, as was actually the case, the engine's name was MARMION.

To compute the size of a crowd in an open field is difficult enough, but to do so at Eglinton Park was almost impossible. Even the press, who were used to multitudes, could hardly so much as guess its proportions or think of an adequate phrase with which to describe it; in the end they could only report that nothing comparable had been seen in Scotland since the coronation of George IV when, in 1822, he had driven in state through Edinburgh.

There were swarms of boys in every tree, countless parties staring at the Castle, innumerable groups on the roofs of carriages, four thousand people in the stands and possibly seventy thousand on the banks of the river. A total of one hundred thousand was thought a conservative estimate. Guesses like these are often exaggerated, but, from its universal adoption, such a figure was probably fairly accurate.

As all could read who had bought a programme (see pp. 249-259), the cost of which was half a crown, and which, in suitable Gothic lettering, revealed the names and titles of the knights, the Tournament was due to start with a procession which was timed to leave the Castle at twelve o'clock. When noon passed and nobody appeared, the crowd began to get restless; after a while a Castle minion, a halberdier in the Eglinton colours with a blue and yellow soup-plate hat, announced that the knights would be late.

The cause of the delay was lamentably obvious to those who were close to the Castle. All who have ever been in the army or any similar professional body will know the problems involved in arranging a parade, and the task was twice as hard at Eglinton because, instead of being experienced, all the participants were amateurs.

The procession consisted of forty different groups and all of them had to march to the Castle, collect an officer, knight or damsel and retrace their steps to halt at a pre-arranged point.

This manoeuvre was difficult enough, easy though it is to describe, but the site of the Castle made it much more complicated. For, being built at the end of a promontory, instead of having a pair of entrances—one for IN and one for OUT—it had only a single drive for all the traffic; and so all the troops who were marching up had to make their way through those who were marching down.

According to Willis—once again at the centre of excitement, the knights were mounted with difficulty. The first, the Earl of Craven, the Knight of the Griffin, was forced in the end to call for a chair, being quite unable in the weight of his armour to manage alone with the stirrup. The next,

Lord Waterford, ascended nobly, although he got up with
such a vault that he nearly broke his charger's back. Lord
Eglinton proved the best of them all, nimbly climbing into
his seat with the skilled address of a "parfit gentil knight."

When finally everyone was ready—the Eglinton Herald
in a massive tabard, the Judge of Peace in crimson velvet,
the Knight Marshal in steel and surcoat on an armed,
plumed, caparisoned horse, the Ladies Visitors in minivered
jackets, the Ballochmyle Archeresses ' a band of nymphs in
Lincoln green', the King of the Tournament in cape and
coronet, Lord Eglinton himself in a suit of gold, and all
the Knights complete in armour, with pages, esquires,
retainers, musicians—more than a hundred of whom were
mounted and more than a hundred of whom were armed—
the procession was half a mile in length and more than
three hours late.

Last to be called to her place was the Queen of Beauty
and, as her horse was led to the porch, as it was announced
by a blast from a trumpeter, as her name was cried by a
chamberlain, as her train was lifted by her pages, as her
ladies brought her to the door, the Park was shaken by a
fearful clap of thunder. In a sudden hush and a strange
darkness, a single flash of lightning parted the sky.

Now a storm of rain began which destroyed the hopes of
everybody. During the morning the sun had shone but
those who had known the Ayrshire weather had looked
across at the mountains of Arran and had seen them much
too clearly. By ten o'clock the warm, moist air from the
Gulf of Florida had once again begun to gather in ominous
condensations; and the first drenching squall struck just
as the procession started.

In the 'good old days' the knights could have called the
Tournament off—no records of jousts in the rain exist—
but a cancellation in Lord Eglinton's case was felt to be

inadmissable; for what had begun as a private fête had become a public festival.

So, in a pelting, icy torrent, the cavalcade without the ladies who, on Lord Eglinton's personal command had been told to shelter and wait for carriages, at last set off for the Lists.

The immediate consequence of this arrangement was that none of the crowd could see the Queen of Beauty, many of whom had waited hours to do so.

Jane Georgiana, Lady Seymour, was the youngest daughter of Tom Sheridan, son of the famous Richard Brinsley, who had married a celebrated beauty, Henrietta Callendar. One of three radiant sisters who were called, inevitably, the Three Graces—the eldest of whom became Lady Dufferin and the second the well known Caroline Norton—she was twenty-nine at the time of the Tournament, the wife of Adolphus, Baron Seymour, the son and heir of the 11th Duke of Somerset.

It tends to be axiomatic in Society that all who are rich or grand are beautiful, but Lady Seymour had, in truth, a rare and appealing loveliness. Willis who, in writing afterwards, had no incentive or desire to flatter and was only concerned with reporting the facts—which was not the case with all the journalists, some of whom were inclined to toady—watched as she crossed the hall of the Castle and was wholly, instantly enchanted.

She was dressed in a long, full, violet velvet skirt which reached to her feet and was covered in golden heraldic wings, 'two wings, conjoined in lure, the tips downwards, or, for SEYMOUR,' to quote their technical description. Above she wore an ermine and miniver jacket, and over her shoulders a superb, voluminous, crimson velvet mantle; round her throat were chains of diamonds and on her head was a crown encrusted with pearls.

She was not tall but she walked with a graceful upright carriage which revealed her figure charmingly; and all agreed on the beauty of her face which, framed by raven hair, had the lily skin and roseate cheek of traditional Celtic colouring. Her manner, too, was all that is said to be Irish—fanciful, gay, spontaneous, witty and amusing.

Why she was given the honour is not recorded. The expected choice had been Lady Londonderry whose puffy features were always said to be fine because she was an heiress, being, the gossips said, Lord Eglinton's mistress; but when her husband agreed to be King of the Tournament she was forced, against her will, to be Queen beside him.

By common consent, Louisa Stuart, the second daughter of Lord Stuart de Rothsay who, at the age of twenty-four married Lord Waterford three years afterwards, was the loveliest woman present; but perhaps for reasons of Victorian etiquette and also possibly to prevent Lord Eglinton having to make an invidious choice, the Knights decided only to offer the post to a married woman.

Whatever the reason, it fell to Lady Seymour, who performed the duties with a sweet and pleasing gaiety. Some thought that Lady Londonderry might have acted with greater fire and theatrical grandeur, having a more imperious temperament, but all concurred that none, in looks, could have equalled Lady Seymour.

There was, however, one fact about her which, in spite of all her virtues, ought to have made her ineligible; at least, that is, to Charlie Lamb and any of the knights who loved him: one of her favourite hobbies was cooking and some of her choicest dishes were made with guinea pigs.*

This taste, had he known about it, would surely have

---

* *Leaves from the Note-Books of Lady Dorothy Nevill;* p. 15. Macmillan, 1907.

turned him against her, for Charlie was one of those whimsical people—sometimes lovable and often tiresome—who carry a childish streak into adult life and only the week before at Beauport, as though to seek a guinea pig blessing, he had paid a visit to the cemetery of Winnipeg and sat by the graves of two of the original Knights of the White Rose: Sir Heliodorus, Prince of Rarribun, and Turkwine, the Earl of Newton.

Happily enough, no one at Eglinton ever knew anything about it and all the knights, and Charlie, too, were dead before, in the next century, anyone beyond her immediate family learned of her predeliction.

The rain cascaded down Charlie's neck as, superb in a Gothic armour, on a white charger, barded and caparisoned, he made his way to the Lists. Only aware of the dream in which he lived, he ignored completely the actual conditions —the cakes of mud on all the trappings, the scowling clouds that obscured the sky, the sheets of water that drummed like thunder on the crouching knots of miserable spectators who lined the procession's route beneath umbrellas.

In his third and last illuminated MS, in a colourful if rather primitive miniature, he depicted himself riding to the contest cheered by groups of tartaned peasants under the lea of Eglinton Castle beneath a cloudless sky.

Now he was clad in a goodly suit of polished steel. Hys surcote covered over with white roses which were also embroidered upon hys belt, whereon was the legend of *une seule*, and one white rose in hys cap, all in token of his Lady love. Hys shield emblazoned with the arms of Burges, hys father's house. The crest of the same upon his helmet, with plumes of his tinctures and a mightie sword in hys hand readye to do battaille with

There were two stages to the Tournament. In the first, two kni
him with his lance. In the second, which is shown above, all
Lord Waterford lost his temper; he is shown here, left, in con
(an engraving of a drawing by Ja

down the Lists and each tried to unhorse the other by striking
ts taking part engaged in hand-to-hand fighting. In this *mêlée*
st Lord Alford. Sir Charles Lamb is on the left with his baton.
y Nixon, published 1843)

all comer, and how he and others sped thereat will be seen in the sequence of thys historie.

For it has seemed as must be known to everyone that a great Tournament was proclaimed to take place on the day I have mentioned at Eglinton Castle. It was talked for a year and a half previous over all England, Scotland and France. That and nothing else. It was now two centuries since such a thing had been seen in Europe. Passages of arms had indeed been attempted on a few occasions in these times such as the one in the United States of America*, where Earl Cathcart presided, also at Malta by some officers of the garrison† where the armour of the Knights of St John was used. An annual joust took place until very lately on the Bridge at Pisa‡ in which all the combatants wore armour but all these were on a trifling scale to present one from the pomp and splendour in which it was held. No one indeed believed that it would take place. Howsoever many gallant young gentlemen prepared to appear in the lists. Those who did appear, for many failed at the appointed time, were Henry Marquess of Waterford, that reckless and gay young nobleman who from a street brawl to daring the lion on ye plain of Africa was ready at home or abroad for all that promised novelty or adventure. He came handsomely equipped with a splendid retinue. He wore a suit of German armour fluted, his horse with caparisons of black and white. He was attended by Lord John his brother, Sir Charles Kent, baronet, Lord Maidstone, Richard Lumley, Mark White-Kerr and Lewis Ricardo Esquires, all mounted wearing his tinctures of black and white with back

* At Philadelphia in 1778. See the *Annual Register* for that year, p. 265.
† On the 19th of February, 1828, at the Palace Square, Valetta.
‡ The last of these was held in 1808.

breast and head pieces of polished steel. With him also were Lord Ingestrie, habited as a Turkish dervise and one in the garb of a friar. These with grooms and footmen armed with pikes completed his train. He himself was tall and handsome and so were his followers. He was known by the name of the Knight of the Dragon, from his crest. The Earl of Craven came next. He was equipped in a very handsome inlaid suit of Milan armour which became him admirably. His colours were red and gold. His brother Frederick and James Macdonald (ye Lord's brother) were his Esquires. Then came Lord Alford, his colours blue and white, followed by his brother Charles and Richard Gascoigne Esquire. He was called the Knight of the Black Lion from his crest. There were with him several men on foot armed with halberds. The Lord Glenlyon came from the highlands to this tournament. Sir David Dundas and Balfour of Balbirnie were his Esquires. He was accompanied by seventy men of Atholl. There were several gentlemen among them and they were all picked men equipped and armed with swords targets after the manner of their country. They marched up the castle with their pipes playing, having a gallant appearance, he at the head of them on foot, having come so thro' the low countries. Mr Edward Stafford Jerningham, son of Lord Stafford, was called the Knight of the White Swan, from his crest. Mr Stevenson was his Esquire who was related to the Laird of Macleod. His colours were white and gold. James Fairlie of the Lion came to break a lance for the honour of the Shire of Ayr. He was a handsome gentleman, skilled at all manly exercises. His appearance when armed and mounted was excelled by none. He wore a suit of gilded armour and over that a surcoat of cloth of gold with a red lion embroidered before and behind. The trappings of his horse were blue and crimson. His banner was borne by Mr Charles Cox, his Esquires John Purvis and Thomas Pettat of Gloucestershire. Fifteen chosen yeomen armed with halberds formed his train. Mr Lechmere, a gentleman of good birth from the West of England, came next. He wore for his cognisance a red rose in memory of the part taken by his ancestors in the Wars of York and Lancaster. He was a big strong man and wore a massive suit of fluted armour with a very handsome plume of crimson feathers and mounted upon a fine grey stallion. Two gentlemen named Smith and Cory were with him. I do not think he had any more. After him came Walter Gilmour who was called the Black Knight. He was a tall and handsome man. His Esquires were Lord Drumlanerig and James Hunter Blair. They were habited as well as the serving men in black attire and the Knight himself wore a suit of black armour. The horses and the trappings were also black, such being the humour of Mr Campbell of Saddel who had intended to have come but at the time he was taken very ill and requested Mr Gilmour to go in his place. Mr Gage, second son of the Lord Viscount Gage, called the Knight of the Ram. His Esquires were Robert Fergusson of the Kilkerran family, and a gentleman named Murray. The Earl of Cassilis appeared also. He was known by his cognisance of the dolphin. He had no retainers but accompanied Mr Gage. He was a sorry representative of his ancient race in appearance, but did not want for gallantry. Sir Francis Hopkins an Irish gentleman of fortune was called from his crest of the burning tower. He had no retinue but I must [word missing] his charger was far more beautifully accoutred than that of any other knight. His trappings were of black velvet, such being the field of his arms, and reaching to the ground, his charges embroidered upon it from the neck downwards. He was a most excellent sitter and a powerful horseman.

All these noble knights and also all the superb officials, similarly described in Charlie's MS., trotted towards the Lists in perfect weather. The shivering multitude which actually watched them only beheld a bedraggled crocodile; and Lord Londonderry riding in the centre of it holding aloft a tremendous green umbrella.

As often happened in genuine tournaments, the King and Queen and other notables were expected to parade round the Lists before they took their places on the throne but—as it was almost four o'clock, as all were soaked and chilled to the bone, and as the crowds were becoming restless—having at last arrived at the gates, they decided to cancel all the preliminaries and go at once to their seats.

As a result, the Knights were denied the romantic ceremony of riding up to the grandstand to choose their paramours and of being given scarves or handkerchiefs to tie to their lances or helmets; the Eglinton Herald was denied the privilege of standing alone in the hushed arena while reading out the rules; and the crowd, too, most unhappily, was denied a glimpse of Lady Seymour, who would have ridden round in state and allowed the expectant world to admire her beauty.

As it was, she arrived in a carriage and entered the dais from the back, and was hardly noticed amongst the others —Lady Londonderry, Lady Montgomerie, Aunt Jane and Louisa Stuart—until her brother, Charles Sheridan, clad in an exquisite suit of plate, took his stance behind her throne and unfurled a crimson parasol over her head.

For now another calamity had happened. The planks of wood which formed the grandstand roof, instead of being tongued and grooved, had only been laid together edge to edge, being merely required temporarily and being, anyway, covered with scarlet cloth. By the time the Queen of Beauty arrived, the rain had begun to filter through them, and long before the jousts began the entire royal box was flooded, as well, naturally, as every corner of the grandstand.

For those who were there as Lord Eglinton's guests this was an absolute disaster. Having been told that their seats would be covered, only a few had brought their overcoats and, as a final touch to their misery, many had come in expensive fancy costumes. The women, especially, suffered agonies. All had planned their hair and dresses for months and, as jets of water fell on their shoulders and gusts of wind removed their hats, young and old were filled with grim despair.

When at length everyone was seated, the only person left in the Lists was the Jester. He was an actor called Robert M'Ian who had made a name for himself portraying Robin Oig M'Combich in *The Two Drovers* and other plays that were drawn from Sir Walter Scott. Riding a donkey, and dressed in cap and bells, he jogged about and made some feeble jokes. But, like many people of the same profession, without a script he was just a bore, and nobody thought him amusing. 'His repartees were like a series of slight electric shocks', wrote one of the journalists, trying hard to be nice about him.

In the end he lost his temper and handed his wand to the Eglinton Herald who had sent the crowd into fits of laughter, striding about in a streaming tabard, trying, in spite of orders to the contrary, to declaim the rules of the joust.

'You take it,' M'Ian snapped at him, 'One fool in the Lists is enough for me.'

All eyes were turned now on the various Knights' pavilions. These, in keeping with everything else, were exact replicas of military tents such as are seen in the illustrations of Froissart—striped according to the owner's colours, a shield of arms above the entrance, and lit by a series of tiny dormer windows on the tops of which were little flags, held open stiff like the tails of weathervanes. Each encampment consisted of three—a marquee and two bell-tents, joined together in a suite; and all were furnished with tables, chairs, wash-stands, carpets and beds.

Pitched at either end of the Lists outside the railings, even under sheets of rain they managed to provide a busy and romantic spectacle. Banners lapped the wind before them, horses pranced and shook their trappings, men at arms bustled in and out, esquires collected and tested lances, poursuivants hurried from one to another and, from time to time, a knight emerged to observe the state of the weather.

All who watched were tense and hushed for the first great climactic moment: the flinging down of the champion's glove and the crying out of the noble terms of the challenge.

For some reason that is not recorded, perhaps simply because of the storm, which had now increased to an absolute tempest, the noise of which would have drowned a megaphone, the first opponents suddenly appeared without the smallest ceremony.

In the good old days, at a friendly Round Table such an event would have mattered hardly at all for, except in the case of an Unknown Knight who would, of course, have concealed his identity, the crowd would have known who the combatants were by their shields.

In the present case the situation was different. Apart

from the fact that to make a challenge had been Lord Eglinton's greatest ambition—the omission of which at the coronation had actually caused him to hold the Tournament—and apart from the fact that the crowd, too, after waiting so long in the rain, had expected to see a complete performance, the whole value of such a ceremony in the changed conditions of the 19th century would have been to announce the names of the competing knights.

Now, as they rode to their places in the Lists, locked inside their suits of steel, their faces hidden by their crested helmets and unproclaimed by any of the heralds, only two or three specialised antiquaries were able to say with any certainty which two of the Knights were about to fight.

For only one per cent of the public had any practical knowledge of heraldry in spite of the wide popular enthusiasm for everything connected with the Middle Ages and, in the case of the people at Eglinton, few, if any, had learnt the arms by heart.

The press who, more than anyone, ought to have known the combatants' names, found themselves completely foxed, their stand being so positioned—far away at the end of the Lists—that even a scribe from the College of Arms could have told them little without the aid of a telescope.

Some had actually brought these instruments; but the wind blew them round and round and they never managed to hold them still enough even to get them focussed.

If, as the crowd watched the Knights who rode slowly to the ends of the barrier, couched their lances under their armpits, and waited for the Marshal to signal the charge, all were sorry to have missed the challenge, almost as many regretted the omission, equally inevitable because of the weather, of another picturesque ceremony.

After the procession had circled the Lists, the King and

Queen had ascended their thrones, and all the officers had taken their positions, the heralds ought to have addressed the contestants and given them a number of instructions.

This spectacle, if not so thrilling would at least have been traditional and would, also, have given the spectators a chance to hear the rules.

These ancient regulations—specially printed copies of which had already been given to all the Knights—were based on a set of 1602, written by Norroy King at Arms for the last jousts held in the reign of Elizabeth. They were, however, drawn from others which had been composed for Edward IV by the Earl of Worcester, in 1465; and they were, therefore, quite as authentic as the words and procedure of the challenge.

The Ordinances, Statutes & Rules, made by John, Lord Tiptofte, Erle of Worcester, Constable of England, by the King's commaundement, at Windsore 29 Day of May, *Anno Sexto Edwardi Quarti;* and commanded in Eliz. 4; to bee observed or kept in all manner of Justes of Peaces Royall, within this realme of England. Reservinge alwaies to the Queen, and to the Ladyes present, the attribution and gifte of the prize, after the manner and forme accustomed: to be attributed for their demeritts according to the Articles ensueinge.*
How many waies the prize is woone.

1. Who so breaketh most speares as they ought to bee broken, shall have the prize.
2. Who so hitteth three times, in the sight of the healme, shall have the prize.
3. Who so meeteth too times, cournall to cournall, shall have the prize.

* *The Triumph holden at Shakespeare's England* by F. W. Cripps-Day, 1912, p. 7.

4. Who so beareth a man downe with stroke of a speare, shall have the prize.

How many waies the prize shall be lost.

1. Who so striketh a horse shall have no prize.
2. Who so striketh a man, his back turned, or dis-garnished of his speare, shall have no prize.
3. Who so hitteth the foile (or tilt) 3 times shall have no prize.
4. Who so unhealmeth himself two times shall have no prize, unlesse his horse doe faile him.

How broken speares shall be allowed.

1. Who so breaketh a speare, between the saddle and the charnell of the healme, shall be allowed for one.
2. Who so breaketh a speare, from the cournall up-wards, shall be allowed for two.
3. Who so breaketh a speare, so as hee strike his adversary downe, or put him out of his saddle, or disarmeth him in such wise as hee may not runne the next course after, or breaketh his speare cournall to cournall, shall be allowed three speares.

How speares shall be disallowed.

1. Who so breaketh on the saddle shall be disallowed for one speare-breakinge.
2. Who so hitteth the toyle once, shall be disallowed for two.
3. Who so hitteth the toyle twice, shall, for the second time, be abated three.
4. Who so breaketh a speare, within a foot to the cournall, shall be adjudged as no speare broken, but a fayre attaynt.

For the prize to be given and who shall be preferred.

1. Who so beareth a man downe out of the saddle, or putteth him to the earth, horse and man, shall have

the prize before him that striketh cournall to cournall 2 times.

2. Hee that striketh cournall to cournall two times, shall have the prize before him that striketh the sight three times.

3. Hee that striketh the sight three times, shall have the prize before him that breaketh most speares.

Item, if there be any man that fortuneth in this wise, which shall be deemed to have abiden longest in the field healmed, and to have runne the fayrest course, and to have given the greatest strokes, and to have holpen himself best with his speare, he shall have the prize.

(subscrybed)
John Worcestre

Although enumerated rather differently and described as 'Actions worthy of Honour', these five paragraphs of rules formed the basis of those for the Eglinton Knights. They were only modified in one respect: because of the warning from the Sheriff of Ayr that anyone causing a fatal accident might be charged with manslaughter, or even murder, the Knights were not allowed to aim at the helmet; the point of attack for the highest score was made the coat of arms emblazoned in the centre of the shield.

The method of marking down the score, to be seen today in the great tournament rolls in the College of Arms, was simple, neat and interesting.

A jousting tally was called a 'Cheque', and this was merely a piece of paper on which was drawn a long rectangle marked in half by a line lengthways projecting beyond one end. On the three parallel lines thus formed, a vertical tick, or sometimes a pinprick was made to note a result: on the top for an 'atteint' or satisfactory hit; on the middle for a spear correctly broken; on the bottom for a fall or penalty. In the middle line beyond the box a tick was put to denote the number of courses.

It is sad to record, when so many medieval cheques exist, that none of the Eglinton ones survive if, that is, they were ever written. The Knights' scores are therefore lost and, because of the awkward seating of the press and because, also, of the poor visibility, the tallies given in the newspapers do not agree.

And by now, when at last the Knights were poised, more than four hours later than scheduled, many of the reporters had fallen asleep, having been up since the peep of dawn, having eaten nothing since breakfast and having swallowed pints of whisky to allay the effects of the weather.

As the Knight Marshal raised his baton, as the heralds shouted 'Laissez les aller', as the Eglinton Trumpeters blew the charge, as the Knights dropped their lances in the rests, as the dripping horses skidded forward, a few of the journalists snored and moved uneasily. But all the designated courses were run before they roused themselves enough to see them.

They only opened their eyes in the end because of a roar of laughter. For the two Knights who had started jousting —who proved to be Swan and Golden Lion, Edward Jerningham and James Fairlie—had thundered down the squelching Lists and merely galloped past each other. Their second course had fared no better and their third had gone even worse. Fairlie again had poked thin air while Jerningham, trying to reach his opponent in a last, frantic exasperated effort, had almost repeated his flight at the rehearsals and, in a fearful struggle to stay on, had dropped his spear, tied to which was his wife's cambric handkerchief.

From this moment, if not before—if not from the very day it was thought of—the Eglinton Tournament was doomed to certain failure.

Nothing in the world is worse than ridicule and the more a pageant aspires to grandeur the more, if it fails, it will sink to bathos. Once the spectators have started to smile, it is almost impossible to stop them.

So now, as the other Knights appeared, as the Knight of the Dragon challenged Lord Eglinton; as Sir Francis Hopkins jousted Mr Lechmere; as Lord Glenlyon ran at Lord Alford; and as, in the last combat of the day, the two lords—Waterford and Alford—clumped together and tried to impale each other, the crowd watched with impatience and contempt or, once in a while, with a rueful grimace of sympathy.

It was far worse than the most boring point-to-point or race meeting. There were long gaps between the courses while the Knights rested and adjusted their armour and when at length they ran again, each time, with few exceptions, they either botched their strokes or missed completely.

The only combat of any reality was between Lords Eglinton and Waterford. Both were exceptionally able horsemen, both had taken their training seriously, both had comfortably fitting armour, both were out to prove their skill and, in spite of increasingly difficult conditions—for every hoofmark had become a puddle and the Lists had become extremely slippery—both dashed at each other as hard as they could. Although on the second course they missed, on the first and last Lord Eglinton engaged, striking the centre of the Dragon's shield and breaking his spear on it perfectly.

He remembered, too, as soon as he had done so to throw away the butt. Such an act was most important for the long splinters of a broken shaft easily penetrate the opponent's visor, the very thing that had actually happened to his own forbear, Count Montgomerie, when he killed the King of France.

There was, finally, by way of a diversion, a fight between two gigantic swordsmen. One was a soldier entitled Redbury and the other an actor called Mackay, the latter having, like the Jester, made his name on the Scottish stage in plays from Sir Walter Scott. Their two-handed swords were formidable and they whacked away at each other like Roman gladiators. But the crowd, now, had seen enough and when the combat came to an end, one of them actually breaking his weapon, no applause greeted the victor and no sound broke the stillness except the patter of the rain.

In the long, depressing pause that followed Lord Eglinton suddenly appeared in the Lists and galloped up to the barrier. It was clear that he wanted to make an announcement and once more the multitude stirred as people dried their ears with handkerchiefs and peered from under their umbrellas.

He began by saying how sorry he was that everyone had got so wet, especially those who had come from a long way off. Speaking as one who lived in Ayrshire, who had known its weather all his life, he wanted to say that he, at least, had never seen anything to equal the present deluge. Not that he wished to make excuses but he felt that the fact might like to be known. Should conditions improve, he would try again, if not tomorrow, then the next day, or else the following week. In the meantime he bade them farewell and wished them all a successful journey homeward.

He then rode closer to the Grandstand and addressed his personal friends and guests, the two thousand people with special tickets. They, he said, through his own carelessness, for which he feared they would never forgive him, were doomed to bear another and final disappointment. The much advertised medieval banquet as well as the costume ball to follow had both, now, at this last minute, been unavoidably cancelled. The magnificent tent behind the Castle in which these functions would have been held had, in the same manner as the Grandstand, having a weakly constructed roof, become the victim of the weather. He had no alternative but to offer his apologies and hope that they, too, would get safely home.

Almost five minutes had elapsed and Lord Eglinton had ridden back to his pavilion before, in the first shock of disappointment, the full portent of what he had said was realised.

Many of his guests lived far away—quite a few on the other side of the county—and most of them had planned, after the Tournament, to rest and change with friends who lived in the district. They had, therefore, sent their carriages away and told them not to come back until after midnight. How, then, could they get in touch with them to explain the change of plan?

As they sat in the waterlogged grandstand and turned this problem over in their minds, the friends with whom they were going to stay became aware of another one. How were they, these lucky locals, to get to their homes themselves? They, naturally, had ordered their carriages to return in the course of the afternoon at such time, whenever it might be, as the jousts were expected to finish. But when they went to the exits to look for them they only observed a single conveyance, one of Lord Eglinton's personal coaches slowly vanishing towards the Castle, bearing away the Queen of Beauty and her suite.

Not another vehicle was to be seen, for, as in all rainy districts, the rivers in Ayrshire rise swiftly, almost as soon as a storm begins, and the Lugton, winding round the Lists, in drought a dancing, shallow burn, had become a raging torrent.

As a result, the Lists had flooded, being really lush water meadows, hardly above the level of the river even during the summer; and the fact was that since lunch time nothing less than a chariot and four, of which Lord Eglinton's was the only one, had been able to return to the Grandstand.

Then began a confused exodus which truly defied description. As one hundred thousand spectators began to make their way from the Lists, forced to head for home on foot, the rain pouring, the wind howling and the mud pulling their shoes from their feet, young and old, rich and poor, jostled together like cattle at a fair and behaved with as little civility.

On the high road beyond the policies the walking should have been easier but instead the slough got worse and worse, for the lucky few who got to the front deposited a trail of slimy mire which had to be traversed by those behind and which, as a result, was carried farther and farther. Any carriages which happened to appear were seized by force by the nearest pedestrians, quite regardless of the person to whom they belonged, and the one train that departed from Irvine had such an extra load of passengers clinging to the coaches, trucks, wagons and even astride the engine itself that some of them had to push it to make it start.

As often seems to happen in life, only the wicked reached their firesides in comfort. Elephant Smith, Bill Caughty and other bigwigs of the Swell Mob had come to the Tournament in suits of armour which, it is fairly safe to assume, they had hired from Samuel Pratt. With helmets on and visors down they had entered the Park with hilarity thinking that, in this disguise, they were safe from all detection.

But a man in armour is like a horse with blinkers, only able to see what is straight in front of him, and so, as they strolled among the crowd, they failed to notice that some-one had started following them.

For although Pratt had made mistakes, he had not forgotten to deal with the problem of burglars and after the rehearsals he had been to Bow Street and retained the services of Goddard and Ballard, two of the country's sharpest police detectives.

Also equipped in medieval style, although in the handier costume of Franklins, they spotted the mobsters in half an hour and long before the jousting started ordered them on to the horse-drawn railway and packed them off to Ardrossan.

Warm and dry but much annoyed, the Mulberry Hawks and Bill Sykes's threw their armour into the harbour and sat in the saloon of the *Royal Sovereign* until, as the sun began to set, they were joined by other parties of spectators, most of whom had been forced to walk from the Lists.

This was the chance for which they had all been waiting. Mingling among them and offering them drinks, they helped themselves to their money and watches and, when they berthed the following morning, legged it down the gangway and vanished in Liverpool.

Many people who lived at a distance—particularly women in fancy dress, and especially those of humble birth—never, never forgot the night that followed. By nine-thirty it was pitch dark, the rain continued to fall in sheets, the roads were still chaotic in all directions. In desperation they sheltered in cowsheds, they burrowed caves in the sides of haystacks, they crouched in the boles

After the disappointment of the actual tournament, the medi
temporary banqueting hall, proved a moderate success. All gu
seated on the dais. (An engraving of a drawing by James He

quet and ball that were held two days later in the specially built
e in medieval dress; Lady Seymour and Lord Eglinton are shown
on, published 1843)

of hollow trees, even returned and huddled beneath the grandstand.

When at last morning came they reached places like Ayr and Kilmarnock, only to find that others had got there before them. There was no food, no drink, no accommodation, no transport, not even a change of clothing for those who could pay for it. In the great rush of the evening before every single thing had been sold and, to the shame of honest citizens, at more than eight times the normal profit. One woman who had come from Edinburgh, a Mrs Stott of Gayfield House, had, it is still recollected in the family, been compelled to give eighty shillings for a single pair of stockings.

At Eglinton itself the Knights had not been happier. No record has come to light, if ever one was made at all, of how they got away from the Lists or what they said or did when they reached the Castle. If, at least, they had warm bedrooms with bright fires stoked high with the finest coal from the Eglinton collieries, attentive servants to bring them hot water, diligent maids to dry their clothing, silent footmen to bring them wine and a company of chefs to cook their dinner, they must have felt they deserved these comforts and must, still, have had to struggle to keep aside their depression.

And when early the following morning they cantered down to inspect the Lists, still lashed by occasional squalls, they must have caught their breaths and gasped with misery.

The scene in the once gay amphitheatre was fit for a troubadour's lament. Although the grandstand had withstood the storm, very little else had managed to survive it. Harness and equipment were strewn about, broken lances eddied in the burn, here and there a piece of armour lay in the mud, already rusting, only heaps of sodden canvas marked the sites of their once magnificent pavilions.

215

If no quantity of time and money had been able to bring to life a tournament, no amount of study and expense, neither by artists at the Royal Academy, nor by Meyrick at the Tower of London, nor by Cottingham at Pratt's showroom, nor by Ducrow at Astley's Arena could have managed to reproduce a scene that was anything like this.

Here was a field of battle and of rout, at one sweep, fulfilling perfectly all the mixed demands of romantic gothicism. Owned by a peer of noble lineage, it was ancient, desolate, inspiring, chivalrous: and for those who had taken part—the most difficult of all conditions—its picturesque and medieval air had been felt and known as something real in their own personal, costly and bitter experience.

# Chapter Twelve

IN THIS way the Eglinton Tournament, held on Wednesday, the 28th of August, in the third year of the reign of Queen Victoria, really came to an end. Failure always requires a scapegoat and so, as the weakest person available was easily the wretched Samuel Pratt, everyone made him the butt of their disappointment.

'I must write you a line of thanks for remembering me at such a moment,' Lady Londonderry scribbled to Disraeli who had just got married to Mary Anne, heading her letter 'From Eglinton Castle, Thursday, August 29th, 1839'

and I beg you will accept my sincere congratulations and very best wishes for your happiness.

You tell me to send you accounts of the Tournament which, alas! has been spoiled by the weather. Nothing could have been more perfect than all the arrangements. The lists all beautiful and most picturesque with all the tents and encampments. The procession was gorgeous and the whole reception splendid, 300 feet of temporary room having been erected, thousands and thousands flocking from everywhere, even from America when as usual in our horrible climate down came that sort of vicious, spiteful pour that never visits other countries except in the rainy season when people know what to expect and make their arrangements accordingly.

My 1st feeling was to sit down and cry—my 2nd to tear Mr Pratt into small pieces, not that he could help the rain, but for putting up tents that would not resist a shower, much less a deluge. The weather however today shows signs of repentance and amendment and tomorrow we hope for better things.

*Adieu*, you should hear again before I leave England, but I would not delay writing one line to assure you of the interest I take in your happiness which I hope is now fixed.

Believe me yours very truly

F. A. Vane Londonderry*

Lady Londonderry, as a woman of fashion and possibly the country's richest heiress, might easily have added her tears to the rain, tears of rage at not being seen for, having failed to be Queen of Beauty, she had hoped, at least, to outshine the latter in appearance. She had, therefore, worn a gown so encrusted with gold and jewels that she might, according to one of the observers, have exchanged the pearls on the headdress alone for two or three German Principalities.

Lewis Mark Mackenzie of Findon, a young officer sitting close to her and one of the few who managed to admire it, wrote to his mother the following week and did his masculine best to convey its effect.

The tilting commenced at $\frac{1}{2}$ past 3 but perhaps before I proceed to give you an account of the tilting you would like to hear a little of the dresses of the ladies who were present and I will first tell you of Lady Londonderry's dress which was by far the most magnificent of all. The headdress was a velvet cap coming down to the shoulders, but as to its further description I cannot tell you but will shew you in your book of costumes, it was covered with pearls and diamonds and presented a most

* Disraeli MS at Hughenden.

splendid appearance. The dress was also of velvet (crimson I think) and across the breast were bands of solid gold about an inch and a half in breadth, set with precious stones, Emeralds, carbuncles and amethysts of a very large size. I should think there must have been about three of these bands besides quantities of diamonds all the way down the front of her dress, hers was certainly the most remarkable of all the ladies dresses, but all the others were very splendid and costly, altho' no one had so great a profusion of jewels about them as her.*

It was not, of course, only Lady Londonderry who wanted to collapse and give way to grief, for apart from all the other women who had spent months and considerable sums planning and perfecting their various dresses, and apart from many of the opposite sex who, like the local Irvine Archers—a band of Ayrshire Robin Hoods—had taken pains to equip themselves suitably, the unhappy host, poor Lord Eglinton, had longed to weep most bitterly.

For as well as the failure of the whole project and aside from the waste of a minor fortune, he, too, had worn an outfit, a superb suit of gilded armour fit, indeed, for a dashing German princling; and without a gleam of sun, let alone in the pouring rain, only a few of his friends had been able to see it.

Like nearly all relics of the Tournament, especially those belonging to the family, later generations of which have failed to realise its social interest and only thought it a monstrous folly, this suit was put to auction and now cannot be traced. Beautifully engraved with leafy scrolls, the breastplate decorated with a pair of wyverns, above which, from the Eglinton crest, was a 'lady dressed in

* The Mackenzie papers, Vol. 19, British Museum 39,200. f. 98.

ancient apparel', every part of it was richly gilt and, in the sun, its effect would have been magnificent. (See plate 16).

That only a handful of people close to him had actually seen how marvellous he looked was a fact that really depressed him. Not without a manly vanity, this was a little pinch of fate he was often heard to bemoan.

Apart from this he bore the fiasco wonderfully. He alone of all the Knights, even including Charlie Lamb, had behaved as though the sun had shone, had bowed and smiled to all the crowd and calmly rearranged the programme as though the curtailments had really been improvements. As befitted a noble leader, he had ridden first among the Knights and been the last to return to the comfort of the castle. And, as behoved the owner of the park, once he had taken off his armour and seen to the comfort of all his guests, he galloped back to the public stands and did what he could to help and cheer the spectators.

The admirable manner in which he behaved, his genuine anxiety and sorrow for others, his absolute lack of pity for himself, his perfect calm and natural cheerfulness were, according to all observers, hardly human or credible; from this moment justly earning him a reputation for invariable sportsmanship which he held for the rest of his life.

When after breakfast on Thursday, having returned from inspecting the Lists he called a conference of all the Knights and suggested they jousted again tomorrow, everyone's spirits rallied and began to rise. Every joiner on the Eglinton estate was employed in sealing the roof of the ballroom, every one of their wives and sisters was put to cleaning and drying the interior, the Lists were drained, the tents put up and as many repairs as possible made to the Grandstand.

Within the castle the activity was just as great. Maids washed and mended frantically, for most of the costumes had shrunk and were stained; armourers hammered and scoured like demons for much of the armour had been dented and was rusty; and after lunch, to keep their hands in, the Knights assembled in the drying ballroom, much to the annoyance of those who were cleaning it, and fought with staves and broomsticks. One of the combats even had to be stopped, Sir Charles Lamb restraining Charlie who, becoming completely involved, lost his sense of what was proper and almost got the better of Louis Napoleon.

The next day, Friday, dawned with a sky that was bright and cloudless. The procession set off in brilliant sunshine, great crowds assembled to watch it, the jousts were held with moderate success, the Knight of the Swan was winged in the arm and had to be attended by a Dr Guthrie, one of the several medical practitioners who, the Tournament letters reveal, had come to the event with their lancets and bone-setters; and although, according to the rules, Fairlie gained the highest score, Lord Eglinton was led to the Queen of Beauty and given the golden circlet reserved for the victor. There was even a form of medieval *mêlée* at which the Knights, divided into teams, charged one another in front of the Grandstand and tried, with a single blow of their swords, to cut off the crests from each other's helmets. They were meant to swipe and gallop on but Lord Waterford, failing to keep his temper, perhaps because he had lost his dragon, suddenly wheeled and pounded after Lord Alford. The two began to fight in earnest, providing the finest combat of the day, and the Knight Marshal, at extreme risk, was forced to rush between them waving his baton.

Then in the evening, in fancy dress, the disappointed guests of Wednesday arrived at last at the Castle. Regaled at first by a medieval banquet with every imaginable ancient dish—they had flagons of malmsey, bowls of syllabub, quarts of hippocras, pints of ping, boars' heads, pots of swan, lamprey pies, prymrose tarts and eight hundred pounds of turtle, escorted personally from London by a chef on the steamer *Sir William Wallace*. The meats were eaten from dishes of silver and the puddings consumed from others of gold, all of which had been specially commissioned from a firm of London goldsmiths. No accounts for the banquet exist but, as four hundred people were invited, the plate alone must have cost a sum that was fabulous.

Quite inevitably, many of the victuals were thought to be totally disgusting. William the Conqueror's favourite dilligrout smelled and tasted like a bran mash and the peacock pie had such a crust that Lady Londonderry was heard to remark that it must have been made of armour and supplied by Pratt. But the Pope's posset and flummery caudle were palatable and more sustaining; and after the usual toasts and speeches, and after the ladies had gone to the saloon, the Knights were able to stretch their legs and wassail.

Last, to the strains of Thompson's orchestra and the band of the 2nd Dragoon Guards, all of whom were dressed like minstrels at, one presumes, Lord Eglinton's expense, two thousand guests and friends danced in Pratt's marquee. Banked with vast quantities of flowers, hung with tapestries, carpeted with velvet and lit by thousands and thousands of candles in coloured lanterns and chandeliers, it moved the prosaic Dr Richardson—perhaps elated by draughts of drangollie—to liken its effect to Fairyland.

Certainly many of the company's dresses were of hardly mortal description. Aunt Jane was in dahlia satin with an Indian veil embroidered with gold; Lady Montgomerie, in

16. The Queen of Beauty, Lady Seymour, standing beside Lord Eglinton's helmet and breastplate. (an oleograph of a miniature by W. J. Newton)

rich cerise, had a headdress 'tastefully adorned with cameos'; Lady Graham, a popular beauty, her jewelled bosom swathed in green, had a string of pearls about her waist which might have been used for a skipping rope; a Mrs Campbell was 'trimmed with bullion'; Lady Charleville, a friend of the Lambs', was 'festooned with bouquets of precious stones'; many an aristocratic waist—like the Duchess of Montrose's in ruby velvet, was hidden beneath a diamond stomacher, fastened with emeralds, amethysts and sapphires in place of hooks or buttons.

Most of the men, too, were dressed magnificently. Lord Chelsea was suited in emerald velvet, Lord Maidstone mantled in golden lace, Lord Saltoun robed in crimson satin, Sir Charles Lamb in sky blue silk—all might have come from Oberon's Court to awaken Sleeping Beauty. In this respect Charlie Lamb was already ahead of the others for, having hidden Charlotte in Edinburgh at 105 Princes Street, he was able to wake her with a kiss whenever he liked. Still romantically and deeply in love with her, he was dressed as a knight of the 15th century in buckskin boots, violet hose, a long black velvet tunic held at the waist by a crimson belt on which was embroidered his chosen motto *'Une Seule'* and a single silver rose.

Friday, in fact, was quite a success although it was only a poor reflection of what Lord Eglinton had dreamed. For although the jousts had taken place, the Lists had been covered with a foot of mud; although the roof of the Grandstand had been mended, all the hangings had been torn to ribbons; and although the spectators had arrived and enjoyed it, many had come in ordinary clothes for their fancy dresses had been ruined.

As for the ball, splendid though it was, it was nothing better than a hundred others to which the people who had

223

Q

supped and danced were already thoroughly accustomed.

'The banquet took place in an immense temporary room', Louisa Stuart wrote in a letter to her friend, Lady Jane Bouverie,

> each knight having his banner held by a page behind him. Then followed a ball in an equally large temporary room. Some of the dresses were most absurd, others beautiful. Lord Fitzharris had a magnificent dress of green velvet and fur, which would have made a good drawing. I did a number of studies, from which I must try to give some idea of the beauty of the sight. The ball and banquet one could easily have dispensed with, being the same as such like in London, but the procession into the Lists, and the tilting, the *mêlée*, were such beautiful sights as one can never expect to see again.*

And Louisa's view of the Knights and the jousts was charmed by awakening love. Strange though it seemed to many of her contemporaries, she became enamoured of the 'Mad Wag Knight',† the dashing, rich but slightly insane Lord Waterford. Seeing him first as he rode to the Lists and from that moment falling in love with him, until she

---

* *The Story of Two Noble Lives*—Augustus Hare, Vol. I. p. 207.

† 'His "eccentricities" as a young man, for which he was notorious, are thus described by Ralph Neville (*Sporting Days and Sporting Ways*, pp. 7-8). 'He painted the Melton toll-bar a bright red, put aniseed on the hoofs of a parson's horse and hunted the terrified divine with bloodhounds. On another occasion he put a donkey into the bed of a stranger at an inn. He took a hunting box in the shires, and amused himself with shooting out the eyes of the family portraits with a pistol. He smashed a very valuable French clock on the staircase at Crockfords with a blow of his fist, and solemnly proposed to one of the first railway companies in Ireland to start two wagons in opposite directions on the same line in order that he might witness the smash, for which he proposed to pay.'

The above quote is from a footnote to Lord Waterford's entry in the *Complete Peerage*.

married him three years afterwards—and, indeed, for the rest of her life—she cared for no one else.

As the moon set on Saturday morning the rain began to fall again with the same tropical ferocity. Vague plans, weather permitting, had been made to joust in the afternoon, but the high wind and thunderous clouds made such hopes impossible. And the fact was that most of the Knights, nearly all the Castle guests and certainly Pratt and the members of the press were frankly extremely thankful.

By Tuesday morning everyone had left and, so far as conditions permitted or were ever likely to do so for months, Lord Eglinton resumed a normal life and the Castle began to revert to its usual appearance.

In the great octagonal hall, however, where the Knights had assembled before the procession and where they had gathered, three days later, to say farewell to their generous host, a change was made in the decoration which was never afterwards altered.

Before they left, in the medieval manner, they presented their banners and shields to Lord Eglinton who hung them up on the walls with his own, their names and titles, in Gothic lettering, suitably painted beneath.

There these knightly trophies hung until in the early 1920's they were sold at auction as curiosities when the Castle was partially demolished.

Today the hall is open to the sky and all that remains of the Eglinton Knights is a faint, fading trace of some of their names.

As Coleridge wrote of Sir Arthur O'Kellyn:
> 'The knight's bones are dust,
> And his good sword rust;—
> His soul is with the saints, I trust.'*

* *The Knight's Tomb*, 1817 (?).

Their names were:

Alford
Beresford
Cassillis
Craven
Eglinton
Fairlie
Gage
Glenlyon
Hopkins
Jerningham
Lamb
Lechmere
Little Gilmour
Waterford

# Chapter Thirteen

## EPILOGUE

Any event which makes a splash which involves the lives of many people invariably affects others, too, by a simple form of chain reaction; and of this sequence of cause and effect the Eglinton Tournament provided an excellent example.

Apart, normally, from newspapers and journals, the most sensitive national sounding board is always the popular theatre; and of those in London, Astley's Amphitheatre was usually far the best. With *The DEAD SEA and The Crocodile's Grot*, which brought to a close *The SEIGE OF JERUSALEM*, even before the Tournament took place Ducrow published the following thrilling announcement. In the only copy which seems to be available, some of the lines at the end are missing but the treat in store for all who read it is clear.

Mr Ducrow is happy to inform the Nobility, Gentry and Visitors of the Amphitheatre, from the great sensation caused by the forthcoming chivalrous pageant of the TOURNAMENT at Eglinton Castle! Has induced him to form arrangements for the veritable Real Armour, and other decorations used on the occasion with complete suits for a Troop of Foot and Mounted Cuirassed men, constructed in Paris by that unequalled Manufacturer Mons. D. Baranger, who executed those so admired in the Jewess. The Theatre is undergoing extensive alterations for the above purpose (when those Ladies and Gentlemen who may not have an opportunity of witnessing the Representation . . . (words missing) . . . of the most extraordinary, faithful and Gorgeous Delineations ever produced in the . . . (rest of the words missing)*

Ducrow's version was a great success and 'attracted immense audiences.'† In a letter to a friend, Wilson in Edinburgh, Sir Walter Scott's biographer, Lockhart, who had been to the rehearsals in St John's Wood and had also seen Ducrow's announcement, wrote what he thought of the one and predicted of the other.

Astley's, to be serious, is a better thing by far than, from witnessing the rehearsals, I expect the performance to prove.‡

Most of the people who went to both agreed that his prophesy came true.

Other take-offs on the subject were equally effective. At Covent Garden the whole Tournament starred in the Christmas pantomime. With all the trimmings of Mother Goose, Puss in Boots, etc., etc., the last and most spectacular scene was a 'Grand Moving Panorama of the Clyde from Glasgow to Eglinton.' With a 'short knight and a long day', a 'short RAIN' for the Queen of Beauty, and heaps of spears which became umbrellas, the lovers at last, luckily for them, were transported to the 'Realms of Sunshine.' On the whole, the critics liked it but, as one of

* Astley's playbills, the Enthoven Collection, Victoria and Albert Museum.

† *The New Monthly Belle Assemblée*, October, 1839.

‡ *Life and Letters of John Gibson Lockhart* by Andrew Lang, Vol. II. p. 211. Lockhart to John Wilson, Professor of Moral Philosophy at Edinburgh University, August 26th, 1839.

them wrote laconically, 'At the fall of the curtain there was much applause, mingled with something that was not applause.' The panorama, however, was 'very beautiful.'

At the Adelphi, the celebrated Yates produced a full length drama.\* Based on Ainsworth's novel *Crichton* with Yates himself as Henri de Valois, the knights appeared on actual horses, the armour and costumes were supplied by Pratt and the stage was lit, in the final scene, by the very turquoise chandeliers that Starr and Mortimer, the London silversmiths, had supplied for the banquet at Eglinton. Entitled *The Knight of the Dragon and the Queen of Beauty*, Lady Seymour's husband went to see it.

India Board
November 20, 1839.

I had no time to write you yesterday, for I went to see some lunatics, and, happy to say, I found a few returned to their senses, and fit to be let out; examining these people took the whole afternoon. In the evening I went with M. Stanley and Byng to the Adelphi, where we saw the latter part of *Jack Sheppard*, and then a piece called the *Tournament*, or, as the actors pronounce it, 'Tournamong'; they also called 'joust' 'a juice'. It was the stupidest thing ever seen; the queen of beauty entangled her hair in the long flowing wig of one of the knights, and they were held fast together, which made us laugh; and Yates, fearful that such laughter might injure the performance, turned to our private box, and begged us not to laugh—rather an impudent request! However, we had no more chance of laughing; it was too dull.'†

\* On Monday, Nov. 18th, 1839.
† *Letters of Edward Adolphus Seymour*, p. 90. Bentley and Son, 1893.

Thus, at last, some of the participants, Knights and Squires, peers and gentlemen, who had taken part in the actual affair, had a chance to see what the world thought of them, and to laugh at themselves as well.

One such who had been to the rehearsals but had not, for an unrecorded reason, taken part in the final event was a Member of Parliament, Colonel Fane, as the papers put it 'yclept the Honest', who lived in Oxfordshire at Wormsley Park. A second cousin of Lord Burghersh whose opera, *The Tournament*, he had much enjoyed, he was very amused at the show at the Adelphi and decided to hold a minor tournament himself.

Less in sympathy with the deeds of old than he was with the struggles of Sancho Panza, he determined to mount his knights on donkeys and make the affair a burlesque. On the 6th of August the following year, almost the Tournament anniversary, he and his friends assembled at his home, armed themselves with kitchen hardware, and, before an immense gathering jousted in front of his house.

For this tournament the weather was cloudless, and five thousand local inhabitants watched it. The Thame band provided the music, led by guardsmen in crimson lace and nine children with penny trumpets; the procession began with a Wormsley Herald; the Knight Marshal was a Colonel Drake; the Lord of the Tournament was Colonel Fane; his son, John, was Knight of the Gridiron; other knights were teapots or kettles; and the Queen of Beauty in Elizabethan costume, although apparently of feminine shape, displayed, the crowd were surprised to observe, above an extremely *décolleté* bodice, a beard and black moustaches.

Then, in the evening, in a nearby barn, three hundred friends and neighbours sat down to a sumptuous banquet. One of the knights had composed a song to the tune of

'The King of the Cannibal Islands' which, as the port went round and round, they began to sing uproariously.

Oh! have you heard the news of late
About a very famous fête,
For if you've not, it's in my pate,
The Tournament at Wormsley:
Where knights did meet their arms to pass,
And each was mounted on an ass,
And Eglintoun it did surpass,
For *that* to this was quite a farce:

*Chorus:*

Houst'em, joust'em, tilt away,
Donkeys gallop, and kick and bray,
I never saw so funny a day
As the Tournament at Wormsley.*

The following day when the knights departed they gave their host a presentation—a pewter inkstand, two feet high, of twelve gallons capacity. The symbolic meaning of this is lost, if, that is, there was any at all, although the article itself survives, almost impossible, indeed, to get rid of, embedded now in the hall at Wormsley, usually filled with umbrellas. Perhaps it stood for nothing at all and was just a final schoolboy dig at the other Knights in Ayrshire; for they, when their own Tournament had ended, had given Lord Eglinton, as a mark of gratitude, a handsome silver trophy.

The Eglinton Trophy, which survives too, was made by Garrard, the London silversmiths, designed by the artist, Edmund Cotterill, whose special bent was creating silver ornaments. Nearly five feet in height, it rose from a wide crenellated base round the sides of which were the shields of the Knights to form an ornate Gothic pulpit beneath a pinnacled canopy. Here stood the Queen of Beauty,

* Family papers, Wormsley.

placing a wreath on the brow of the Lord of the Tournament. Beside him rode the Knight Marshal with squires and halbardiers.

Much praised at the time of its construction, much ridiculed, inevitably, afterwards as a gross piece of Victorian materialism, it is once again widely approved as a fine example of the type of work of the period. Certainly no one who likes the Gothic and enjoys a display of Victorian skill can fail to admire its robust romantic magnificence.

Two hundred and thirty-nine of Lord Eglinton's friends subscribed to it, the maximum amount allowed being twenty guineas.

'You hear, I suppose that we have entered into a subscription to present Eglinton with a piece of plate, to commemorate the revival of the days of chivalry!' wrote Jerningham's Esquire, W. Stephenson, to Lady Shelley of Michelgrove.*

I don't know if our ancestors were equally pugnacious, but we cannot even carry this through without quarelling! A committee had been formed to carry this into effect; at the head of it was Lord Londonderry (not to promote the pugnacity, but the subscription), and till he left the Castle all went smoothly. But, after his departure the names of Burghersh and Lord Chelsea were added, which was no sooner made known to the King of the Lists than he wrote a most frantic letter, declaring they ought to have nothing to do with it, and withdrawing his own name. I have not heard since if the matter has been set right, but I believe the first intention was to take him at his word!

* *The Diary of Frances Lady Shelley.* Ed. Richard Edgcumbe. 1913. Vol. II, p. 261.

Four years were needed to complete the trophy which now stands, for all to admire, in the County Hall at Ayr.

No one can read of an item like this, let alone of the Tournament itself, without considering the cost; and although the bill for the Trophy survives—£1,775:0:7d—all the principal accounts for the Tournament are missing. Nothing remains in the family archives, now safe in the Edinburgh Register House, except the following sundry and minimal items:

Expenses in connexion with the Tournament, 1839:—

| | | | |
|---|---:|---:|---:|
| Sawing Timber | £98 | 8 | 5½ |
| Carriage of do. | 42 | 11 | 0 |
| Timber bought | 11 | 5 | 4½ |
| Sundries | 20 | 3 | 8 |
| Constables and Others | 184 | 7 | 6 |
| Joiners and other workmen and labourers paid by Gardener per separate Account Book | 486 | 2 | 0 |
| | £842 | 18 | 0 |
| Value of Timber from Estates | 666 | 9 | 0 |
| | £1,509 | 7 | 0 |

Expenses in connexion with the Tournament, 1840:—

| | | | |
|---|---:|---:|---:|
| Timber | £942 | 16 | 6 |
| Joiners | 90 | 3 | 11 |
| Carriage of Timber | 33 | 6 | 3 |
| Sundries | 149 | 4 | 3 |
| Constables Expenses of distributing tickets, etc. | 35 | 12 | 6 |
| | £1,251 | 3 | 5 |

Beyond these trivial details one has to fall back on the estimates given by the press. The average figure is £40,000 and taking everything into account such a sum is reasonable. With this amount, at that period, Lord Eglinton might have built a church—like, for example, St Luke's in Chelsea—or, like Lord Acland before the Reform Act, he might have spent it in rotten boroughs, virtually buying a couple of seats in Parliament. In either case, had he done so, history now might have said he had spent it better.

For except for the silver testimonial, the Knights' shields and banners at the Castle and a couple of suits of armour and dresses retained by one or two of the Knights, everything else went back to Pratt and after twelve months had passed nothing remained of the Eglinton Tournament at all.

Pratt decided to hold a sale which gave him another excuse for an exhibition. Everything left was put on view; the suits of nearly all the Knights, their esquires' armour, their retainers' costumes, their lances, gonfalons, crests, caparisons; even Little Gilmour's sword still bearing the stains of Jerningham's blood.

Then in June all was sold, Lord Waterford's equipment fetching the most—£240 with £20 in addition for its plaster horse.

As *entrepreneur* of the Tournament itself, Pratt undoubtedly made a profit, nearly all at Lord Eglinton's expense, for many of the others were slow in paying him and a few, even, never did so at all; Lord Eglinton, being the man he was, eventually settled their accounts. But the sale afterwards was not a success and most of the items, especially the dresses, went for sums that were trifling.

A knight's black velvet costume, slashed with white and bound with silver, including a cloak that was lined with satin—the bill for which had been £100—made only ten guineas; an even finer geranium robe, actually worn by Louis Napoleon, fell to Ducrow, the only bidder, for a mere seventy shillings.

Many of the clothes, of course, had been spoiled by the weather and in this connection it is worth considering whether, knowing the climate in Ayrshire, such a party in the open air should ever have been considered. The average rainfall in August at Eglinton for the first quarter of the present century was one inch every week and although Lord Eglinton was bored by statistics and did not, in fact, record the rain, he knew, naturally, as well as anybody, the extreme likelihood of at least some heavy showers. A few miles away at Rothesay the rainfall in August, 1839, was more than five inches; compare this with the fall in Edinburgh which, during the same period, was rather less than two. It was bad luck, nevertheless, that nearly the whole of the monthly average seems to have fallen on the very day that was scheduled for the opening of the Tournament.

If he should not be considered rash to have chanced so much on his native climate, he must, at least, be severely criticised for having shown such extravagance. This, with a certain natural vanity, was the one really serious weakness he displayed throughout his life. And of this span, after the Tournament, he had more years than his present descendants—still trying to recoup his losses—might perhaps have wished. Not that he lived long, however, for he died suddenly when forty-nine, but in these last twenty-two years he spent money at such a rate that any sums defrayed on the Tournament were entirely insignificant. But he never paused to consider finance, leaving that to factors and solicitors, and even the locked pages of his diary reveal not a single worry about his debts.

What they disclose, in a way, is infinitely worse. At the

time of the Tournament he was still a bachelor but shortly afterwards, in 1841, with needless haste and reckless obstinacy, against every caution of sense and judgement, he became engaged to the widow of a naval officer.

One of eight natural children of the second and last Viscount Newcomen, and perhaps because of this unhappy status—non-existent in the legal sense so that, on paper, her father was childless—she was so determined to maintain her position as the wife of a normal, legitimate nobleman that she made his life a pilgrimage of misery and Eglinton Castle a gaol.

'It was the great, the most important, error of my life,' he wrote of his marriage to Theresa Cockerell.

Hardly in one respect did we suit. She had many good qualities. She was good hearted, conscientious, resolute, truthful to the highest degree, devoted to me throughout, but she was irritable and domineering, she was of a most suspicious disposition and her jealousy amounted to absolute madness. There was not a servant whom she did not suspect of cheating her, there was not a woman under 70 who she did not fancy was making love to me. At church I was accused of ogling someone, in a Country house I was sometimes goaded to desperation by her jealousy, when I could not guess which of the party was the object of her suspicions, if I was absent for a few hours I found her generally in tears and pacing about the room in a species of frenzy, and I was called on to give an account of how I had spent my time, if I was detained later than usual at the House of Lords, I was forthwith accused of the worst conduct. I have had to carry her upstairs to her room in hysterics, because she was jealous of an ugly woman of 50, I have had to run out of the room to prevent a scene which would have disgraced us both. The greater portion of our nights used to be spent in fierce altercation; I have known her dash herself against the wall and beat her head on the floor, I snatched my razor away when it was at her throat, I struck a bottle of laudanum out of her hands when it was at her mouth. All this too went on without the shadow of a cause for it. I never during the 13 years we lived together was faithless to her in thought, word, or deed.

His avowal of chastity is almost certainly honest for although in his teens and early manhood he had lived as promiscuously as anybody else, he changed entirely after his marriage, gave up hunting almost at once, sold his stud within the decade and, whenever he managed to escape from home, devoted himself to politics. For this, in the end, he received his reward, twice serving as Viceroy of Ireland under Conservative governments.

There were plenty of sneers at this selection and all the obvious jibes were quickly made about him. The year was 1852, the Gothic Revival was still in force—indeed more so than ever before—and the front cover of *Punch* for January showed the British Lion as King of a tournament, Britannia as Queen of Beauty beside him, and Mr Punch, the triumphant victor, receiving a wreath for defeating Humbug and Folly.

With great pleasure the DIRECTOR of the NEW PALACE THEATRE, WESTMINSTER respectfully announces to the Nobility, Gentry and Clergy that the Performances at this establishment have recommenced under new management. The Company has been completely reorganised. The comic entertainment of *Dublin Castle* will be revived for Mr.

EGLINTOUN, and the splendid real armour will be introduced, as worn at the Scottish Tournament.*

Thus, with jokes of a similar caste, *Punch* and others announced Lord Eglinton's appointment. Everyone lived to eat their words for he proved to be the best Viceroy there had been for a generation.

'Sociable, jovial, frank, open,' he was always ready to talk to the humblest, perfectly impartial on the question of religion, entirely fair in domestic politics, and grandly hospitable to all.

He even managed, on certain occasions, to score a point on his wife. Whenever he gave an official Drawing Room he had, in accordance with established protocol, to bow gravely to all the gentlemen and to greet their wives and daughters with a gentle kiss. He once, according to a note in his diary, embraced nine hundred and thirty in a single evening. It was almost more than Theresa could bear and if he approached them rather warmly, as he sometimes did, at the end of the evening she used to hiss nervously behind him and once was heard to mutter, 'It is too much.'

She died unexpectedly the following year, meeting a sudden and painful death courageously. Of middle height, handsome figure, dark hair which fell in ringlets and, in repose, an agreeable face, she was well aware of her destructive weakness and had always managed, at least, to control herself in public. She bore Lord Eglinton four children, one daughter and three sons, from the second of whom, George Arnulph, the present male line of the family descends.

With such an unfortunate marriage behind him, endured with gentleness for thirteen years, Lord Eglinton swore he would never attach himself again but when in Ireland in

* Feb. p. 123.

17. Cartoons in *The Tournament* by Richard Doyle

| | | |
|---|---|---|
| Pratt arming Jerningham | Marquess of Londonderry and Jester. M'Ian | Mackay and Redbury |
| Heralds | Lord Glenlyon and the Railway Knight | Jerningham and Esquire |

18. 'The Eglinton Tomfooleryment'
(cartoon from *Cleave's Penny Gazette*)

1858 on his second tour of duty as Viceroy he fell in love with Adela Capel, the eldest daughter of the 6th Lord Essex and married her within the year. With her, sixteen years his junior, he was instantly intensely happy; and her death in childbirth two years later caused him a greater depth of anguish than any he had known before.

He, too, though unaware of it, had only months to live. On the 1st of October, 1861, he was having dinner with a friend at St Andrew's, Whyte-Melville, the father of the novelist, when he suffered a fit of apoplexy. During the day he had played some golf and had seemed in excellent health although for some months before he had been complaining of minor hallucinations. He never regained consciousness again and died on October the fourth.

He was so widely known in Scotland, so popular with every class, even amongst his political opponents, such a grand and familiar figure at every public and sporting event, always fit, cheerful and vigorous, that when the news of his death was published people could hardly believe it; and the warmth and sincerity of all his obituaries moved many who had hardly known him to feel a personal bereavement.

'What a loss Lord Eglinton was!' exclaimed the editor of *Blackwood's Magazine* in a conversation recorded later.

Of him it may emphatically be said that honour was his polar star, and no consideration whatever could induce him to swerve one step, to the right or the left, from what he believed to be the path of duty.*

To his large circle of personal friends the loss was infinitely greater. His finest quality was generosity; many people whom he hardly knew often stayed at Eglinton for weeks, and those whom he loved—like his natural sister

* *Blackwood's Magazine*, Nov. 1861.

239

R

and the three daughters of his wife's first marriage, each of whom he dowered nobly—missed him bitterly with all their hearts and were never again, in the head of the family, to find such a sympathetic patron.

'I remember as a little boy my father's poignant regret at the death, at the age of fifty, of the thirteenth Earl of Eglinton,' wrote Abbot Hunter Blair.*

The Abbot's father was the son of Sir David, then approaching his eightieth birthday, who, thirty years before, had refused to allow Lord Eglinton a horse at Eton. It is pleasant to observe such a happy ending to what must have been a strained neighbourly relationship, and pleasant, too, to record how it came about.

On the 10th of March, 1856, five years before his death, Lord Eglinton wrote to Sir David the following letter:

St James's Sq.
March 10, 1856

Dear Sir David,

I have this morning been informed by Messrs Hunter, Blair and Cowan that the Trust created by my grandfather has been closed, and that you are at last released from the duties imposed on you by it.

While I congratulate you on this escape from a business which must have caused you so much trouble and anxiety during the many years it has endured, I beg that you will receive my very sincere thanks for the kindness and assiduity which have distinguished you in the performance of your duties.

May I trust that you have long since forgiven any hastiness, and even rudeness, of which I may have been guilty during the earlier portion of our connection, and

* *A Medley of Memories.* Sir D. Hunter Blair, 1919, p. 113.

that you have had little cause to complain of me since I have attained to years of discretion.*

With best regards to Lady Hunter Blair, believe me,

Very sincerely yours,

Eglinton & Winton.

Sir David answered him three days afterwards:

My Dear Lord,

I don't think I ever in my life received a more gratifying and pleasing letter than your's of the 10th of March just received. I shall keep it as a treasure to my dying day.

I assure you I have long since entirely forgotten any little *contretemps* that may have formerly happened in the management of the Trust in its early days. The uniform kindness & friendship you have constantly evinced to me & my whole family since you became your own master have been a source of great delight to me, and I shall ever deeply feel that the cordial expressions of regard you bestow upon me deserve my best gratitude.†

Thus, with characteristic sincerity, Lord Eglinton achieved the Trustees' blessing and, so far as they were concerned, atoned for the sins of his youth.

No one reading the Eglinton history and learning the appalling cost of the Tournament can fail to wonder what, if anything, the Trustees did to prevent it. Dealing as they were with a headstrong nobleman, the answer is that whatever they attempted was bound to come to nothing; for as a result of the Act of Parliament, all Lord Eglinton's money was his own and their only legal responsibility was to clear the debts at Ardrossan.

* Family Papers, Blair.
† Family Papers, Blair.

And during the first half of his life, that is to say until he got married, he always behaved exactly as he chose and absolutely refused to listen to criticism. Such an attitude was almost inevitable, given his upbringing by his aunt' and mother, both of whom spoilt him hopelessly, given the fact that he held a peerage—a tremendous asset in the 19th century—and given his enormous wealth. Having decided to hold a tournament, and having all the means to do so—the place, the money and the organisation— nothing in the world except the law or, of course, an act of nature, certainly not a former Trustee, could have made him agree to stop it. Remaining cheerful, polite, hospitable, even inviting Sir David to attend it which, in fact he actually did, his son squiring Little Gilmour, dressed in the style of Henry VIII, Lord Eglinton brushed aside his advisers and refused to be warned of its cost. For this he must take the full responsibility; only his step-father and his brother Charlie can reasonably be said to share a little of the blame.

Apart from failings in this direction and apart from a certain lack of ambition which, at least in early manhood, enabled him to live without a care—only hunting, shooting and racing, all of which were harmless enough but hardly worth his exclusive attention—his character was sociable, open, manly and immediately attractive to all who came to know it. He was never heard to show his temper, never seen to be rude or unkind, always ready to help his friends, just as gay when he lost a game as he was when he usually won it. For, from his very earliest manhood, he had been extremely athletic; and few could manage better on a horse, run so tirelessly behind a hare, master him at tennis, squash or racquets or beat him at fives or billiards.

The happiest part of his life was spent on the turf and here he made a genuine contribution. Apart from winning all the classics, and apart from owning a magnificent stable which, with typical impetuosity, he sold suddenly for 2,500 guineas, hardly a fifth of what it was worth, his personal example of sportsmanship and honour at a time when doping and swindling were rife, helped to achieve that standard of honesty of which the racing world is proud today.

After his marriage he changed, naturally, but far from being embittered by unhappiness he merely lost a little of his gaiety and turned his mind to those duties for which by birth he was placed. Not endowed with outstanding intellect but full of judgement and common sense which made him an invaluable chairman of committees, he was by conviction a profound Conservative and was one of the Whips of his party in the House of Lords. At home in Ayrshire he was Lord Lieutenant, patron of innumerable sporting events and Lord Rector of Glasgow University; always proud of his family history, he engaged Sir William Fraser, the antiquary, to write the *Montgomerie Memorials*.

But, in the hearts of his family today, all these excellent qualities are blurred by his terrible extravagance. This weakness was perhaps inherited for many of his ancestors had led the way; but they at least had died with something to show for it. At least his grandfather had built a harbour and at least all his other forbears—from 'Greysteel' to Mundegumbri—had either actually increased their wealth or left a promise of substantial capital improvement.

But Archibald William, Earl of Eglinton, Earl of Winton, Lord Montgomerie, Lord Seton and Tranent in Scotland, Baron Ardrossan in the United Kingdom, Hereditary Sheriff of the County of Renfrew, Knight of the Thistle and Doctor of Laws only left an honoured name, substantial debts as Viceroy of Ireland, many others for racing and hunting and one of £40,000 for the whim, at the age of twenty-seven, of holding a friendly tournament.

When, in 1872, Disraeli was planning to write *Endymion*, an historical novel of the 1830's, he decided to include an account of the Tournament and wrote to the former Lady Seymour to ask for anecdotes and souvenirs.

'My Dear Mr Disraeli,' she answered from 30 Grosvenor Gardens on October 31st:

> I am very unwell or I would have answered before your letter of Oct. 26th. I do not know what I can find of the Eglinton Tournament, except a colored print which I will send you—I had all sorts of relics, points of splintered spears with the colours of the Knights but a stupid old house-maid considered them as 'rubbish' as she said, and burnt them together with a Blessed Palm that I had caught in mid air from the Pope's own hands, but I will certainly look out whatever I can find.
>
> Ever most truly yours
> Jane G. Somerset.*

Such a reply must have struck Disraeli as symbolic, and although the book was a fair success and is still useful to students today it had only a short and inaccurate account of the Tournament.

Yet, in regard to the event itself, what indeed can be said about it? Genuine tournaments must have been thrilling when the knights were tough and used to jousting and were able to ride and fight with skill and ferocity. But the Eglinton Tournament, for all its cost, for all the care that was taken to arrange it, for all the practice put in by the Knights, never really came to life and was never more than an aristocratic pageant.

Viewed now in the telescope of history, it throws an interesting light on the period and the way in which the Gothic image, like Rebecca's charms in the Lists at Ashby,

* Disraeli MSS, Hughenden, E/VI/T.1.

drove frantic the wisest men that lived. But as an attempt to revive the past it was plainly a total failure.

During the reign of Charles VII in the first half of the 15th century when jousts were still extremely savage, a Turkish ambassador at the Court of France is said, when watching a certain tournament, to have made the following comment: that if it was in earnest it was not enough, and if it was a game it was too much.*

This remark was remembered and quoted when, in 1559, Lord Eglinton's kinsman, Count Montgomerie, fatally wounded the King of France.

Three hundred years later it was used, too, for the Eglinton Tournament. For naturally, after a little while—especially when the costs were known—as the sun rose on the Age of Steam while the Gothic spirit blossomed in architecture and reached sublime heights in poetry, some harsh facts had to be faced by all who actually wished to be shining knights.

For those who had tried it, the *preux chevaliers* who had left their shields and banners in Ayrshire, had found out from their own experience that the Turk's verdict was only too correct.

* '*Si c'etait tout de bon, ce n'etait pas assez, et que si c'etait un jeu, c'etait trop.*' (Leber - *Coll. des Dissertations* XI, 363).

# APPENDIX I

The following is a list of some 18th and 19th century tournaments:

| Date | Place | Remarks |
|------|-------|---------|
| 1750 | Berlin | Held by Frederick the Great. See Carlyle Vol. V. p. 262. |
| 1769 | Parma | In honour of the marriage of Ferdinand, Duke of Parma, to Maria Amelia, Archduchess of Austria. A splendid affair, magnificently recorded in a book by Bodoni. B.M. Pressmark 650:c:6. |
| 1777 | Sweden | Given by Gustavus III who wrote that he wished to revive tournaments of the age of chivalry in order to counteract the present day effeminacy. Journal of the Royal Armoury of Stockholm, V. iv:4. |
| 1778 | Philadelphia | In honour of the retirement of General Sir William Howe. Known as the 'Mischanzia', it was organised by Lord Cathcart, a young officer. His family seat was in Ayrshire, and he lived to see his grandchildren take part in the Eglinton Tournament 61 years later. It is well described in the *Annual Register* for 1778. |

| Date | Place | Remarks |
|------|-------|---------|
| 1781 | Sweden | |
| 1785 | Sweden | |
| 1788 | Sweden | |
| 1791 | Copenhagen | |
| 1791 | Dresden | |
| 1799 | Sweden | |
| 1800 | Sweden | This was the last of these tournaments in Sweden (until 1894) because they were felt to be unlucky. Many spectators were injured on this occasion. Some were shot by two excited knights; others were squashed when the Grandstand collapsed; the rest were laid out by an epidemic of measles. |
| 1800 | Vienna | At about this time the Emperor Francis I built a special Gothic Tilt Yard at Laxenburg and held tournaments there. |
| 1814 | Vienna | On the 20th November in honour of the Allied Sovereigns. A MS account of this is possessed by the Duke of Atholl. |
| 1827 | Firle Place | A tilting party by Viscount Gage. |
| 1828 | Malta | Held by the officers of the Garrison in the Palace Square, Valetta. |
| 1833 | Barcelona | Held in honour of the accession of Isobel as Queen of Spain. |
| 1839 | Turin | Held by the King of Sardinia in honour of a visit by the Hereditary Grand Duke Alexander of Russia. |

| Date | Place | Remarks |
|------|-------|---------|
| 1839 (June) | New Orleans | This and many other tournaments were held in the southern states of America during the 1840's and 1850's. They were inspired by the same Gothic fever that was over-running Europe. See R. G. Osterweis, *Romanticism and Nationalism in the Old South*, Yale Historical Publications, Vol. XLIX, 1949. |
| 1839 (August) | Ayrshire | The Eglinton Tournament. |

[APPENDIX II — A FACSIMILE]

# Programme

OF

# THE PROCESSION

FROM THE CASTLE TO THE LISTS,

AT

# The Tournament,

AT

# Eglinton Castle,

AUGUST 28th and 29th, 1839.

LONDON: PRINTED BY J. DAVY, QUEEN STREET,
KING STREET, NEAR LONG ACRE.

# Programme.

## MEN AT ARMS,

In demi Suits of Armour and Costumes.

## MUSICIANS,

In rich costumes of Silk—their Horses trapped and caparisoned.

## TRUMPETERS,

In full costume—the Trumpet and Banners emblazoned with the Arms
of the Lord of the Tournament.

BANNER BEARERS of the LORD of the TOURNAMENT.

## TWO DEPUTY MARSHALS,

In costumes, on Horses caparisoned.
Attendants on foot.

## The Eglinton Herald,

In a Tabard, richly embroidered.

TWO POURSUIVANTS.

In emblazoned Surcoats.

## The Judge of Peace,

### (LORD SALTOUN.)

In his Robes, and bearing a Wand, on a Horse richly caparisoned.

RETAINERS,

On foot, in costumes, carrying heavy Steel Battle Axes.

## Officer of the Halberdiers,

On horseback, in a Suit of demi Armour, with a Gilt Partizan.

HALBERDIERS,

On foot, in Liveries of the Lord, carrying their Halberds.

MEN AT ARMS,

In demi Suits of Armour.

## The Herald of the Tournament,

In his Tabard, richly emblazoned with emblematical devices.

---

## The Knight Marshal of the Lists,

### (SIR CHARLES LAMB, BART.)

GROOM.    In a rich embroidered Surcoat, and embossed    GROOM.
and gilt Suit of Armour—his Horse richly
caparisoned, &c.

Esquire,

LORD CHELSEA.

Esquire,

MAJOR McDOWAL.

## ATTENDANTS OF THE KNIGHT MARSHAL,
In Costumes of his Colours, Blue, White and Gold.

## HALBERDIERS OF THE KNIGHT MARSHAL,
In Liveries of his Colours, with their Halberds.

### Ladies Visitors,

LADY MONTGOMERY,          LADY JANE MONTGOMERY,

MISS MACDONALD,

On Horses, caparisoned with blue and white Silk, embroidered with Gold and Silver, each led by a GROOM in costume of their colours.

---

## The King of the Tournament,
### (MARQUIS OF LONDONDERRY,)

HALBERDIER.   In his Robes of Velvet and Ermine,   HALBERDIER.
and wearing his Coronet—his Horse
richly caparisoned.

Esquire,

COLONEL WOOD.

Esquire,

H. IRVINE, Esq.

### HALBERDIERS,
In Liveries, as before.

---

# The Queen of Beauty,

GROOM.   **(LADY SEYMOUR.)**   GROOM.

In a rich Costume, on a Horse richly caparisoned—a Silk Canopy borne over her by Attendants in costumes.

## LADIES ATTENDANTS ON THE QUEEN,

In rich costumes.

## PAGES OF THE QUEEN,

In costumes of her colours.

Esquire,            Esquire,

F. CHARTERIS, Esq.

---

# The Jester,

In a characteristic costume, bearing his sceptre, on a Mule, caparisoned and trapped, with bells, &c.

## RETAINERS,

On foot, in Liveries of the colours of the Lord of the Tournament.

---

# The Irbine Archers,

In costumes of Lincoln Green, black Velvet Baldric, Rondelle, &c.

### CLAUDE ALEXANDER, Esq.

| | |
|---|---|
| LORD KILBORN | A. CUNNINGHAM, Esq. |
| SIR ROBERT DALLAS | C. S. BUCHANAN, Esq. |
| CAPTAIN BLAIR | SIR A. HAMILTON, Bart. |
| STUART HAY, Esq. | CAPT. MONTGOMERIE |
| J. BROWNLOW, Esq. | J. BURNETT, Esq, |
| — HAMILTON, Esq. | HONBLE. J. STRANGWAYS |
| CAPTAIN BLANE | GEORGE RANKIN, Esq. |

---

RETAINERS of the LORD OF THE TOURNAMENT.

HALBERDIERS of the Lord, in Liveries of his colours.

MAN AT ARMS,     THE GONFALON,     MAN AT ARMS,
in Half-Armour.     Borne by a Man at Arms.     in Half-Armour.

# The Lord of the Tournament,

### (EARL OF EGLINTON.)

GROOM.     In a Suit of Gilt Armour, richly chased;     GROOM.
on a barded Charger—caparisons, &c.
of Blue and Gold.

### The Banner

Borne by LORD A. SEYMOUR.

Esquire,     Esquire,     Esquire,

G. DUNDAS, Esq.     F. CAVENDISH, Esq.     G. McDOUAL, Esq.

RETAINERS of the LORD, as before.

---

S

8

HALBERDIERS OF THE KNIGHT OF THE GRIFFIN,
In Liveries of his Colours.

MAN AT ARMS,    THE GONFALON,    MAN AT ARMS,
in Half-Armour.    Borne by a Man at Arms.    in Half-Armour.

## The Knight of the Griffin,

### (THE EARL OF CRAVEN.)

GROOM.    In a Suit of engraved Milanese Armour, inlaid    GROOM.
with Gold; on a barded Charger—caparisons
&c. of Scarlet, White and Gold,

Esquire,    The Banner    Esquire,
THE HON.    Borne by a    THE HON.
F. CRAVEN.    Man at Arms,    F. MACDONALD.
in Half-Armour.

RETAINERS.

---

HALBERDIERS OF THE KNIGHT OF THE DRAGON.
In Liveries of his Colours.

MAN AT ARMS,    THE GONFALON,    MAN AT ARMS,
in Half-Armour.    Borne by a Man at Arms.    in Half-Armour.

## The Knight of the Dragon,

### (MARQUIS OF WATERFORD.)

GROOM.    In a Suit of polished Steel Fluted German    GROOM,
Armour; on barded Charger—caparisons, &c.
of Blue and White.

Page,
LORD JOHN BERESFORD.

Page,
MARK WHYTE, Esq.

Esquire,
Sir CHARLES KENT.

The Banner
Borne by a
Man at Arms.

Esquire,
L. RICARDO, Esq.

RETAINERS.

---

HALBERDIERS OF THE KNIGHT OF THE BLACK LION.

MAN AT ARMS,
in Half-Armour.

THE GONFALON,
Borne by a Man at Arms.

MAN AT ARMS,
in Half-Armour.

## The Knight of the Black Lion,

### (VISCOUNT ALFORD.)

GROOM.

In a Suit of polished Steel Armour, on a
Charger—caparisons of Blue and White.

GROOM.

Esquire,
THE HON. MR. CUST

The Banner
Borne by a Man
at Arms.

Esquire.
T. O. GASCOIGNE, Esq.

RETAINERS.

---

HALBERDIERS OF THE KNIGHT OF GAEL.

MAN AT ARMS.
in Half-Armour.

THE GONFALON,
Borne by a Man at Arms.

MAN AT ARMS.
in Half-Armour.

## The Knight of Gael,

### (VISCOUNT GLENLYON.)

GROOM.

In a Suit of polished Steel Armour, on a
barded Charger—caparisons, &c. of Green,
Blue, and Crimson.

GROOM.

Esquire,                 The Banner                Esquire,
SIR DAVID DUNDAS.    Borne by a Man       JOHN BALFOUR, Esq.
                         at Arms.

RETAINERS.

---

RETAINERS OF THE KNIGHT OF THE DOLPHIN.

MAN AT ARMS,      THE GONFALON,      MAN AT ARMS,
in Half-Armour.    Borne by a Man at Arms.    in Half-Armour.

## The Knight of the Dolphin,

### (EARL OF CASSILLIS.)

GROOM.    In a Suit of engraved Steel Armour, inlaid    GROOM.
          with Gold, on a barded Charger—caparisons,
              &c. of Scarlet, Black and White.
Esquire,                                              Esquire,

---

## The Knight of the Crane,

### (LORD CRANSTOUN.)

In a Suit of polished Steel Armour, on a
barded Charger—caparisons, &c. of Red
and White.
Esquire,            The Banner            Esquire,
                    Borne by a Man
                    at Arms.

---

RETAINERS OF THE KNIGHT OF THE RAM.

## THE GONFALON,
Borne by a Man at Arms.

# The Knight of the Ram, *✗ Swan —*

## (THE HON. CAPT. GAGE.)

GROOM.　　In a Suit of polished Steel Armour, on　　GROOM.
a barded Charger — caparisons, &c. of
Blue, White and Crimson.

Esquire,　　　　　The Banner　　　　　Esquire,
R. MURRAY, Esq.　　Borne by a Man　　J. FERGUSON, Esq.
at Arms.

---

## HALBERDIERS OF THE BLACK KNIGHT.

MAN AT ARMS,　　THE GONFALON,　　MAN AT ARMS,
in Half-Armour.　　Borne by a Man at Arms.　　in Half-Armour.

# The Black Knight,

*Mr. Johnstone*
## (JOHN CAMPBELL, ESQ. OF SADDELL.)

GROOM.　　In a Suit of Black Armour, on a barded　　GROOM.
Charger—caparisons, &c. of Black.

Page,　　　　　　　　　Page,
MASTER J. FLETCHER.　　　　MASTER FLETCHER.

Esquire,　　　　The Banner　　　　Esquire,
CAPT. BLAIR.　　Borne by a Man　　CLANRANALD.
at Arms.

### RETAINERS.

---

## RETAINERS OF THE KNIGHT OF THE SWAN.

MAN AT ARMS,　　THE GONFALON,　　MAN AT ARMS,
in Half-Armour.　　Borne by a Man at Arms.　　in Half-Armour.

*[the programme continues for another five pages]*

# BIBLIOGRAPHY

*PART ONE*

1. The Eglinton family papers, the Scottish Record Office, Edinburgh.
2. *The Memorials of the Montgomeries*, by Sir Wm Fraser, Edinburgh, 1859.
3. *Historical Memoir of the House of Eglinton and Winton*, by John Fullarton, 1864.
4. *Origin and History of the Montgomerys*, by Count Bo Gabriel de Montgomery, 1948.
5. *History of the House of Seton*, by Viscount Kingston, 1829.
6. *Kay's Edinburgh Portraits*, by James Paterson, 1885.
7. *Chapters from family chests*, by Edward Walford, 1887.
8. *Ayrshire families*, by G. Robertson, 1823.
9. *History of the County of Ayr*, by James Paterson, 1847.
10. *Survey of Ayrshire*, by W. Aiton, 1811.


*PART TWO*

1. *The Eglinton Tournament*, text by 'B', Drawings by Edward Courbould. Published by Hodgson & Graves, London, 1840.
2. *The Eglinton Tournament*, text by the Rev. John Richardson, LL.B. Drawings by James Henry Nixon. Published by Colnaghi & Puckle, London, 1843.
3. *The Tournament.* Drawings by Richard Doyle. Published, London, 1840. The related text is in his *Journal for* 1840, published by Smith, Elder & Co. London, 1885.

4. *The Passage of Arms at Eglinton.* Anon. Published by Stewart and Murray, London, n.d.

5. *The Field of the Cloth of Gold of Eglinton,* by H. Curling. Published by Sampson Low, London, 1839.

6. *The Grand Tourney,* by James Bulkeley. Published by Saunders and Otley, London, 1840.

7. *The Eglinton Tournament,* by Peter Buchan. Published by Simpkin, Marshall & Co. London, 1840.

8. *An Account of the Tournament at Eglinton,* sketches by W. Gordon. Text by James Aikman. Published by Hugh Paton, Edinburgh, 1839.

9. *Grand Tournament at Eglinton Castle.* A Broadsheet sold for one penny in Edinburgh by N. Bowack, 46 Leith St. J. Neilson, Printer.

10. *Guide to the Tournament.* Published by Maxwell Dick, Irvine, 1839.

11. *The Tournament.* A mock heroic ballad with eight illustrations by Alfred Crowquill. Published by Thomas M'Lean, Haymarket, London, 1839.

12. *Backward Glances,* by James Hedderwick, LL.D. Wm. Blackwood & Sons, Edinburgh, 1891.

13. *Autobiographical Reminiscences,* by James Paterson. Maurice Ogle & Co. Glasgow, 1871.

14. *Kilwinning,* by Wm. Lee Ker, M.A. Published by A. W. Cross, Kilwinning, 1900.

15. *Through the Long Day,* by Charles Mackay; W. H. Allen & Co. London, 1887.

16. *Recollections,* by John Richardson, Published 1856, by C. Mitchell, London.

17. *Memoirs of a Bow Street Runner,* by Henry Goddard, Ed. Patrick Pringle, Museum Press, London, 1956.

The files of the following newspapers for 1838/39 at the following places:

| | |
|---|---|
| *The Aberdeen Journal* | Aberdeen University Library |
| *The Ayr Advertiser* | Ayr Public Library |
| *The Ayr Observer* | Glasgow Mitchell Library |
| *The Dumfries and Galloway Courrier* | Glasgow Mitchell Library |
| *The Glasgow Argus* | Glasgow Mitchell Library |
| *The Glasgow Chronicle* | Glasgow Mitchell Library |
| *The Glasgow Courrier* | Glasgow Mitchell Library |
| *The Glasgow Herald* | Glasgow Mitchell Library |
| *The Perthshire Courrier* | Perth Public Library |
| *The Paisley Advertiser* | Paisley Public Library |
| *The Stirling Journal* | Stirling Public Library |
| *The Scotsman* | National Library of Scotland, Edinburgh |

At the British Museum Newspaper Library, Colindale:
*The Age*
    *Bell's Life in London*
    *Bell's New Weekly Messenger*
    *Bell's Weekly Messenger*
    *Cleave's Penny Gazette*
*The Court Journal*
*The Court Gazette*
*The Evening Chronicle*
*The Evening Mail*
    *Franklin's Miscellany*
    *John Bull*
*The Morning Chronicle*
*The Morning Herald*
*The Morning Post*
*The Observer*
*The Penny Satirist*

*The Social Gazette*
*The Spectator*
*The Times*
*The Weekly Despatch*

American papers at the above library:
 *Daily National Intelligencer*, Washington
 *New York American*
 *National Gazette*, Philadelphia

# Select Index

265

*By Permission of the Earl of Eglinton.*

STEAM CONVEYANCE

FROM

# ARDROSSAN TO LIVERPOOL.

THE GLASGOW and LIVERPOOL ROYAL STEAM-PACKET CO. have made arrangements to SAIL their splendid and powerful Steam Ships from ARDROSSAN to LIVERPOOL:—

ROYAL GEORGE,......SATURDAY, 31st AUGUST, at 6 o'clock, Evening.

ROYAL SOVEREIGN,..SATURDAY, 31st AUGUST, at 10 o'clock, Evening.

FARES—Saloon, 25s.; Steward's Fee, 2s.

Carriages, 30s. a wheel; Horses, 63s. each. Goods of every description, 6d. per foot.

For further particulars, apply to

JOHN TASSIE, Agent,
16, ST. ENOCH SQUARE.

Glasgow, 22nd August, 1839.